AFRICAN ENCOUNTER OF FAITH & CULTURE

RITUAL & SYMBOL FOR YOUNG PEOPLE IN TIV SOCIETY OF CENTRAL NIGERIA

Clement Terseer Iorliam, Ph.D.

PACEM IN TERRIS PRESS

Devoted to the global vision of Saint John XXIII,
author of the famous encyclical letter "Pacem in Terris"
and prophetic founder of Postmodern Catholic Social Teaching,
and devoted to the search for a regenerative and postmodern
Global Ecological Civilization
that will draw on the
spiritual and philosophical wisdom-traditions
of our global human family.

www.paceminterrispress.com

*Pacem in Terris Press publishes scholarly and inspirational books
directly or indirectly related to Catholic Social Teaching's
commitment to ecology, justice, peace, and spirituality,
on behalf of the search for a Postmodern Ecological Civilization.*

*To support ecumenical and interfaith dialogue,
Pacem in Terris Press also publishes scholarly and inspirational books
from other Christian perspectives, from other religious perspectives,
and from perspectives of spiritual seekers,
which promote ecology, justice, peace, and spirituality,
for our global human family and for our wider family of all creatures.*

*Opinions or claims expressed in publications from Pacem in Terris Press
do not necessarily represent the official position of
Pacem in Terris Press, the Pacem in Terris Ecological Initiative,
Pax Romana / Catholic Movement for Intellectual & Cultural Affairs - USA
or their officers, directors, members, or staff.*

PACEM IN TERRIS PRESS
*is the publishing service of the Pacem in Terris Ecological Initiative,
which is a central project of*

PAX ROMANA
CATHOLIC MOVEMENT FOR INTELLECTUAL & CULTURAL AFFAIRS
USA
*1025 Connecticut Avenue NW, Suite 1000,
Washington DC 20036
www.paceminterris.net*

ABOUT THIS BOOK

F aith and culture should enjoy a harmonious relationship. In past centuries of Catholicism, however, evangelization often did not take into cognizance the culture of a people. Until recently, the translation and adaptation approaches were the dominant models that missionaries used for evangelization.

Sadly, those approaches failed to create an adequate relationship with the local cultures where the faith was transplanted. The resulting distance between faith and culture caused the Catholic faith to be foreign to many cultures across the globe including North African countries and Japan. In Tiv society of central Nigeria too, Catholicism has yet to take concrete root in the local culture.

Building on the worship experiences of educated emerging adult Catholics in institutions of higher education in Tivland, this book uses the circle method and other related contextual approaches to contextualize Catholicism in Tiv culture.

In making this work truly contextual, Tiv students in institutions of higher education in Benue State, Nigeria were interviewed. The information gathered was narrowed to what most connects emerging adults with Catholic worship, and what the Catholic Church needs to know about them. *The information given by these young people revealed a constantly recurring notion of unappealing worship and inadequate catechesis on core doctrinal issues.*

One way to make their experiences of faith worship more meaningful is by synthesizing Tiv cultural symbols with Catholic worship symbols. Community faith gatherings, intensive catechesis, and service to the church are the three practical strategies that can synthesize faith and culture and ground the Catholic Church in Tivland. Pious organizations that bring emerging adults together as community can serve as forum to adequately catechize them by synthesizing Catholic symbols with cultural texts that are already familiar to them.

This synthesis will lead to a mutual enrichment of both Tiv cultural practices and Catholic worship symbols. That will ultimately form Tiv Catholic emerging adults as community theologians who can effectively articulate the faith to others, including those in rural communities.

ABOUT THE AUTHOR

REVEREND CLEMENT TERSEER IORLIAM, born to Abraham Iorliam Gyata and Agatha Mbaduun Iorliam, is from Benue State, central Nigeria. He studied at St James Junior Seminary, now in Yandev, Gboko, and he studied philosophy at St Thomas Aquinas' Major Seminary, Makurdi and theology at St Augustine's Major Seminary, Jos, all in Nigeria.

Having earned a Diploma and a Bachelor of Sacred Theology, he was subsequently ordained priest in 1997. He was ordained originally for the Diocese of Makurdi, but with the creation of the Diocese of Gboko in 2012, he became an incardinated priest of Gboko diocese. There, Reverend Iorliam provided ministry in parishes and educational institutions in Nigeria as associate pastor, pastor, school chaplain and lecturer.

His passion for knowledge led him to further his education, as a result of which he earned a Graduate Diploma (PGDE) in Education, a MA in Religious Studies at Benue State University, Makurdi, and a Ph.D. in Practical Theology at St Thomas University, Miami, Florida, USA. During his studies at St Thomas University, he was mentored by renowned professors including Doctors Joe Holland, Bryan Froehle, and Mary Carter Warren.

His research interests include faith and culture, young people (emerging adults), education, social justice and domestic violence. Reverend Iorliam loves to read, teach, write, listen to news, and workout. He also loves working with young people and has a passion for pastoral ministry.

DEDICATION

This work is dedicated to my deceased friends
who promoted the course of young people:

Fr. Herbert Bulbwa
Fr. Edward Igboko

It is also dedicated to my deceased brothers and sisters
who died young:

Mr. Innocent Aondover Iorliam
Miss Regina Tersôr Iorliam
&
Catherine Ternenge Iorliam
James Gwaza Iorliam

I also dedicate this work to
educated young people in Tiv society

TABLE OF CONTENTS

DIALOGUE OF FAITH & CULTURE

S cholars[1] who write on the encounter between Christianity and Tiv culture underscore the tension that existed between the two religions. For instance, they state that Christian missionaries did not agree with *tsav* (witchcraft) and *akombo* (magic). African religion and culture on the other hand, saw Christianity as intruding and thwarting African belief systems and practices.[2] In Tiv society, witchcraft and magic, and other practices are constitutive aspects of religion and culture. Such scholars argue that the encounter demonstrated a dialectical relationship of the practices of both.

The goal of the pioneer missionaries to save the souls of Africans in general resulted to a continual appeal to Africans to renounce cultural practices that opposed the Christian religion if they were to be Christians. As the faith was increasingly accepted by Africans, the call to substitute cultural practices with Christian beliefs was criticized by African scholars[3] on the basis that the substitution theory

---

[1] See Dominic V. Yuhe, "The Encounter of Tiv Religious and Moral Values with Catholicism in the Time of Secularization" (Ph.D. dissertation, Pontifical St Thomas University, Rome, 1978), and James Moti and Francis S. Wegh, *An Encounter between Tiv Religion and Christianity* (Enugu: Snaap Press Limited, n.d).

[2] This encounter is demonstrated by Achebe. See Chinua Achebe, *Things Fall Apart* (New York: Anchor, 1994). Themes of Orobator's theology are based on the content of this book. He focuses on God, Trinity, creation, grace and sin, Jesus Christ, church, Mary, communion of saints, inculturation, and spirituality. Building on the literary narrative of this text suggests that the themes have analogies in most African cultures. See Agbonkhianmeghe E. Orobator, *Theology Brewed in an African pot* (Maryknoll: Orbis, 2009).

[3] Luke Mbefo, "Theology and Inculturation: Problems and Prospects – The Nigerian Experience," *The Nigerian Journal of Theology* 1, no.1 (December 1985).

deprived Africans of their cultural heritage. Such tension revealed that the Christian missionaries had little or no knowledge of indigenous rituals and cultural practices as inherently possessing primal religious systems that could enrich the Christian faith.

Today, a discussion about Christianity in Africa transcends the tension that was observed between the two religions. It also goes beyond the casting of blame on foreign missionaries who have been accused of "destroying" African practices seen as a way of life.[4] Rather, theological discourse explores the mutual enrichment of the practices of Christianity and those of African cultures. It also explores ways the gospel message and Christian ritual resonate with Africans in their situation.

In exploring ways by which the Christian faith can be meaningful and take root in African cultures, one has to understand that Africa is a vast continent that cannot be studied as a whole. With a population of over one billion people, it is the second most populous continent with 54 recognized sovereign states and countries, nine territories and two de facto independent states.[5]

Each of the countries or territories has many different cultures, languages and peoples. Nigeria for example, has over two hundred and fifty tribes. Taken as a whole, these factors express the difficulty of talking about "Africa." Diversity characterizes Africa's geographical, cultural, and religious maps.[6]

In this context therefore, this practical theological investigation centers on Catholic worship, and uses Tiv culture of central Nigeria as a case study. The investigation also enriches the discussion with experiences from other African societies.

The central argument is to explore the relationship between faith and culture drawing from the worship experiences of emerging adults in institutions of higher education in Tivland. As a theology of inculturation, the goal is to explore Tiv cultural symbols that make Catholic worship meaningful and rooted in Tiv culture. This

---

[4] John Mbiti, *African Religions and Philosophy* (London: SPCK, 1969), 16
[5] "Africa Population 2014," *World Population Review*, 2015, accessed January 27, 2015, http://worldpopulationreview.com/continents/africa-population/
[6] Orobator, *Theology Brewed in an African pot*, 140.

is a practical theological investigation with a goal to transform strategies of evangelization that would root Catholicism in Tiv culture. Emerging adults are the primary agents of this mission.

Two things are involved: inculturation and contextualization. In rooting the faith in a culture, the context in which the Christian community lives cannot be ignored. While inculturation deals with dialogue between cultures, contextualization is an encompassing terminology that takes into consideration the socioeconomic, political, cultural, religious, and geographical factors.[7] This discussion limits the context to education, family, socioeconomic, and religious factors as they present enormous challenges to emerging adults' practice of the Catholic faith. The dearth of intensive catechesis since the coming of Catholicism to Tivland is what makes the religious factor critical to this discussion.

The Catholic faith was formally introduced in Tivland when the first Mass was celebrated in Makurdi town in 1930. Close to one hundred years since the establishment of the Catholic Church, the faith has permeated all of Tivland. However, it has yet to take concrete root in Tiv culture as the doctrines and practices of Catholicism appear to be alien to the people.

The issue of the contextualization of Catholicism is a global problem that has raised serious concerns among theologians. Catholicism did not take root in North Africa (even though the territory was part of the origins of the Catholic faith).[8] Those who transmitted the faith did not explore the possibility of synthesizing it with the culture of the people.

The story of the split of faith with culture was also true of Japan.[9] Today, this gap can be bridged by taking seriously Pope Francis' recognition that not all discussions of doctrinal, moral or pastoral

---

[7] Anscar J. Chupungco, "Inculturation of Worship: Forty Years of Progress and Tradition," Valparaiso University, Indiana, 226, accessed January 28, 2015, http://scholar.valpo.edu/cgi/viewcontent.cgi?article=1109&context=ils_papers

[8] John Paul II, *Ecclesia in Africa* [Post-Synodal Apostolic Exhortation], sec. 31, October 1, 2014, http://www.vatican.va/holy_father/john_paul_ii/apost_exhortations/documents/hf_jp-ii_exh_14091995_ecclesia-in-africa_en.html

[9] Robert J. Schreiter, *Constructing Local Theologies* (New York: Orbis Books, 2006), 155.

issues need to be settled by interventions of the magisterium. Each country or region, moreover, can seek solutions better suited to its culture and sensitive to its traditions and local needs. For 'cultures are in fact quite diverse and every general principle... needs to be inculturated, if it is to be respected and applied.'[10]

The failure of the missionaries in the past to inculturate has led to a phenomenon of many cultures including Tiv culture experiencing a distant relationship between faith and culture. This raises the question of the factors that were responsible for this state of affairs. These factors are most often identified with evangelization approaches.

The model of transmitting faith in a culture determines to a large degree how the faith is received. Scholars identify the translation, adaptation, and contextual models as the three basic models that missionaries often use in their missionary work. Contextual models are the most enduring of the three models.[11] Embedded in inculturation approaches, these models can effectively dialogue with Tiv culture that has undergone several cultural permutations. In discussing the relationship of faith and culture in Tiv society, it is important to sketch an overview of the trajectories of the development of Tiv society within which the theological investigation is located.

Trajectories of Development in Tiv Society

The argument of this investigation is located within pre-colonial, colonial, and post-colonial Tiv society. The present generation of emerging adults is not grounded in Tiv culture. Retrieving cultural resources and putting them side by side with Catholic practices can be mutually enriching. The resources can ground them in Tiv culture and enrich the Catholic faith as well. This claim is supported by

---

[10] Pope Francis, Amoris Laetitia [Apostolic Exhortation on the Joy of Love], sec 2, http://w2.vatican.va/content/dam/francesco/pdf/apost_exhortations/documents/papa-francesco_esortazione-ap_20160319_amoris-laetitia_en.pdf

[11] Schreiter, *Constructing Local Theologies*, 16. Stephen B. Bevans, *Models of Contextual Theology* (Maryknoll: Orbis, 2010). Bevans expands the discussion to cover six specific areas of contextual models. He identifies translation, anthropological, praxis, synthetic, transcendental, and countercultural models as contextual models.

the following assumption. "If it is true that today's African young people are not grounded in their traditional cultures, then a relevant African Christianity is challenged to speak also to the new generation and new African values."[12]

This integration approach uses analogies and symbols that advance the relationship between faith and culture. Faith cannot be separated from the culture where it is planted. Situating the investigation within three epochs of Tiv society is critical in identifying different cultural patterns.

The missionaries who brought the Catholic faith to Tivland were not grounded in the practices carried out in the pre-colonial and colonial epochs. Consequently, they were unable to use cultural resources to advance their work of evangelization. An overview of Tiv society helps in understanding cultural practices that were dominant in the past.

In the first place, Tiv society was not a vassal territory to any foreign authority until colonial occupation of Tivland began in 1900. The pre-colonial Tiv society for the most part was known for egalitarian practices and young people played significant roles in furthering communal practices. Tiv society was known for community life practices.

The concept of *hyumbe* (exchange labor), *kwa ruam* (squatting round a bowl of meal) in the *ate* (common sitting area), strongly emphasized communality among Tiv people. Young people, women and men carried out these practices based on gender. Young people were at the center of agricultural work, which was very much facilitated by *hyumbe* (cooperative work). They cleared the land and tilled the soil communally.

Women had their separate associations that helped them to weed and harvest their crops on a rotational basis. They went to the stream together to fetch water in groups. This was particularly important since they offered mutual support to each other in the process of lifting the pots or basins of water on each other's head.

---

12 Joseph Healey, mm and Donald Sybertz, mm, *Toward an African Narrative Theology* (Maryknoll: Orbis, 1996), 39.

Predominantly, in the past, people used their heads to convey goods from one point to the other. Today, this practice is still in use, but at a reduced rate. The practice has endured for ages due to lack of money to use modern means of transportation, and inaccessible roads to most rural communities in Tivland. In some communities, women are still using their heads to convey water from the source mostly a stream to the home.

It was very common to see women offer this kind of support in mutual exchange. In the case of two women who went to the stream, one helped the other lift her basin of water on the head. With her water on the head, she could bend gently and use one hand to assist the other lift hers too.

A woman who went to the stream alone encountered a problem of having to wait anxiously for assistance from someone who came to the stream or was passing-by at that moment. She also appeared strange, as it was often said of her, *soon ye kwagh azua un a or ga*, (she does not want to have anything to do with another person). Such cooperative exercise of domestic duties was another way of showing their fidelity in marriage.

Women did such things together as tangible evidence of their fidelity to their husbands. Being in the company of other women in the community was sufficient testimony that they were not involved in adulterous relationships. These and other community practices were deeply entrenched in Tiv life. Those cultural practices are potent theological sources that need to be revisited.

Second, colonialism, cross-cultural contact and other factors brought changes that affected various aspects of Tiv culture including community life, which was a potential tool for the contextualization of Catholicism. Money was introduced in the economy, and it became the medium for the exchange of goods and services.

During this era too, young men became more involved in the colonial government through agriculture, commercial labor, and their role as tax officials. Some became independent wealthy people, and no longer subjected themselves to the authority of the elders.

During this period, individualistic tendencies conspicuously made inroads into Tiv society disrupting the communitarian spirit. Young people who became rich no longer depended on the community to accomplish their tasks. These changes were not entirely negative since they introduced a higher level of prosperity among the Tiv.[13]

Third, in the post-colonial era, rural agrarian areas that provided the context for community practices have been deserted by young people. They move in large numbers to urban areas for higher education and to search for better opportunities. Those who fail to secure admission into institutions of higher education or cannot find jobs begin to remake themselves in strange ways. Even those admitted into institutions of higher education go through experiences of all kinds. Some are computer literate, which can be beneficial to the contemporary work of evangelization.

Scope of the
Theological Inquiry

This book argues that analogical correlation of the resources of the past in conjunction with the present digital and cyber culture of educated young people can make the Catholic faith meaningful and contextual. To do this effectively requires breaking down the theological inquiry into a series of related specific questions that narrow down to the issue of what most connects emerging adults to Catholic worship, and what the Catholic Church needs to know about them. In this way, the book addresses three basic questions.

1. *How does culture provide clues for the understanding of Catholic ritual in a Tiv context?*

The answer to this question is helpful in identifying the role of culture toward understanding Catholic ritual on the one hand. On the other hand, an analogical relationship between ritual and cultural practices leads to the contextualization of Catholicism. The answer to this question helps in developing a positive view of culture rec-

---

[13] See Laurenti Magesa, *Anatomy of Inculturation: Transforming the Church in Africa* (Maryknoll: Orbis, 2004), 192.

ognizing that culture has both negative and positive aspects. The positive aspects of culture provide a source for the grounding of the Catholic faith in Tiv culture.

2. *What analogies provide a mutual enrichment between culture and worship?*

This question brings culture and worship in a reciprocal dialogue. It is a give and take relationship. What will Tiv culture give to Catholicism, and what will Catholicism receive in return? The question identifies cultural practices that are analogous to catholic worship. The answer to this question is helpful in making Catholicism at home in Tiv culture.

3. *What are emerging adults' experiences of worship in institutions of higher education in Tivland?*

Answering this question requires exploring the context of emerging adults, their ages, clans, and educational levels. It also identifies the most salient aspects of worship, the practices and symbols often taken for granted. The question investigates what most connects them with worship, and what the Catholic Church needs to know and do. Paying attention to institutions of higher education is helpful in effectively engaging them on what it means to be educated emerging adult Catholics, and what their experiences mean to them.

The scope of this book is within the precincts of the above questions. Offering appropriate solutions to the questions will help Catholicism to take root in Tiv culture. This can be done using the circle method, Browning's strategic practical theological method and Tracy's method of analogical correlation. In particular, the circle has been most effectively used in transforming pastoral situations. In this context, the experiences of educated emerging adults in relation to worship is a pastoral issue that needs to be addressed.

Their experiences can help in doing three things. First, identify cultural practices that can lead to the understanding of Catholic ritual in a Tiv context. Second, explore analogies that synthesize cultural practices or symbols with Catholic beliefs and practices. Third, examine their role as community theologians who will articulate the faith to others. In this way, Catholicism can take root in Tiv culture. The changes in Tiv society require theologians to identify new ways of making Catholicism at home in Tiv culture.

As new questions constantly spring from the human situation, a contextual theological model is the most appropriate model to use in responding to the challenges of evangelization in Tivland. Contextual models recognize changes in cultural contexts and identify the most appropriate ways to respond. Institutions of higher education provide the context for the dialogue between faith and culture, and ultimately offer effective response to the present state of Catholicism in Tivland. Educated young people can use Tiv cultural symbols to explain Catholic doctrines and practices thereby enhancing the community's self-understanding, and the understanding of the Catholic faith.

Doing theology in Africa is not an individual enterprise, but a community event.[14] This community of emerging adults is the theologian, and it is a key source for theology's development and expression in Tiv context.[15] The predilection to engage emerging adults as pastoral agents arises from two main reasons.

Firstly, they represent the future of Catholicism in Tivland as educated people who will act as community theologians by interpreting the faith to others particularly those in rural communities.[16] Education is a key factor because, in pre-colonial Tiv society, uneducated young people were involved in a variety of ritual practices that moved Tiv society forward. Educated young people can create greater impact in the contemporary Tiv society, which supports the Tiv claim that *or u fan takerada saan she ga* (an educated person can never be a useless person).

Secondly, history is replete with instances of young people spearheading changes in other societies. This supports the view that they

---

[14] Orobator, *Theology Brewed in an African Pot*, xi.

[15] See Schreiter, *Constructing Local Theologies*, 17.

[16] See Schreiter, *Constructing Local Theologies*, 17. Also see Orobator, *Theology Brewed in an African Pot*, xi. The author says doing theology in Africa is not an isolated enterprise, but a community event.

can also help to contextualize Catholicism in Tiv culture by interpreting the faith using analogical correlation. They can also relate Catholic worship analogically with Tiv cultural practices to make worship authentically Tiv and authentically Catholic. As an inculturation theology, the notion of inculturation is explored in the following section from the historical, anthropological, and theological perspectives.

Perspectives on Inculturation

Inculturation has been viewed from three basic perspectives, historical, anthropological, and theological.

Historical Perspective

The term inculturation was not known in church circles. Anthropologists often used enculturation (the learning of a new culture) and acculturation (the encounter between cultures)[17] in discourse about cultures. In the early part of the twentieth century, Protestant missions had used the term 'indigenization' to describe their aim of establishing churches that would be authentically indigenous in governance, financial viability, and take ownership of their own mission.[18] In contrast, the Catholic Church preferred adaptation approach to evangelization.

Adaptation suggests a situation whereby a foreign missionary announces the gospel message to suit the circumstances of the receiving culture.[19] Faith adapts or accommodates itself in a limited fashion to the exigencies of cultural expression for the sake of the communication of the message. The idea behind this concept goes back to the patristic period, but the term itself became popular in missiological circles between the two world wars, and it continued to be used down to the time of the 1974 Roman Synod on Evangelization.

---

[17]Robert J. Schreiter, "Faith and Cultures: Challenges to a World Church," *Theological Studies* 50 (1989): 747.

[18]Brian Stanley, "Inculturation: Historical Background, Theological Foundations and Contemporary Questions,"*Transformation* 24, no 1 (2007): 22.

[19] See Barth Chidili, *Inculturation as a Symbol of Evangelization* (Jos: Mono Expressions, 1997), 4.

In regard to liturgy, the Second Vatican Council approved adaptation of the liturgy to different groups, regions, and peoples, especially in mission lands, provided that the substantial unity of the Roman rite is preserved.[20]

Today, the term is considered inadequate because of its simplistic and too static understanding of culture as if a culture can be so easily read that an adaptation can be readily prescribed, and that this process takes place once and for all in an unchanging culture.[21] Its inadequacy led to the use of other terms such as incarnation that penetrate culture in a deeper way.

Incarnation came to be popular in missiological thinking prior to and during the Second Vatican Council. The analogy is with the incarnation of Christ, who emptied himself and took on flesh as a human being in a particular culture. Christian faith must imitate its Lord in becoming truly part of a human culture.[22] Incarnation has a close link with inculturation.

Inculturation is not mentioned in any of the documents of Vatican Council II. It came to be used in relation to the gospel in 1962 by the French writer Joseph Masson who used the phrase '*Catholicisme inculturé.*' Following extensive discussion of the concept at the 32nd General Assembly of the Jesuit order in 1974, the Superior-General of the Jesuit order, Pedro Arrupe, introduced the term 'inculturation' to the Synod of Bishops in 1977.[23] It first appeared in a papal document of John Paul II in 1979.[24] Inculturation is different from mere external adaptation as it signifies an interior transformation of authentic cultural values through their integration into Christianity and the rooting of Christianity into various human cultures.[25]

---

[20] Vatican Council II, "Constitution on the Sacred liturgy [Sacrosanctum Concilium]," section 38,
http://www.vatican.va/archive/hist_councils/ii_vatican_council/documents/vat-ii_const_19631204_sacrosanctum-concilium_en.html.
[21] Schreiter, Faith and Cultures, 746.
[22] Schreiter, Faith and Cultures, 746.
[23] Stanley, "Inculturation: Historical Background, Theological Foundations and Contemporary Questions," 22.
[24] Keith F. Pecklers, *Worship: A Primer in Christian Ritual* (Collegeville: Liturgical Press, 2005), 123-125.
[25] Pecklers, *Worship: A Primer in Christian Ritual,* 126-127.

It has the advantage of echoing the concept of incarnation, while at the same time emphasizing the importance of culture and lifting up the relationship of faith and cultures as an ongoing process rather than a once-for-all encounter. It often gets confused, however, with "enculturation" and "acculturation."[26] The term inculturation is preferred to adaptation since what is required is more than a cursory adaptation of the gospel or the liturgical rites to the particular group.[27] Inculturation takes place within a particular cultural context. Therefore, context if taken seriously can advance the rooting of the Catholic faith in a local culture.

In a situation where emerging adults are losing interest in Catholic worship, context is important in determining what is responsible for the loss of interest. Factors that ignite lack of enthusiasm can affect the contextualization of the Catholic faith in Tiv culture. Originally, the term contextualization was not identified with the Catholic Church.

Protestant mission theory began in 1972 to employ the concept of 'contextualization.'[28] It suggests the interweaving of the gospel with the experiences of people in a particular context. Contextualization speaks of present context or situation in Tiv society into which the gospel must be planted.[29] It emphasizes the importance of the context of Tiv emerging adult Catholics. This includes their worship experiences in particular contexts of higher education chaplaincies within Tivland.

While the term has a slightly different theological resonance than does inculturation, many authors have come to use the two terms interchangeably.[30] Both terms do not discuss culture as an abstract concept, but in relation to the human person. In this regard, inculturation is viewed from the perspective of anthropology.

---

[26]Schreiter, Faith and Cultures, 747.
[27] Pecklers, *Worship: A Primer in Christian Ritual*, 124.
[28]Stanley, "Inculturation: Historical Background, Theological Foundations and Contemporary Questions," 22.
[29] Chidili, *Inculturation as a Symbol of Evangelization*, 19.
[30]Schreiter, Faith and Cultures, 747.

Anthropological Perspective

Theology is broadly understood as faith seeking understanding. The shift of theology to make particular claims about Christian life has led practical theologians to adopt the anthropological model in the theological enterprise to advance the work of inculturation.

Anthropological model is understood in two senses. In the first place, the model centers on the value and goodness of the human person. Second, the model makes use of the insights of ethnography to understand human culture in which God is present and seen as acting.

The term ethnography most preferred in Europe is another name for anthropology. It is in studying human culture that one finds the symbols and concepts with which to construct an adequate articulation of a people's faith. [31] Terms such as indigenization and inculturation are associated with anthropology. Indigenization is concerned with what is indigenous or proper to a people and their culture. Inculturation on the other hand is often proposed as well as express the importance of culture in the construction of a true contextual theology.[32]

Anthropologists dwell on the particularity of cultures to seek out answers to core questions of Christian life.[33] In studying the culture of a local congregation in African societies with a focus on emerging adults, one discovers that emerging adult Catholics ask questions bothering on their ritual experiences.

For instance, they question why Catholic ritual is dull, why Catholics "worship" Mary, and why incense is burned during worship. It is only by penetrating the context of emerging adults and interviewing them that anthropologists make contact with their world. Anthropological studies help to identify their feelings and what they are thinking to bring something fresh to theological reflection.[34]

---

[31] Bevans, *Models of Contextual Theology*, 55.

[32] Bevans, *Models of Contextual Theology*, 55.

[33] See Christian Scharen and Aana Marie Vigen, eds., *Ethnography As Christian Theology and Ethics* (New York: Continuum, 2011), 28.

[34] Scharen and Vigen, eds., *Ethnography As Christian Theology and Ethics*, 29.

Priests who minister from the sanctuary may not know what those who sit in the pews are feeling or thinking. Ethnography can be employed to gather the experiences, thoughts and feelings of the local Christian community on a variety of issues.

One positive aspect of anthropological model is that it starts where people are with people's real questions and interests, rather than by imposing questions asked out of other contexts.[35] By undertaking a field work, the anthropologist is in touch with questions asked by local Christian communities. Field work helps anthropologists to collect data and make a "thick description" of cultures. The anecdotal 'armchair' approach to the study of other cultures has been replaced by direct inquiry and participant observation. The anthropologist's task is to describe in detail a culture or society, 'to record as accurately as possible the modes of life of the other people.'[36]

Listening to university students narrate their experiences of worship helps to fashion strategies that explicate the meaningfulness and practice of Catholicism for the ultimate goal of making the faith contextual in Tiv culture. The theological basis of inculturation is critical in making the faith take root in Tiv culture.

Theological Perspective

The term "inculturation" entered the official Catholic Church language in Pope John Paul II's address to the Pontifical Biblical Commission in 1979, and has since been used regularly as a theological term in church documents.[37] Inculturation acknowledges that the seed of the word is present in different cultures and religious traditions. Christ is already present in African culture. Missionaries do not bring him to Africa.[38] This claim implies that the whole body of the Christian message, not just its external wrapping, needs to take flesh, become incarnate, in the patterns of thought, language, and

---

[35] Stephen B. Bevans, *Models of Contextual Theology* (Maryknoll: Orbis, 2010), 60.

[36] Nathan D. Mitchell, "New Direction in Ritual Research," in *Foundations in Ritual Studies: A Reader for Students of Christian Ritual*, eds., Paul Bradshaw and John Melloh (Grand Rapids: Baker Academic, 2007), 119.

[37] Joseph Healey, mm and Donald Sybertz, mm, *Toward an African Narrative Theology*, 26

[38] Healey and Sybertz, *Toward an African Narrative Theology*, 25.

symbols of a particular culture.[39] Inculturation acknowledges the relationship between faith and culture. The integration of faith and culture is like the skin that one carries along wherever one goes, not like the cloth that could be removed the next moment.[40]

Faith and culture need each other. The former needs to find a vehicle to express its content, the latter to find the substance for its very existence.[41] Like a tree that cannot bear fruit unless it takes root in the soil where it has been planted, so too faith needs to be planted and contextualized in the culture where it takes root so that it can bring forth fruit. To do this, faith needs to dialogue with the culture wherein it is contextualized. Faith must initiate and promote this dialogue. Dialogue demands the difficult discipline of reciprocal listening: and not just listening with the ear, but rather listening with the heart. It is precisely in the reciprocity of this listening that both faith and culture are enriched.[42]

This means faith and culture are harmoniously related. Paul VI observed that the Gospel and evangelization are not identical with culture. They are independent in regard to all cultures. Nevertheless, the kingdom which the Gospel proclaims is lived by men and women who are profoundly linked to a culture, and the building up of the kingdom cannot avoid borrowing the elements of human culture or cultures. Therefore, every effort must be made to ensure a full evangelization of culture, or more correctly of cultures.[43]

However, Vatican II warns against every appearance of syncretism and of false particularism in such a way that Christian life will be

---

[39]Stanley, "Inculturation: Historical Background, Theological Foundations and Contemporary Questions," 22.

[40] Healey and Sybertz, *Toward an African Narrative Theology*, 25. This striking image of the relationship of faith and culture was demonstrated by Archbishop Peter Sarpong of Ghana.

[41]Paul Cardinal Poupard, "The Dialogue Between Faith and Culture: Keynote Address at the University of Santo Tomás" (Manila: Colloquium of the Federation of Asian Bishops' Conferences, January 14, 1996), accessed March 23, 2014, http://www.inculturacion.net/phocadownload/Autores_invitados/Poupard,_The_dia logue_between_faith_and_culture.pdf.

[42]Poupard, "The Dialogue Between Faith and Culture."

[43] Paul VI, *Evangelii Nuntiandi* [Apostolic Exhortation], sec. 20, http://www.vatican.va/holy_father/paul_vi/apost_exhortations/documents/hf_p-vi_exh_19751208_evangelii-nuntiandi_en.html.

accommodated to the genius and the dispositions of each culture.[44] It can be argued that syncretism is inevitable because there has never been any pure Christianity. It is a religion that borrowed from the faith and culture of Israel and the Roman culture.[45]

Since the Second Vatican Council, the church has viewed the split between faith and life as a serious error of our age.[46] This disharmony is one of the major obstacles to a real contextualization of the Catholic faith. When faith is separated from daily life, it does not take into cognizance the reality of the incarnation of the son of God in our human nature and life.[47]

The Second Vatican Council encourages dialogue between faith and culture, thus connecting culture and theology, and culture and ritual. "[I]f cultures need Christ in order to experience the fullness of their own cultural existence, in a certain sense it is also true to say that Christ needs culture to contextualize the gift of the incarnation in specific historic epochs and places."[48]

Christ needs Tiv culture as a context to plant the faith, and Tiv culture needs Christ to illumine its cultural practices for Catholicism to take root in Tivland. Tiv culture has to be regenerated by an encounter with the Gospel. But this encounter will not take place if the Gospel is not proclaimed.[49] In the past, the church neglected local

---

[44] Vatican Council II, "Ad Gentes" [On the Mission Activity of the Church], sec. 22, http://www.vatican.va/archive/hist_councils/ii_vatican_council/documents/vat-ii_decree_19651207_ad-gentes_en.html. On the problems and other issues associated with syncretism, see Schreiter, *Constructing Local Theologies*, 144-158.

[45] Gerald A. Arbuckle, *Culture, Inculturation, Theologians: A Postmodern Critique* (Collegeville: Liturgical Press, 2010), 184.

[46] Vatican Council II, "Gaudium et Spes[Pastoral Constitution of the Church in the Modern world]," sec. 43, accessed January 24, 2014, http://www.vatican.va/archive/hist_councils/ii_vatican_council/documents/vat-ii_const_19651207_gaudium-et-spes_en.html.

[47] Juan José Luna, "The Pastoral Circle: A Strategy for Justice and Peace," in *The Pastoral Circle Revisited: A Critical Quest for Truth and Transformation*, ed. Frans Wijsen, Peter Henriot, and Rodrigo Mejia (New York: Orbis, 2005), 30.

[48] Pecklers, *Worship: A Primer in Christian Ritual*, 121.

[49] See Paul VI, *Evangelii Nuntiandi* [Apostolic Exhortation], sec. 20, http://www.vatican.va/holy_father/paul_vi/apost_exhortations/documents/hf_p-vi_exh_19751208_evangelii-nuntiandi_en.html.

cultures, but in the post Vatican II era, the church integrates culture in its evangelization strategy.[50]

The church in Tivland recognizes the role of culture in the propagation of the faith. Cultural aspects including, vernacular, clerical vestments made of traditional clothes, and musical instruments are integrated in liturgy. However, inculturation is not just about external matters such as ecclesiastical dress, church music, or church architecture, it is more about exploring ways in which the faith is received, understood, and expressed in corporate worship and personal devotion.[51] To effectively explore the issue of faith and culture in the worship experiences of emerging adults, the following three interrelated methods are helpful in addressing the question.

Combination of
Three Practical Theological Methods

To effectively respond to the practical theological problem that explores the worship experiences of educated emerging adults, three methods have been selected. The methods are a combination of 1) Browning's strategic practical theological model, 2) the circle method rooted in the Cardijn's "see, judge, and act" method, and 3) Tracy's method of analogical correlation.

These three methods are interrelated. They are all praxis-oriented, and they are appropriate in contextual situations. Inculturation of worship in Tiv society is a contextual issue that falls within strategic practical theology, encompassing catechesis, preaching, liturgy, and social ministries.[52]

As a congregational issue, it is appropriate to observe worship in Tiv culture, and to gather data from stories that describe emerging

---

[50] See Josef Elsener, "Pitfalls in the Use of the Pastoral Circle," in *The Pastoral Circle Revisited: A Critical Quest for Truth and Transformation*, eds. Frans Wijsen, Peter Henriot, and Rodrigo Mejia (New York: Orbis, 2005), 45. The author says, the church regrets having hurt other people by not respecting their culture for many years.
[51] Stanley, "Inculturation: Historical Background, Theological Foundations and Contemporary Questions," 23.
[52] See Don S. Browning, *A Fundamental Practical Theology: Descriptive and Strategic Proposals* (Minneapolis: Fortress, 1991), 8.

adults' worship experiences. What are they undergoing, what are they feeling, what stories are they telling, how are they responding to the teaching of the Catholic Church?[53] These questions resonate with the "see" step of the three-step method, and it underscores the importance of a thick description of the situation.

For theology to be practical, it must describe and interpret both contemporary situations and classic Christian resources. The "thick" description of contemporary practices within the church and between church and world is one of the most essential features of any theology that purports to be practical.[54]

After gathering data and describing the problem in its situated thickness, the investigator moves to analysis, identifying at the same time causes of the problem and primary actors in what is happening. Drawing from the circle method, the analysis dwells on education and family as social and cultural factors that affect the worship experiences of emerging adults. Analysis leads to theological reflection that arises from a sound judgment based on appropriate biblical and ecclesiastical wisdom.

Theology is a careful and systematic reflection on the self-understanding of the Catholic tradition that expresses its self-understanding in the language of myth, story, symbol, and metaphor.[55] Catholic worship is shrouded in symbols. In offering theological reflection, these symbols cannot be adequately deciphered except with the help of hermeneutics. Catholic worship in Tiv culture provides the context to analogically correlate such symbols with Tiv cultural practices.

The revised method of correlation takes cultural practices seriously, not only as sources of questions to be answered by theology, but also as potential generators of alternative answers, which practical theology must critique and, in light of which, practical theology

---

[53] See Frans Wijsen, Peter Henriot, and Rodrigo Mejía, eds., *The Pastoral Circle Revisited: A Critical Quest for Truth and Transformation* (Maryknoll: Orbis, 2005), 229.

[54] Don Browning, "Practical Theology and Political Theology," *Theology Today* 42, no. 1 (1985): 16-17.

[55] Browning, *A Fundamental Practical Theology*, 5

must be critiqued.[56] The revised correlational approach to practical theology is open to the possibility that there might be a variety of relations between Christian praxis and contemporary cultural praxis. The relation can be a matter of *identity* (the two might be highly congruent), one of *non-identity* (they might be vastly different and perhaps antagonistic), or one of *analogy* (the two might be different but have many overlapping analogies).[57]

In the perspective of inculturating worship in Tiv culture, the analogical framework considers a simple language of similarities and differences with a focus on the criteria of adequacy, criteria of appropriateness, and the criteria of internal coherence. These criteria are the framework of interpreting analogies. The interpretative interests of hermeneutics are not ends in themselves but processes of understanding and self-interpretation toward the goal of orienting individuals and communities toward action.[58] Ultimately, the triad methods of strategic practical theology, the circle, and analogical correlation methods share a common goal of providing pastoral response that is praxis oriented and contextualizes the Catholic faith in Tiv culture.

To develop practical strategies for the contextualization of Catholicism in Tiv culture, the case-study approach gathered data using a triad method of participant observation, one-on-one interviews and focus group discussions to gain information on the situation in question. As a qualitative work,[59] these data collection approaches fit the inquiry. The best way to do a qualitative work is to make contact with the situation, sit with the people involved, and listen to their experiences.

The investigator made contact with the contexts, the subjects of the investigation, and observed worship in two institutions of higher education Catholic Chaplaincies. A total of twenty-seven people participated in three focus group interviews. University students

---

[56] Browning, "Practical theology and Political Theology," 18.
[57] Browning, "Practical theology and Political Theology," 18.
[58] Browning, "Practical theology and Political Theology," 16.
[59] See John Swinton, and Harriet Mowat, *Practical Theology and Qualitative Research* (London: SCM, 2007).

participated in two of the groups, while the third group was organized for priests. Those who participated in one-on-one interviews were fifty-five. The data generated from these interviews was analyzed using the social sciences. The following concepts are at the center of this discussion.

Recurrent Concepts

Local Theology

Local theology is a kind of theology that pays attention especially to the immediate, the concrete and the specific. It springs from a particular context and addresses the burning questions of that place. Local theology is aware of the environment in which it operates.[60]

In this book, local theology refers to a distinctively Catholic theology that explores the worship experiences of Tiv emerging adult Catholics. It is a response to the invitation to enter a serious and respectful dialogue with faith and culture with a focus on emerging adults in Tiv culture.[61]

Theology needs to engage cultures because the origins of Christianity are to be found in a particular culture. Dialogue with culture is helpful in understanding the person and message of Jesus Christ in particular, and of the Holy Scriptures in general.[62]

The need for dialogue between theology and Tiv culture supports the claim that Christian identity is constantly negotiated within local cultures. Christians live within local cultures and not within a

---

[60]In this discussion, local theology and contextual theology are used interchangeably. Local theology is a theology that springs from a particular context or a local culture. Tracy categorizes practical theology as fundamental practical theology. In this sense, therefore, local theology and contextual theology would be specialties of practical theology. Many scholars including, Don S. Browning, and Terry Veling have asserted that all theology is practical. Veling observes that practical theology is always attentive to the context of human culture and human experience in its unique singularity and concrete particularity. See Terry Veling, *Practical Theology: On Earth as It Is in Heaven* (Maryknoll: Orbis Books, 2005), 8-9. See also Clemens Sedmak, *Doing Local Theology: A Guide for Artisans of a New Humanity* (Maryknoll: Orbis, 2002), vii.

[61] See Sedmak, *Doing Local Theology*, 79.

[62] Sedmak, *Doing Local Theology*, 80.

Christian culture. Christian religion does not exist on a culturally neutral ground.[63] Local theologies spring from human cultures.

Human cultures are shaped by implicit theologies.[64] Doing theology is an attempt to bring the implicit theologies of emerging adults to the surface by making the hidden values explicit.[65] In their everyday life, for example, Tiv people express public symbols that sustain intersubjectivity and are organized as a meaning-giving system, which are implicit, and are often taken for granted.[66]

Tiv people commonly express many of those symbols in their thinking and everyday life. In a changing Tiv context, implicit theologies can shape Catholicism in Tiv culture. The traditional local communities such as families, clans, tribes, villages, various groups and associations stemming from social contacts, experience more thorough changes every day.[67] This local theology encourages contact that would make emerging adults develop a strong sense of community living.

Community Life

In the past, practices of community life advanced integration in Tiv culture as they emphasized interdependence, solidarity, and sharing. From the perspective of emerging adults in institutions of higher education, community is defined as an undergraduate experience that helps students go beyond their private interest, learn about the world around them, develop a sense of civic and social responsibility, and discover how they, as individuals, can contribute to the larger society of which they are a part.[68] Although every individual is autonomous, human beings are deeply dependent upon one an-

---

[63] Sedmak, *Doing Local Theology*, 80.
[64] Sedmak, *Doing Local Theology*, 74.
[65] Sedmak, *Doing Local Theology*, 79.
[66] See Manuel A. Vasquez, *More Than Belief: A Materialist Theory of Religion* (New York: Oxford University Press, 2011), 213.
[67] Vatican Council II, "Gaudium et Spes," sec. 6.
[68] George M. Schroeder, "The Quest for Wisdom: Reflections on Campus Ministry and the Relationship Between the Church and Higher Education," in *The Gospel on Campus: A Handbook of Campus Ministry Programs and Resources 2ndEdition*, ed. Michael Galligan-Stierle, (Dayton: Catholic Campus Ministry Association, 1996), 13.

other.[69] The strength of such a community on campus produces community theologians, enriched by Catholic practices, dual symbols (Catholic symbols and cultural symbols), and cultural values that can help them to effectively articulate the faith of the Catholic Church.

Symbols

Theology as public enterprise cannot do adequate reflection without taking into cognizance the importance of symbols. This is particularly true of Tiv society that needs a contextualization of Catholicism. Tiv symbols are expressed in a variety of cultural texts including, practices, proverbs, stories, myths, riddles, and idioms. These texts, expressed in Tiv language, contain powerful messages.

Contextual theology recognizes the language of Tiv people by expressing some of their sayings in the local language. Using local language in theology is a sign of respect for the local culture because the most important expression of culture is language.[70] Language as system of language games is part of life. The way people talk is linked with the way they live.[71] Using symbolic sayings to express the beliefs and practices of Tiv people corroborates the understanding that religion is a cultural system and a system of symbols.[72]

Symbols are as important to us as water is to fish.[73] Whatever Christians say about God has a symbolic meaning. It points beyond itself while participating in that to which it points.[74] In no other way can faith express itself adequately than through symbols because the language of faith is the language of symbols.[75] Theology operates

---

[69] Schroeder, "The Quest for Wisdom," 13.

[70] Sedmak, *Doing Local Theology*, 81.

[71] Sedmak, *Doing Local Theology*, 82.

[72] Clifford Geertz, *The Interpretation of Cultures* (New York: Basic, 1973), 90.

[73] Gerald A. Arbuckle, *Culture, Inculturation, and Theologians: A Postmodern Critique* (Collegeville: Liturgical Press, 2010), 19. Also see Victor Turner, *The Forest of Symbols: Aspects of Ndembu Ritual* (London: Cornell University Press, 1967).

[74] Paul Tillich, *Dynamics of Faith* (New York: HarperCollins, 2009), 51. Also see David Tracy, *The Analogical Imagination: Christian Theology and the Culture of Pluralism* (Crossroad, 1981), 176, and Elizabeth Johnson, *Quest for the living God: Mapping Frontiers in the Theology of God* (New York: Continuum, 2012).

[75] Tillich, *Dynamics of Faith*, 51

within three publics, the church, the academy, and the society. Incorporated in the public of society is the realm of culture within which both participation in and critical reflection upon symbols, including religious symbols principally occur.[76]

Symbols mean different things to different people. As a symbol system, the Catholic faith centers on the Christian classic of the God proclaimed to be manifested and represented in a myriad of symbols, images, genres, concepts, and doctrines. God's self-manifestation is decisively in the event and person of Jesus Christ.[77] Symbols are important classics in both culture and the Catholic tradition. Tiv people have symbols that promote different values. Some Tiv symbols resonate with the Catholic faith, and potently synthesize the ritual experiences of emerging adult Catholics, making their practice of faith alive, meaningful, and contextual.

Ritual

Ritual is broadly defined "as a more embracing category of social action, with religious activities at one extreme, and social etiquette at the other."[78] This definition does not limit ritual to religion or the sacred, but loosely refers it to a wide spectrum of formalized but not necessarily religious activities. Therefore, ritual is concerned with society and social institutions, not just religion or religious institutions.[79] Like symbols, rituals also have various interpretations and meanings.

Regardless of how one defines it, ritual is essential to human life and holds a particular function within society. It preserves both cultural traditions and bridges transitions, leading to change in the community.[80] Ritual brings people together as a group. It functions to "strengthen the bonds attaching the individual to the society of which he or she is a member."[81] Religion is a critical medium

---

[76] Tracy, *The Analogical Imagination*, 11.
[77] See Tracy, *The Analogical Imagination*, 248.
[78] Catherine Bell, *Ritual Perspectives and Dimensions* (New York: Oxford University Press, 1997),39.
[79] Bell, *Ritual Perspectives and Dimensions*, 39.
[80] Pecklers, *Worship: A Primer in Christian Ritual*, 5.
[81] Bell, *Ritual Perspectives and Dimensions*, 25.

through which shared social life is experienced, expressed, and legitimated.[82] Religion provides the clue for a deeper understanding of the connection between worship and social life.

While ritual is loosely defined, worship as ritual experience is exclusively concerned with the sacred. "Worship entails rites, rituals, sacred stories, songs, symbols, and creeds that express the fundamental claims about who God is and what God has done for the people."[83] Christian worship is fundamentally God's work in or on us as God's salvific purpose is worked out and accomplished. It is an event of tremendous grace at which the community encounters God in holy mystery not as passive spectators, but rather as active participants.[84]

In this context, the terms ritual and worship are used interchangeably to show the relationship of the human person to the sacred, and how this relationship connects social life. This suggests the importance of ritual symbols that make Catholicism relevant to the contemporary Tiv person.

Catholic worship is replete with symbols of light and darkness, bread and wine, water and oil, and bodily acts of standing, kneeling, bowing, eating, and drinking. As these symbols are transformed within the liturgy, they take on a deeper significance for the worshipping community.[85] These symbols resonate with Tiv culture in various ways. The Eucharistic symbols of bread and wine resonate with the inclusive image of common table in Tiv culture.

Like the symbol of common table in Tiv culture, worship too is inclusive. It connects people on the margins of human society. In Catholic understanding, people belong to the church by belonging to its worship and liturgy.[86] Therefore, as a social reality, worship brings people together, and expresses the communal nature of

---

[82] Bell, *Ritual Perspectives and Dimensions*, 25.

[83] Kathleen A. Cahalan, *Introducing the Practice of Ministry* (Collegeville, Minnesota: Liturgical Press, 2010), 84.

[84] See Pecklers, *Worship: A Primer in Christian Ritual,* 23.

[85] See Pecklers, *Worship: A Primer in Christian Ritual,* 4.

[86] Nathan D. Mitchell, "History of the Relationship Between Eucharist and Communion," *Liturgical Ministry* 13 (Spring 2004), 63.

church. People come to Sunday worship to pray together as a community. Praying together enhances a sense of community that depends on the presence of other individuals.[87]

In Tiv culture, such communalism is expressed by the concept of *tema imongo* (sitting together), a symbol that binds the Tiv together.[88] Emerging adults who come together for worship can promote community life through symbols that contextualize the Catholic faith in Tiv culture.

Emerging Adult

Emerging adulthood as a distinctive life period is a relatively new concept that has opened conversation among scholars as recent scholarship appears to be moving in this direction.[89] However, more social scientists seem to be studying young people than theologians, which results in a dearth of theological literature. Using emerging adults as theological subjects helps to further the conversation on emerging adulthood.

Emerging adulthood is increasingly defined as a distinctive life period between adolescence and adulthood from ages 18 and 25, and in some cases extending to the late twenties.[90] In contrast to what obtained in industrialized societies in the 1970s, what determines young adulthood is no longer graduation from college, marriage, and parenthood, but when one reaches the point of accepting responsibility for one's actions, taking independent decisions, and becoming financially independent.[91] This change in cultural markers has necessitated the development of a new period of life for young

---

[87] Pecklers, *Worship: A Primer in Christian Ritual*, 12.

[88] Edward Terkula Atel, *Dynamics of Tiv Religion and Culture: A Philosophical Theological Perspective* (Lagos: Free Enterprise, 2004), 23.

[89] See works by Christian Smith and Patricia Snell, *Souls in Transition: The Religious and Spiritual Lives of Emerging Adults* (New York: Oxford University Press, 2009); Sharon Daloz Parks, *Big Questions Worthy Dreams: Mentoring Emerging Adults in Their Search for Meaning, Purpose, and Faith* (San Francisco: Jossey-Bass, 2011); David P. Setran and Chris A. Kiesling, *Spiritual Formation in Emerging Adulthood: A Practical Theology for College and Young Adult Ministry* (Grand Rapids: Baker, 2013).

[90] Jeffrey Jansen Arnett, *Emerging Adulthood: The Winding Road from the Late Teens through the Twenties* (New York: Oxford University Press, 2004), 4.

[91] Arnett, *Emerging Adulthood*, vi.

people in the United States and other industrialized societies, lasting from the late teens through the mid to late twenties.[92] This is necessitated by the desire to acquire higher certificates that would pave the way for better paid jobs.

The term *emerging adult* was coined to describe a distinctive life period that is different from adolescence, youth, and the young adult stage. It is not a transition to young adulthood, but a period of life with distinctive features that make emerging adults who they are rather than what they will become. Five features unique to this life stage include;

1. The age of identity exploration, of trying out various possibilities especially in love and work.
2. The age of instability.
3. The most self-focused age of life.
4. The age of feeling in-between, in transition, neither adolescent nor adult.
5. The age of possibilities, when hopes flourish, when people have an unparallel opportunity to transform their lives.[93]

Features of emerging adults in African societies are almost the same with those of advanced societies. By the age of 25, most emerging adults in advanced societies are graduates. However, in African societies, many are still undergraduates in their late twenties and early thirties. Cultural factors, economic status, and educational challenges are responsible for the late attainment of adulthood in most African societies.

Emerging adult is not a familiar concept in African cultures. Tiv language for instance, has no nomenclature with a specific rendering of the concept for youth, teenager, adolescent, emerging adult, or young adult. In the language and culture of the Tiv, one is either *wanye* (a child), *gum or/gum kwase* (young man/young woman), or *gyanden or/gyanden kwase* (elderly man/elderly woman. In the past, certain rites of passage in Tiv culture determined transition to an-

---

[92] Arnett, *Emerging Adulthood*, 4.
[93] Arnett, *Emerging Adulthood*, 8.

other stage of life. A young male became a matured person when he was able to *ande ba sule* (complete a line of heaps) on the farm in a day. Circumcision also determined his maturity.

In former times, the Tiv did not circumcise early. Some boys were circumcised at sixteen while others reached eighteen years before they were circumcised. The Tiv were afraid that if circumcision was done too early, the child would be sickly. When all the rites associated with circumcision were performed, the child became a man, and started going after women. By implication, he was also ripe for marriage.[94] The Ndembu of northwestern Zambia, also have a similar understanding of the rite of circumcision. The main purpose of the Ndembu Mukanda rite is to turn boys into men.

The critical mechanisms of this transformation are the removal of the boys from the care of their mothers. By this act, the boys assume new duties and social identities that reinforce their relationship to their fathers. The rite culminates in a communal celebration that acknowledges the changed status of the young men as they return to places in the larger society.

Circumcision for the Ndembu signifies that the uncircumcised boy is unclean, effeminate in his dependence on women, and outside the formal male governing structure of the tribe. The circumcision rite is an act to purify him, break his connection to the world of women, and induct him in the male hierarchical power system.[95] In most African cultures, the circumcised qualifies as an adult, and is eligible to marry.

---

[94] Rupert East, trans., *Akiga's Story: The Tiv Tribe as Seen by One of Its members* (London: Oxford University Press, 1965), 29-38. Transition from one stage to the other was marked by a series of milestones. The earliest was the visible sign of ear piercing performed as soon as a boy started to go about with arrows in his hands (see pages 26-28). The next was teeth-cutting. Those whose teeth were not cut were perceived as kids (see pages 28 and 29). Circumcision was the most important stage that determined a boy's maturity. After circumcision, the next big event in a man's life was marriage (see page 41). An interesting aspect of these practices was that, those who had undergone the painful rites taunted those who were yet to have them performed. The taunting challenged them to summon courage and go through the passages. Also see Arnold van Gennep, *The Rites of Passage* (London: Routledge, 2004).
[95] Bell, *Ritual Perspectives and Dimensions*, 53.

The criteria for determining young girls' maturity for marriage was based on their ability to effectively carry out domestic chores such as filling the house pots with drinking water every morning, cleaning the kitchen, cooking and clearing the farm.[96] In African societies today, the term emerging adults can be associated with educated young people who are struggling to acquire higher education to lay the foundation for a better future. The struggle to acquire higher education comes with several challenges. In view of emerging adults' challenges, this life period has become critical in practical theological reflection. This discussion uses emerging adults as theological subjects in exploring the theological inquiry.

Conclusion

This investigation is about rooting the Catholic faith in Tiv culture by means of inculturation. The central argument examines the relationship between faith and culture, narrowed to the worship experiences of emerging adults in institutions of higher education. The theological argument is located within the pre-colonial, colonial and post-colonial Tiv society. In exploring ways of solving the problem of the tension between faith and culture, three praxis-oriented methods that are interrelated are appropriate for use.

Catholicism cannot take root in a culture if it fails to establish contact with the culture. In this regard, the Catholic faith can take root in Tiv culture when it effectively dialogues with Tiv culture. How to achieve the overall goal is shown in subsequent chapters. The next chapter discusses the encounter of the Catholic faith with Tiv culture.

---

[96] See East, trans., *Akiga's Story: The Tiv Tribe as Seen by One of Its members*, 309.

2

ENCOUNTER OF CATHOLICISM
WITH TIV CULTURE

T he Catholic faith came into an encounter with Tiv culture in 1930. But one cannot talk of this encounter without identifying the role of Africa in the development of the Catholic faith before the faith came to Tivland. Africa is part of the origins of Catholicism. For Africans to say that Christianity or Catholicism is a western religion is to ignore the role Africa played in the development of the Catholic faith. The encounter of Catholicism with Africa took place in three phases.

Phases of the Encounter

First Phase: Apostolic Times

In ancient times, and during the time of Jesus, Egypt was very strategic. Israel, Egypt, and the then known world were inextricably tied together. In the Old Testament, Egypt was seen as a land of abundance (Genesis 41:47-49). The New Testament refers to it as a land of security and protection. God used Egypt to preserve the life of the infant Jesus (Matthew 2:13-15).

Also, Catholicism is connected with Africa, as th debate about Simon of Cyrene who was compelled to carry Jesus' cross shows. One argument about the debate is whether Simon was a Jew living in Cyrene (modern Tripoli in Libya). It is not clear whether he was an African by birth or habitat. He is however depicted as the true disciple who carries the cross and follows after Jesus, a precept that Jesus repeatedly emphasized in his teaching.

Drawing from these examples, Catholicism cannot be said to be "a colonial leftover." The faith was certainly in Africa before it reached other parts of the world.[1] Missionaries were instrumental in taking it to other parts of Africa. From the earliest beginnings, Africa had a glorious experience of Catholicism. In the development of Catholic theology too, Africa played a leading role.

Catholicism was associated with the churches of Africa whose origin goes back to the times of the Apostles and is traditionally associated with the name and teaching of Mark the Evangelist. From the second to the fourth centuries, Christian life in the North of Africa was most vigorous, and it had a leading place in theological study and literary production. Renowned personages like Origen, Saint Athanasius, and Saint Cyril, leaders of the Alexandrian school, were in the forefront of developing the theology of the church. At the other end of the North African coastline were Tertullian, Saint Cyprian and above all Saint Augustine.[2]

Even though the church flourished for several centuries, the passive contact between the church of North Africa and the Berber world and Kabyle culture rendered the faith vulnerable, and it eventually disappeared almost completely, leaving behind only elements of indigenous Coptic Christians.[3]

The story of the split of faith was also true of Japan that experienced a lack of sufficient or sustained contact. The missionaries never achieved the linguistic ability to bring about a genuine contact. In such a situation, Catholicism may be allowed into a culture, and even be tolerated; but it never becomes part of the culture.[4] Missionary activity in Japan began in the sixteenth century coinciding with the second phase of Christian missionary penetration of Africa.

---

[1] Laurenti Magesa, *Anatomy of Inculturation: Transforming the Church in Africa* (Maryknoll: Orbis, 2004), 110.

[2] John Paul II, *Ecclesia in Africa* [Post-Synodal Apostolic Exhortation], sec. 31, http://www.vatican.va/holy_father/john_paul_ii/apost_exhortations/documents/hf_jp-ii_exh_14091995_ecclesia-in-africa_en.html.

[3] Augustine Ogar, "Inculturation of African Traditional Reconciliatory Values," *Abuja Journal of Philosophy and Theology* 2(2012): 52.

[4] See Schreiter, *Constructing Local Theologies,* 155.

Second Phase:
Early Modern Portuguese Explorations

The second phase of Christianity took place in the fifteenth and sixteenth centuries during the exploration of the African coast by the Portuguese that was soon accompanied by the evangelization of the regions of Sub-Saharan Africa. That endeavor included the regions of present-day Benin, São Tomé, Angola, Mozambique and Madagascar. During this time, moved by the Holy Spirit, the great King of the Congo, Nzinga-a-Nkuwu, asked for missionaries to proclaim the Gospel in his land.[5]

The Tiv are said to be connected with the Congo. Scholars have not agreed on the original home of the Tiv. Some argue that Tiv are of Bantu stock and may have migrated from some part of central Africa. Though it may be is difficult to associate the Tiv with a particular tribe or nation in central Africa, a thesis basing its argument on a 67-word list suggests that the words are of Congo origin. The word list shows a similarity between Tiv language, and the language of the Bantu Nyaza found in the present-day Malawi.[6] Scholars however agree that the Tiv may have migrated from their original home and settled around the *Swem* area in the southern part of the Cameroon before proceeding to their present location in the Benue area.

Third Phase:
Beginning in Nineteenth Century

The third phase of Africa's systematic evangelization began in the nineteenth century, a period marked by an extraordinary effort organized by the great apostles and promoters of the African mission. It was a period of rapid growth. Since then, Africans have responded with great generosity to Christ's call. In recent decades many African countries have celebrated the first centenary of the beginning of their evangelization.

---

[5] John Paul II, *Ecclesia in Africa,* Sec. 32.
[6] Shagbaor F. Wegh, *Between Continuity and Change: The Tiv Concept of Tradition and Modernity* (Enugu: Snaap Press, 2003), 36-38.

Indeed, the growth of the Church in Africa over the last hundred years is a marvelous work of divine grace. The growth of the church in Africa is manifested in the list of Saints that Africa has given to the Church. These include, Blessed Clementine Anwarite, Virgin and Martyr of Zaire, Blessed Victoria Rasoamanarivo of Madagascar, Blessed Josephine Bakhita, and Blessed Isidore Bakanja, Martyr of Zaire.[7]

Tiv people share in this glorious history as Father Cyprian Michael Iwene Tansi, a Nigerian was proclaimed "Blessed" in the very land where he preached the Good News of salvation. He is a prime example of the fruits of holiness which have grown and matured in the Church in Nigeria since the Gospel was first preached in Nigeria.[8] In the three phases of the missionary enterprise in Africa, the primary goal was to respond to the mandate to make disciples of all nations as commissioned by Jesus (Matthew 28:19).

Tiv people said to be connected with the Congo[9] were also introduced to the Catholic faith during the third phase of missionary enterprise in Africa. The early missionaries communicated the salvation won by Jesus Christ to the Tiv. Their conversion to Catholicism did not introduce them to a new God unrelated to their African traditions, but to one who brings to fulfillment the highest religious and cultural aspirations of the African heritage.[10] Their existing primal religious systems such as their belief in God made it easy for them to accommodate the new faith manifesting itself in the growth of the population of Catholics.

---

[7] John Paul II, *Ecclesia in Africa*, secs. 33 and 34.

[8] See John Paul II, "Homily at the Mass for the Beatification of Father Cyprian Tansi," secs. 2 and 4,

http://www.vatican.va/holy_father/john_paul_ii/travels/documents/hf_jp-ii_hom_22031998_nigeria-beatification_en.html. Also see Akpenpuun Dzurgba, *On the Tiv of Central Nigeria: A Cultural Perspective* (Ibadan: John Archers, 2007), 26. The third phase of missionary work in Africa coincided with the migration of the Tiv to their present location in the Benue trough.

[9] See Wegh, *Between Continuity and Change,* 146.

[10] Kwame Bediako, *Jesus in Africa: The Christian Gospel in African History and Experience* (Glasgow: Regnum, 2004), 21.

As of 2013, the population of Catholics in Tivland was estimated at 2,032,829.[11] This shows that the Tiv have accepted the new religion that infiltrated their world. Out of this figure, Makurdi diocese has a total of 978,188. The figure representing the population of Catholics in Makurdi diocese is a contentious issue among some Tiv priests. They argue that the creation of the two dioceses out of Makurdi has drastically reduced the size of the present Makurdi diocese. The Diocese of Gboko has more parishes, educational and health institutions, and therefore the population of Catholics should be more. This argument can be sustained if a census of the three dioceses is conducted.

Tivland is made up of three dioceses located within fourteen Local Government Areas. Nigeria operates a three-tier system of administration, the federal, state, and local governments. A local Government is a third-tier level of administration at the grassroots level. It focuses on the development of local communities.

For several years, the Diocese of Makurdi covered a vast expanse of land. When Oturkpo and Lafia Dioceses were created in 1995 and 2001 respectively, its territorial scope was limited to the Tiv area. On December 29, 2012, Gboko and Katsina-Ala dioceses were further carved out by Pope Benedict XVI.

Population figures confirm the vitality of the church in Tivland, but the degree to which Catholicism has taken root in Tiv culture is the main subject of this discussion. Contemporary discussion about Catholicism in Africa and Tiv society in particular is gradually taking a new direction. It is shifting from membership drive, and the much discussed "clash of the Catholic faith with African cultures,"

---

[11] The total population of Tiv people is over 5,000,000. The population of Catholics in the present Makurdi Diocese is 978,188. See Athanasius A. Usuh, "A Brief History of Makurdi Diocese," accessed March 17, 2014, http://makurdidiocese.com/about_us.php. Gboko Diocese has a Catholic population of 708,641. See William Avenya, "Diocese of Gboko," accessed March 17, 2014, http://www.dioceseofgboko.org/about-us/. The population of Catholics in Katsina-Ala Diocese is 346,000. See Peter Iornzuul Adoboh, "Diocese of Katsina-Ala," accessed March 17, 2014, http://www.catholic-hierarchy.org/diocese/dkats.html.

to exploring ways of contextualizing the faith in particular cultures. Tiv society was a fertile environment for contextualization.

Before the advent of Christianity, the Tiv were already believers. They recognized and believed in *Aondo* (God).[12] *Aondo* is the one to whom there can be no comparison or representation.[13] The Christian missionaries acknowledged that Tiv people had already known God. In their talk about God, the missionaries retained the name *Aondo* and filled it with Christian meaning.[14]

They started work among the Tiv by establishing schools, health care facilities, and other social services. These were introduced prior to government engagement in social services.[15] Medical and educational institutions to a large degree replaced the traditional way of doing things: Education was informal, healing and religious practices were all traditional. Tiv religion, with basic central beliefs, is the traditional way of worship by the Tiv people. But Catholicism failed to dialogue adequately with these aspects of Tiv culture because of the tension that existed between the two religions.

The issue of the clash of cultures is as old as Christianity. In the first century of Christianity, tensions between faith and cultures arose when Paul confronted the Judaizers over the issue of Hellenistic converts. The Council of Jerusalem mediated on the issue and resolved that gentiles did not have to be Jews before they could be Christians (Acts 15).

Paul's cross-cultural missionary enterprise left several examples to be emulated for effective pastoral ministry. In his mission to the gentiles, Paul encountered the Athenians who erected an altar for the "unknown god." While introducing the Athenians to the God of the Christians, he began by appreciating their recognition of God symbolized in the altar of the unknown God. Paul argued that the unknown god to whom the altar was dedicated had not only been

---

[12] James Shagba Moti, *The Early Jerusalem Christian Community: A Biblical Model for Basic Ecclesial Communities* (Rome: Urbaniana University Press, 1983), 90.

[13] Moti, *The Early Jerusalem Christian Community*, 91.

[14] Moti, *The Early Jerusalem Christian Community*, 90.

[15] Shagbaor F. Wegh, *Marriage, Family and The Church in Tiv* (Decon Computer Services, 1994), 87. Also see Moti, *The Early Jerusalem Christian Community*, 115.

revealed through nature and human reason, but also in the unique revelation of Jesus Christ.[16]

By identifying the altar of the unknown god as adumbrating the God revealed in Jesus Christ, Paul introduced a new strategy in missionary work involving other cultures. Paul's strategy would have been helpful in the context of the Tiv who were encountering the Christian message for the first time.

The encounter of Catholicism with Tiv culture rather undermined some Tiv cultural practices. Tiv elders saw the Christian message contradicting the time-honored traditions of Tiv culture as it disregarded the tribal taboos, sacrifices and rituals. For Tiv elders, disregard for Tiv culture accounts for why the present generation of Tiv is not rooted in Tiv culture.[17] Theology needs to identify aspects of Tiv culture that can engage Catholicism in a reciprocal dialogue. This requires paying particular attention to the dialogue between faith and culture.

The dialogue of faith and culture is important in making Tiv people truly Catholic and truly Tiv. The acceptance of the Catholic faith by the Tiv led to the erosion of some cultural practices, making the present generation of Tiv people to lack cultural grounding. In addition, Catholicism is yet to take concrete root in Tiv culture even though many Tiv families are Catholics. The older generation of Tiv people who live in rural communities cannot be said to have been born into a Christian culture, embedded completely in Catholic values because Catholicism came to Tivland in 1930.[18] Typically, adults and youth were converts to the Catholic faith.[19]

---

[16] Elaine Graham, Heather Walton, and Frances Ward, *Theological Reflection: Methods* (London: SCM, 2005), 141.

[17] See Moti, *The Early Jerusalem Christian Community*, 116.

[18] See Clement Mato, "The Catholic Church in Tivland," in *Catholic Diocese of Makurdi at 50: A Celebration of Service to Humanity*, ed. Shagbaor F. Wegh (Makurdi: Selfers Academic Press, 2010),39

[19] See Moti, *The Early Jerusalem Christian Community*, 108. The church in Tivland continues to receive converts to the faith through the Rites of Christian Initiation of Adults (RCIA). This rite prepares people in stages for a period of three years before they are baptized.

The dialogue between faith and culture was initiated when indigenous priests started work among the Tiv. They communicated the Christian message to the catechumens in part through analogies.[20] The analogy of Israel as a tribe led by Abraham, an elder, was used to evoke sharper understanding, because in the experiences of the people, the tribal community under the custodianship of elders was already familiar.[21] This approach easily brought faith and culture in dialogue.

Paul VI's 1967 letter to the bishops of Africa, *Africae Terrarum*, recognizes the link between faith and culture. The letter was a landmark in the development of African theology. The supreme pontiff identifies a number of positive values in African cultures (pervasive concept of God, concern for human dignity, profound sense of the family) that may form the basis of an African theology that would be both genuinely African and authentically Catholic.[22] The missionaries were not grounded in the values and practices of African cultures even though some of the practices were profound and resonated with Catholicism.

Encountering
a Familiar Terrain

Pre-colonial Tiv cultural practices resonated with Catholicism in significant ways. However, the experience of colonialism, cross-cultural contact, and other factors have changed Tiv society.

Such contact is possible as a result of globalization. Globalization connotes the practice of everyday life that is becoming standardized around the world. Factors that have contributed to globalization include colonialism, increasingly sophisticated communications and

---

[20] Moti, *The Early Jerusalem Christian Community*, 120.

[21] Moti, *The Early Jerusalem Christian Community*, 120. Also see Shagbaor F. Wegh, "The Emergence of the Catholic Diocese of Makurd," in *Catholic Diocese of Makurdi at 50: A Celebration of Service to Humanity*, ed.Shagbaor F. Wegh (Makurdi: Selfers Academic Press, 2010),32-33. The first indigenous priest was ordained in 1970. Seven others were ordained the following year. They were popularly called the seven sons of Tiv. They constituted the nucleus of the indigenous church. They were also a good omen and symbol of hope for the Tiv nation.

[22]Schreiter, "Faith and Cultures, 750.

transportation technologies and services, and mass migration and movement of peoples.[23] Globalization affects standards of living, as well as cultures and values. These factors are responsible for the cultural changes that have occurred or are occurring in Tiv society.

Contextual theology recognizes the culture of a particular nation or region, and social change that occurs in that culture, due both to technological advances on the one hand, and struggles for justice and liberation on the other. [24] A practical theology of emerging adults takes the context of Tiv society seriously, and the social change taking place in that culture. Other factors responsible for this change include trade, colonialism, Christianity, Islam, Western education, medicine, mass media, and politics.

Traditional Tiv society cherished cultural values that promoted egalitarianism. However, this does not mean that there were no cultural deviants in the practice of those cultural values. Some members certainly did not subscribe to the acceptable practices. Through contact with other cultures, Tiv society is experiencing new ways of living out their values. These factors have affected various aspects of Tiv life, including the edifying practice of community life. Community life was a practice that emphasized among other things, the community's unity and cohesion, and negated the pursuit of individual goals.[25]

---

[23] See the work of John Reader, *Reconstructing Practical Theology: The Impact of Globalization* (Hamsphire: Ashgate, 2008). Intensive colonial engagement in Tivland began in 1900. The British colonizers introduced new ways of living to replace the traditional life-styles of the native people. For instance, money was introduced in the economy, and traditional practices like exchange marriage were abolished. At present, the world has become a global village, and movement to other parts of the world is easier. The Tiv no longer trek long distances on bad roads as was the case. See Akpenpuun Dzurgba, *On the Tiv of Central Nigeria: A Cultural Perspective* (Ibadan: John Archers, 2007), 16. Modern means of communication too have great influences on culture. These factors to a large extent affect Tiv society.

[24] Change as understood here builds on the work of Stephen Bevans, *Models of Contextual Theology* (New York: Orbis Books, 2002. Akpenpuun Dzurgba, *On the Tiv of Central Nigeria*, 10, for instance says, community life was expressed in different ways, but how that value is expressed among emerging adults in the contemporary Tiv society is one of the areas to explore for the rooting of Catholicism in Tiv culture.

[25] Dzurgba, *On the Tiv of Central Nigeria*, 129.

This practice was profound in the same way Christians uphold the principle of edification that encourages Christians to minister to both the material and spiritual needs of those in fellowship. Edification emphasizes mutuality or a fundamental sense of oneness that binds Christians together encompassing relational dimensions of sympathy, compassion, and empathy.[26] These dimensions are crucial in consolidating communal life among members.

In the past, Tiv society practiced community life, which manifested itself in solidarity, interdependence, and village cohesion. This was demonstrated in the way the Tiv built their compounds. In traditional societies, family members comprising the old, young people of various age-grades, and children lived together in large compounds. Age-grades or age-sets were common in traditional Tiv societies. These were group formations of people that mobilized themselves for community work and carried out social activities together. They also enhanced relations among themselves.

A typical polygamous Tiv family lived in a cluster of round huts with thatch roofs to accommodate all, including extended family members.[27] The *Ate* (common sitting area), constructed at the center of the compound was a symbol of unity and communality.[28] Visitors were received in the *Ate,* and family members shared a common meal, discussed family issues, and solved problems that affected the family. Communality offered a great opportunity for immediate and extended family members to come together and work as a community.

The unity demonstrated in eating together was also extended to farm work symbolized by the practice of *hyumbe* (exchange labor). Through *hyumbe,* those who came from the same family or a conflation of different families did farm work together, offering their labor through a system of exchange. It was a rotational peasant system very common in rural agrarian areas guided by the principle of

---

[26] Stanley J. Grenz, *Theology for the Community of God* (Nashville: Broadman & Holman, 1994), 645.

[27] See Wegh, *Between Continuity and Change,* 98.

[28] Andrew Philips Adega, "Ate: (Living Room) As the Centre of Unity in Tiv Compounds," *Journal of African Religion and Culture* 1 (December 2010): 7.

equity "if you work for me today, I will work for you tomorrow." In practice, community life brought different people together under one course in the same way the Eucharist brings different people together. Indeed, the Eucharist is an archetypal model of community.[29]

A strong feature of community was the practice of eating together. As children grew up in these contexts, they imbibed the values of eating together and other virtues that enhanced community life. However, the continuous interaction of Tiv society with other cultures has led to increasing changes through diffusion and adaptation of new ideas, beliefs, knowledge, skills, tools, goods and services.[30] These changes tend to promote individualistic values among young people including, emerging adults who leave the rural areas in large numbers to urban centers for higher education and public sector employment.

The movement of young people to urban centers is leading to the decline of community life. This is apparent in the symbolic sayings of emerging adults. For example, the saying *hanma or nana ma atemba a ngo u nan* (everyone should suck his or her mother's breasts) symbolically encourages individualistic living. This saying contradicts Catholic principles of interdependency, solidarity, and sharing.[31] The principle of solidarity recognizes that human beings are

---

[29] See Tracy, *The Analogical Imagination*. The author discusses the Christian classic, the event of Jesus Christ mediated through particular forms and through particular traditions. He recognizes that the interpretation of symbols must resonate with the criteria of adequacy (interpretation must resonate with human experience), criteria of appropriateness (interpretation must accurately represent the tradition of which it speaks), and the criteria of internal coherence (interpretation must resonate with the truth or meaningfulness of the tradition).

[30] Dzurgba, *On the Tiv of Central Nigeria,* 9.

[31] See Pontifical Council for Justice and Peace, *Compendium of the Social Doctrine of the Catholic Church* (Washington: United States Conference of Catholic Bishops, 2005), 81 and 84. The following papal documents discuss the concepts of subsidiarity and solidarity as they apply to human beings.

Ioannes Paulus II, [*Sollicitudo Rei social-*
*is,*http://www.vatican.va/holy_father/john_paul_ii/encyclicals/documents/hf_jp-ii_enc_30121987_sollicitudo-rei-socialis_en.html; John Paul II, *Centesimus Annus,*http://www.vatican.va/holy_father/john_paul_ii/encyclicals/documents/hf_jp-ii_enc_01051991_centesimus-annus_en.html;John Paul II, Post-Synodal Apostolic

connected with one another. It also upholds the relationships of interdependence between individuals and peoples.

Subsidiarity is understood as the sum relationships between individuals and intermediate social groupings. Subsidiarity stresses that it is gravely wrong to take from individuals what they accomplish by their own initiative and industry and give to the community. It is also an injustice and at the same time a grave evil and disturbance of right order to assign to a greater and higher association what lesser and subordinate organizations can do. The analogical relationship between community life, and the principles of interdependence, solidarity, and sharing reveals in a profound way the truth that community life in Tiv culture significantly resonates with those Catholic values and principles.

How can Catholicism take root in Tiv culture now witnessing significant changes and the movement of young people from the rural areas? This can be done by concentrating on experiences of emerging adults who have moved to institutions of higher education by retrieving the value of community life.

Coming together as community on campus will help to integrate young people both in cultural values, and the Catholic faith. This synthesis will equip them to return to their local communities, and effectively minister as community theologians. This discussion builds connections between Catholic theology and Tiv culture that is marked by the contemporary socio-historical dynamism.[32] These dynamisms require contextual approaches to evangelization recognizing that, at the initial encounter of the Catholic faith with Tiv culture, missionaries used the translation model of evangelization.

Exhortation *Ecclesia in America*on the Encounter with the Living Jesus Christ: The Way to Conversion, Communion and Solidarity in America, http://www.vatican.va/holy_father/john_paul_ii/apost_exhortations/documents/hf_jp -ii_exh_22011999_ecclesia-in-america_en.html; Paul VI, *Populorum Progressio* [The Development of Peoples], sec 7, http://www.vatican.va/holy_father/paul_vi/encyclicals/documents/hf_p-vi_enc_26031967_populorum_en.html; Pius XI, *Quadragesimo Anno* [on Reconstruction of the Social Order], http://www.vatican.va/holy_father/pius_xi/encyclicals/documents/hf_p-xi_enc_19310515_quadragesimo-anno_en.html.
[32] Jean-Marc Éla, *My Faith as an African* (Maryknoll: Orbis, 1993), 170

Two Models of Evangelization

Translation Model

Most foreign missionaries caught up in a new pastoral situation adopt the translation model as the first approach to evangelization. [33] This model frees the Christian message from its previous cultural accretions and translates it into a new situation without losing the essence of the message.

This model was used by the missionaries who worked in Tivland. Through this model, they translated Catholic concepts into Tiv language. The "natures" of Christ and other similar words for example, were and are still difficult concepts to explain to Tiv Catholics. For example, grace is rendered in Tiv as g*racia or gratia;* the word sacrament translated as *Sacramentu;* nature was rendered *natura;* while the word Trinity simply returned as *Triniti,* and Christmas as *Kirimishi.*

The more incomprehensible is that, Holy Order was translated as *Cighian Ordoo.*[34] In spoken Tiv language, *Cighian Ordoo* carries a different meaning. It conveys the meaning that a consecrated person is a good person.

Thus. as a result of the non-existence of appropriate words to capture the concepts in Tiv, the missionaries resorted to the use of improvised terms. That shows the deficiency of the translation model apparent in limit expression. However, one recognizes that "[t]ranslation models are generally the first kinds of models to be used in pastoral settings, because pastoral urgency demands some

---

[33] Robert J. Schreiter, *Constructing Local Theologies,* 6. Schreiter sees the translation model as the first approach to use in a pastoral situation. Stephen B. Bevans, *Models of Contextual Theology: Faith and Cultures* (Maryknoll: Orbis Books, 2010), 37, building on the work of Schreiter, expands the discussion to include, translation, anthropological, praxis, synthetic, transcendental, and countercultural models as contextual models.

[34] See Daniel Ude Asue, "Remodeling Catechesis in Post Vatican II African Church," *Asian Horizons* 6, no. 3 (September 2012):529. These concepts feature prominently in *The Simple Tiv Catechism of Christian Doctrine* (Enugu: Eastern Nigeria Printing Corporation, 1962), and other religious literature and discourses.

kind of adaptation to local circumstances in ritual, in catechesis, and in the rendering of significant texts into local languages."[35]

The missionaries lacked a full understanding of the language, way of life, and cultural practices of Tiv people. It was a difficult task for them to find equivalent concepts in Tiv language as well as symbols in Tiv culture that could adequately explain great theological categories. This shows their limitations in cultural expressions particularly of the language, traditions, arts, symbols, and images of Tiv people.

Their insufficient grasp of the language in part, accounts for the reason why Catholicism could not go deeper into the culture of the people from its earliest encounter. The gospel can only be relevant to a people when it is able to speak to the life and thoughts of the people in languages and images that are comprehensible.[36] In this regard, the use of symbols is an important element in the dialogue between faith and culture.

The centrality of symbols in contextual theology makes hermeneutics an important tool.[37] The recognition and use of cultural symbols is a contextual way of doing theology.

Contextual Model

Cultures are dynamic. The encounter of the Catholic faith with Tiv culture has brought further changes. The goal of such changes is to transform Tiv culture. Contextual models are the most appropriate approaches in this regard. Such models recognize changes in the context.

For example, Liberation theology as a contextual model has been effective in addressing the conflictual situation in Latin America, conscientizing the marginalized to become artisans of their desti-

---

[35] Schreiter, *Constructing Local Theologies*, 7.

[36] Zablon Nthamburi, "Making the Gospel Relevant Within the African Context and Culture," *AFER* 25, no. 3 (1983): 163.

[37] See Tracy, *The Analogical Imagination*. Tracy's hermeneutical approach is a valuable tool in interpreting Tiv symbols.

ny.[38] Liberation approaches have generally been helpful in the theological enterprise.[39]

Similarly, feminist perspectives address issues of women liberation. Chopp discusses feminism from the position of marginality and argues for emancipatory transformation of feminist language and theology. Ross addresses women's ambiguity. She observes that despite the contribution of Catholic women to sacramental theology, their role in ministry is still ambiguous as it lacks clarity. A woman can act as a parish administrator, conduct communion service, visit and anoint the sick, but cannot administer the sacraments. Gebara's work focuses on the evil women do, the evil they suffer, and the redemptive experiences of God and salvation.[40]

Even in the contemporary Tiv society, such approaches can address the challenges confronted by emerging adult males, as well as address the challenges peculiar to females. In Tiv culture, young women are coerced into premature marriage, denied the right to formal education, and subjected to other forms of marginalization and abuse, including female circumcision.[41] Contextual models are effective in transforming situations encountered by Catholicism.

---

[38] See Gustavo Gutiérrez, *A Theology of Liberation* (New York: Orbis, 2010), 9, who says theology reflects upon pastoral activity." Joe Holland and Peter Henriot, *Social Analysis: Linking Faith and Justice* (New York: Orbis, 1983), join the conversation by saying theological reflection produces pastoral action. As a contextual theology that reflects on the experiences of educated Tiv emerging adult Catholics, the goal is to produce pastoral actions capable of contextualizing Catholicism in Tiv culture and ultimately shaping Tiv society.

[39] See liberation approaches by James H. Cone, *God of the Oppressed* (MaryKnoll: Orbis, 1997), written from the perspective of African American religion and culture, and their experiences of struggle and survival. James H. Cone, *The Cross and the Lynching Tree* (Maryknoll: Orbis, 2011). The event of the crucifixion of Jesus is played out again in the experiences of African Americans whose cross is the lynching tree.

[40] See the following liberation approaches from the perspective of women. Rebecca Chopp, *The Power to Speak: Feminism, Language, God* (Oregon: Wipf and Stock, 2002). Susan A. Ross, *Extravagant Affections: A Feminist Sacramental Theology* (New York: Continuum, 1998), 92. Ivone Gebara, *Out of the Depths: Women's Experience of Evil and Salvation,* trans. Ann Patrick Ware(Minneapolis: Fortress Press, 2002).

[41] Eugene T. Aliegba, "Violence Against Women: Its nature and Manifestations," in *Perspectives on Violence Against Women in Nigeria,* ed., Charity Angya (Makurdi: Aboki, 2005), 114.

This book uses contextual models that consider the experiences of emerging adult Catholics in institutions of higher education. Catholicism has made strong contact with universities or colleges in Tivland with a strong Catholic ministerial presence in all institutions of higher education in Tivland. Higher education students in Nigeria go through experiences of all kinds. This is affecting the training of young people who can impact both the church and Tiv society.

Students experience endless years of education due to incessant strikes by faculty and staff. Many students are unable to pay their tuition, which leads to fear of a bleak future. Others are victims of nocturnal activities of secret cult members that have led to the torture and murder of some on campus, maiming and killing of rival cult members and elimination of real and perceived enemies.[42] Some drop out of school, and are left with no focus in life. Generally, university students in Nigeria are confronted by personal challenges, including often overwhelming challenges of sustenance.

Those who fail to gain admission into institutions of higher education and cannot find jobs roam the streets unemployed. They are effectively excluded from mainstream society, unable to achieve self-reliance. Some turn to escapism through drugs and alcohol.

The youth in Nigeria comprise 85 million people or 68% of the population. Of these, two million are educated, having gained admission into institutions of higher education. The other 83 million are on the farms, streets in crime, and anti-social activities. They fall prey to drugs, prostitution, and political thuggery or join rebel groups.[43] Others attempt to remake themselves in other anonymous urban settings.

---

[42] See abstract of paper by Abdulrazaq Kilani, "The Changing Faces of the Terror of Cultism in Nigerian Society: An Islamic Perspective," *Comparative Islamic Studies* (2010), doi:10.1558/cis.v4il-2.97.

[43] Paul Iyorpuu Unongo, "The Imperative of Youth Leadership Development in the Current Millennium," a lecture delivered to the Community of Tiv Students (CTS) and the community of the Benue State University, Makurdi, October 16th 2010, 13 and 21. The author uses "youth" as a term to refer to people between ages 6 and 24. The percentage of educated youth has increased since then.

In areas of political and social fragility, some join rebel groups or armed militant gangs. Many young Nigerians have become involved in ethnic militia and other forms of militancy because these promise a more secure means of employment than life on the streets.[44] The phenomenon of ethnic militia is true of the Tiv particularly when their security is threatened by external aggressors. Young people voluntarily offer to defend their clannish territory in times of communal clashes. These factors are denying the Tiv church of sound community theologians.

Contextual models can address unpleasant situations by initiating a dialogue with faith and culture. This dialogue is helpful in transforming the present praxis of young people to a life of community living that leads to the emergence of community theologians. The task of the community theologians to root Catholicism in Tiv culture includes the missiological and ecclesiological dimensions of ministry. It is missiological because in interpreting the faith to others, they are involved in the mission of the church by propagating the good news. It is ecclesiological as the emphasis on community life strengthens the understanding of the church as community.

Community begins when emerging adults come together for worship. Catholicism needs to vigorously pursue such a community on campus to promote dialogue with faith and culture. A religious community that promotes the relationship of faith and culture helps Catholicism to speak in the language and symbols of the Tiv. Such communities take the worship experiences of emerging adults in higher education contexts seriously. What are their worship experiences? What does culture say to those experiences? These questions can also be addressed in the reverse order: What are their experiences of culture? What does the Catholic faith say to those experiences?

---

[44] Venatus Kakwagh, and Agnes Ikwuba, "Youth Unemployment in Nigeria: Causes and Related Issues," *Canadian Social Science* 6, no. 4 (2010): 231, http://proxy.stu.edu/docview/756031488/fulltextPDF/1370F6DfE94569D6B2C/1?accountid=14129.
Also see Clement T. Iorliam, "Recreating Community Life Among Young People in Tiv Society, Nigeria: "The New Heavens and the New Earth" (Is 65:17-25)," *International Journal of African Catholicism* 3, no. 2 (Summer, 2012): 9, http://www.saintleo.edu/media/411882/young_people_in_nigeria_final.pdf.

Pursuing these questions as a community project helps to explore faith and culture in a way that leads to the construction and expression of a local theology in Tiv context. The greatest achievement is that it produces community theologians who are grounded in both the Catholic faith, and Tiv culture, and can most effectively articulate the faith. To be effective, community theologians need to understand Tiv culture and the various permutations that have taken place since its contact with colonial authorities and Christian missionaries.

Conclusion

In the encounter of Catholicism with Tiv culture, the special role of Africa as part of the origins of Catholicism has been identified. The Catholic faith did not take root in some parts of the world because it ignored the relationship of faith and culture. The encounter of the Catholic faith with Tiv culture brought tension of a dialectical relationship. The faith can take root in Tiv culture when it effectively dialogues with Tiv culture recognizing that Tiv society has practices that resonate with Catholicism.

Today, the conflict young men and women are experiencing requires pastoral agents to use contextual approaches for evangelization. Given a healthy environment, emerging adults can be effective pastoral agents just as young people were effective during the pre-colonial and colonial era. The next chapter discusses the ritual practices of young people in the past as a background to explore present day emerging adults.

3

YOUNG PEOPLE IN
PRE-COLONIAL & COLONIAL TIV CULTURE

T his chapter reviews Tiv life during the pre-colonial and colonial periods, and especially in terms of youth. It serves as a prelude to examining in the next chapter the involvement of young
people in educational and religious institutions, and the religious
experiences of emerging adults in the contemporary Tiv society.

Pre-colonial and colonial Tiv society had different patterns of of life
that relate to ritual practices. Young people were deeply involved in
those practices at various levels. The structure of Tiv society before
colonial rule was one of communality. Its socio-political life was
cohesive. Farming was easily carried out as people formed associations that offered exchange labor.

The success of everyone was guided by the philosophy of corporate
existence among Tiv people. "I am, because we are; and since we
are therefore I am." It defined to a large degree the interconnected-
ness of the Tiv in the social, political, religious, and economic institutions of Tiv society.[1]

Tiv religion does not separate religion from public life. The Tiv take
their religion to social and political gatherings, to the farm, and to
their economic engagements.

---

[1] See Simeon Tsetim Iber, *The Principle of Subsidiarity in Catholic Social Thought: Implications for Social Justice and Civil Society in Nigeria* (New York: Peter Lang, 2010), 28.

This chapter also makes us recall that the earliest form of Christian community life was identified with the Jerusalem community (Acts 2:42-47). Drawing from the archetypal model of communality practiced by the early Christian community in Jerusalem, subsequent Christian movements in the early church were also known for the practice of *theosis* and community.[2] *Theosis* involves the deification and transformation of human nature and existence such that "deified" human beings participate and share a union with God and divine attributes. It came to be associated with deified members of a Christian community, who undertook a collective activity.

Precolonial Tiv Society as Egalitarian & Communitarian

Tiv society in central Nigeria had a simple, egalitarian, political and social organization during the pre-colonial period before 1854 This was also true of most African societies in pre-colonial days, as Africans strongly upheld egalitarian principles. Before the rise of the modern state, extended family system and the clan system were the vehicles through which the needs of every member were taken care of by the whole community, resulting in non-cases of extreme poverty or excessive wealth in the hands of a few.[3]

Acephalous Familial Communities

The Tiv lived in acephalous communities with no traditional chiefs, let alone kings. They lived in compounds with an average of ten

---

[2] See Lewis Ayres, "Deification and the Dynamics of Nicene Theology: The Contribution of Gregory of Nyssa," *St Vladimir's Theological Quarterly* 49, no. 4 (2005):375- 394. *Theosis* is a doctrine that was propounded by the Church Fathers such as Gregory of Nyssa. Also See, Rita Nakashima Brock and Rebecca Ann Parker, *Saving Paradise: How Christianity Traded Love of This World for Crucifixion and Empire* (Boston: Beacon Press, 2008), 178. *Theosis* was a collective activity of the whole church community embodied in love, which is always a social reality and never an individual achievement. As a group process, individual commitment and effort were required. The movements attracted slaves, peasants, women, the disaffected and other ordinary people. The church expected them to share their goods in common so that every member of the community would have a decent life.
[3] Victor Zinkuratire, "Isaiah 1-39: Life Context of the Interpretation," in *The Global Bible Commentary*, ed. Daniel Patte (Nashville: Abington Press, 2004), 186.

people.[4] In African tradition generally, community consists of the family, household and the individual.[5] The family set-up includes both the immediate family and the extended family relations. The extended family made up of two or more brothers (in patrilocal societies) or two or more sisters (in matrilocal societies) set up families in one compound.[6] The individual exists for the community and community for the individual, sharing in the individual's joys and sorrows.[7] The autonomy of the individual was recognized insofar as he or she existed for the community, which was gerontocratic.

Tiv society was governed through *ijir tyo* (traditional council,) an egalitarian system without an elite class that took decisions on behalf of families in the community. In their formal meetings, the traditional council members, who were mainly elders representing their various communities arrived at decisions by consensus.[8] Typically, such gatherings were exclusively for elders, but the Tiv make allowance for responsible young people to participate and contribute to the discussion. Such responsible young people were recognized following the saying that *wanye ka nan ôô ave tsebelee yô nan ya kwagh vea mbaganden,* (a child who washes his or her hands clean can eat with elders).

This understanding corroborates the Akan people of Ghana who have an adage that says, 'when a child knows how to wash his/her hands s/he sits at table with the royal class. This implies that what determines maturity includes responsibility, independence, and cultural good sense. One who is a child (in terms of age) may be an

---

[4] Atel, *Dynamics of Tiv Religion and Culture,* 12.

[5] John S. Mbiti, *African Religions and Philosophy* (London: Heinemann, 1985), 106.

[6] See Iber, *The Principle of Subsidiarity in Catholic Social Thought*, 28. Today, the notion of extended family does not necessarily mean members must live together in one compound. Family members who share a consanguineous relationship but live in different places are still part of the extended family system.

[7] Iber, *The Principle of Subsidiarity in Catholic Social Thought,* 28.

[8] See Dominic V. Yuhe, "The Encounter of Tiv Religious and Moral Values with Catholicism in the Time of Secularization" (Ph.D dissertation, Pontifical St Thomas University, Rome, 1978), 85, and Wegh, *Between Continuity and Change,* 51.

adult (in terms of maturity) and an adult may still be a child (because of dependence on parents).[9]

Maturity was a major criterion of admitting a young person to participate in the council of elders' meeting. The *ijir tyo* governing system resonates with the Christian principle of equality as all members who participated in such meetings acted as equals. The *ijir tyo* system is also analogous to the collegial role of the apostles who took unanimous decisions after intensive deliberations (Acts 15:6-7).

Another important duty of the council of elders was to decide on other issues of common good such as setting up of local community markets and execution of projects through communal labor. The community responded to the call to construct wooden bridges at strategic locations across a stream, and the construction of road paths to link various compounds.[10] Young people were at the center of such community projects.

Cooperative Work

During the pre-colonial and early part of the colonial period, labor was a ritual practice organized on the basis of age grades or *kwav*.[11] At the age of 18 to 20, young men began to form associations of people in a common age group.[12] The phenomenon of *kwav* was typically a production-oriented device of Tiv society that emphasized the interdependence of group members. The *kwav* group was cohesive to the degree that individual members knew details about others, including details of who was older or younger.

The various age sets also knew quite a lot about their locality, and this knowledge greatly enhanced their level of cohesion. One outstanding feature of the group was that, it was repugnant to the ex-

---

[9] Emmanuel Y. Lartey, "Globalization, Youth and the Church: Views from Ghana" in *Youth Religion and Globalization: New Research in Practical Theology,* eds. Richard R. Osmer and Kenda Creasy Dean(New Brunswick U.S.A/London UK: Transaction Publishers, 2006), 63. The Akan people constitute 45% of the population of Ghana.
[10] Moti, *The Early Jerusalem Christian Community,* 100.
[11] Baver Dzeremo, *Colonialism and the Transformation of Authority in Central Tivland: 1912-1960* (Makurdi: Aboki, 2002), 83.
[12] Dzeremo, *Colonialism and the Transformation of Authority in Central Tivland,* 27.

istence of class among the Tiv, and negated individualism and exclusiveness. It promoted egalitarian principles.[13] These and other practices of young people constituted their *habitus*,[14] a system of operation in the pre-colonial and early part of the colonial period.

The overall goal of the age-sets was to help members carry out their activities successfully including their economic pursuit.[15] The group assisted individual members at different times on the farm, and in the construction of a new building. They also improved the community by constructing new roads to link one community to another. No remunerations were paid for the services they rendered. The beneficiary only supplied liquor and food. Labor activities were non-coercive because the purpose was to cultivate a sense of friendship that fosters unity among the people.[16]

The age grades phenomenon was only found among men. Women had an indirect association to the group by virtue of their husbands who were members. Members offered support to widows whose husbands were members by rebuilding their huts and cultivating their farms.[17] As the phenomenon of *kwav* has declined, few widows enjoy this privilege.

Cooperative Agriculture

In general, organized cooperative work greatly enhanced agricultural activities in Tivland. The divine command to cultivate and care for the earth (Genesis 2:15), offers a powerful incentive to cultivate the land. By this command, the human person has been given the mandate to co-create. The greatest resource of co-creating the

---

[13] Dzeremo, *Colonialism and the Transformation of Authority in Central Tivland*, 83.

[14] See Pierre Bourdieu, *Outline of a theory of Practice*, Trans. Richard Nice (Cambridge: University Press, 1999). The author discusses the summons to participate in collective work, repairing roads, digging drains, transporting flagstones, etc. (159). Division of labor was between sexes, ages, and occupations (163). The author discusses an entire system of schemes of perception, appreciation, and action as the dispositions that constitute *habitus*. Habitus brings order to customary social behavior by operating as the generative basis of structure, and objectively unified practices. Practices are products or habitus and they are seen as the right way of doing things.

[15] Dzeremo, *Colonialism and the Transformation of Authority in Central Tivland*, 28.

[16] Dzeremo, *Colonialism and the Transformation of Authority in Central Tivland*, 84.

[17] Dzeremo, *Colonialism and the Transformation of Authority in Central Tivland*, 28.

world at the disposal of the Tiv is the land. The Tiv do not conceive their land simply as a track of the earth on which they live. It is the land of their fathers. It is sacred land. It took them long distance trekking, suffering attacks from their neighbors before they finally acquired their land.

In precolonial Tiv society, agriculture as the mainstay of the economy followed a simple, but serial ritual practice. It involved ordinary economic activities (like planting and cultivating) that resulted to the accumulation of goods.[18] The basic unit of production was the household made up of several families.[19] Men, women, and young people had distinct roles in the cultivation of the land. Production was orderly, and it defined the various stages of the year into agricultural phases. The agricultural process followed a sequence of bush burning, bush clearing, cultivation, tilling, sowing, weeding, harvesting, threshing, and storing.[20] Older men and young people were responsible for clearing, cultivating, and tilling, while women typically did the sowing, weeding, harvesting, threshing, and storing.

In their practice of shifting cultivation, the Tiv cultivate a parcel of land and return to it after several years. The head of the home usually starts the farming process by selecting a piece of land from a vast area of farmland that had been left to fallow over the years. Young people did the clearing and tilling, and women sowed the crops. Bush burning was another way of clearing the land in preparation for farming. Most of all, it was a strategic avenue for hunting. The Tiv are not accustomed to the practice of animal husbandry. Some families practice extensive horticulture. A few raise animals. In this regard, hunting and fishing provided the opportunity to gain access to meat and fish.

Men, women, and young people were involved in hunting by typically coming behind the direction of the burning bush to hunt ani-

---

[18] Elochukwu E. Uzukwu, *Worship as Body Language: Introduction to Christian Worship an African Orientation* (Collegeville: The Liturgical Press, 1997), 224.

[19] Dzeremo, *Colonialism and the Transformation of Authority in Central Tivland,* 16.

[20] Dzeremo, *Colonialism and the Transformation of Authority in Central Tivland,* 16.

mals of all kinds.[21] The hunters either sold or consumed their game. Fishing was carried out by both men and women, but this was seen mostly as the role of women. Tiv are not traditional fishermen. From time to time, women set aside a day for fishing. It was a fishing festival that attracted all women within the locality.[22] Fishing supplemented meat that was a luxury lacking in most Tiv homes, and also it was an economic means of survival in a challenging poverty situation. This level of poverty made some people to explore different avenues for survival.

Impact of British Colonialism in Tivland

The contact of the Tiv with a British expedition that spanned between 1854[23] and 1860 brought significant changes to the sociopolitical structure of Tiv life[24] that affected the Tiv communitarian spirit. Some of the policies affected the family unit that hitherto

---

[21] See Dzeremo, *Colonialism and the Transformation of Authority in Central Tivland*, 17. This style of hunting was mostly for animals that burrow including rats, rabbits and grass-cutters. The hunters used sticks to level ash heaps as they walked through the ashes to identify burrow holes. Hoes were used in digging the holes, occasionally peeping through, and using sticks to access the extent of the holes. There was a very high danger of dipping one's hands or fingers inside the holes because in some cases the holes were occupied by poisonous snakes. Many casualties have been witnessed as people who risked using their hands have been beaten by such poisonous snakes. Poor people who struggle to survive are usually exposed to a lot of dangers as was, and still is the case with the rural Tiv. It was expected that animals that did not burrow would run from their hiding places to escape the wildfire and would eventually be attacked and killed by the hunters.

[22] Dzeremo, *Colonialism and the Transformation of Authority in Central Tivland*, 17. The practice was done by entering into the stream, and in a swift manner participants simultaneously dispersed a body of water with their bowls or calabashes in order to get hold of the fish that got trapped at the base. This practice was popularly known as *sua kohol* (dispersing water).

[23] Atel, *Dynamics of Tiv Religion and Culture*, 8.

[24] See Zinkuratire, "Isaiah 1-39: Life Context of the Interpretation," 186. The Hebrew society too went through similar changes. Biblical evidence in the eighth century BCE shows that in pre-monarchical times, tribal confederation was a political system that held the Hebrew people as a single unit. The majority of the population was peasant living in egalitarian communities under the leadership of elders who tried to guarantee the welfare of everyone especially the weak members of the society such as widows and orphans. When kingship was introduced in Israel, the situation changed with the existence of economic classes, the poor and the rich living side by side.

enjoyed communality. In particular, the introduction of money brought changes in the economy. Perhaps the introduction of taxation during the colonial regime may have been responsible for the decline of the communitarian spirit of executing community projects. The decline of this value as a consequence of the colonial administration of Tivland has led to the high expectation on government to provide infrastructure from the revenue accrued from taxes.

Initial Resistance
to Colonial Occupation

The intensive colonial occupation of Tivland began in 1900, and it led to the loss of other cultural values as well. To curtail the further decline of values, colonialism was aggressively and violently resisted between 1900 and 1906.

On January 8, 1900 angry farmers attacked and routed a group of government sappers who were building a telegraph line across northern Tivland to link it with other parts of the province.[25] These sappers constituted a group of people recruited to defend the position of the British colonial government. Although it is not clear the category of people who were responsible for this attack, it can be argued that the mention of farmers presupposes that it may have been strong people, and young people fit this description.

This assumption corroborates the proactive role played by young people in other places. In societies undergoing modernization, young adults have played a key role in bringing changes. Today, educated young adults are the primary troops of change.[26] They speak out against arbitrary rule, they demonstrate in the streets demanding reforms, they volunteer to lead social movements, and sometimes clash with established authorities in the streets.[27]

For example, the 1947 riot in Makurdi town was a violent resistance to stop the British from the successive imposition of leaders from

---

[25] Dzurgba, *On the Tiv of Central Nigeria*, 39.
[26] Dean R. Hoge, et al, *Young Adult Catholics: Religion in the Culture of Choice* (Notre Dame: University of Notre Dame Press, 2002), 21.
[27] Hoge, et al., *Young Adult Catholics*, 21.

other ethnic groups on the Tiv.[28] As a symbol of their cultural identity, the Tiv requested an indigenous leader.[29] The riot spearheaded by young people in resistance to foreign leadership eventually resulted in changes within the political system with the emergence of the stool of the *Tor Tiv* (the Tiv paramount ruler).

The military reprisals ushered in a six-year period of intermittent strife between the Tiv and the British.[30] The use of force by the colonial government to bring the Tiv under their control failed.[31] They eventually explored the imperial policy of cultivating friendship with the Tiv through peaceful persuasion and negotiations.[32] This policy appealed to the Tiv, and eventually the native authority administration was instituted.

Native Authority Administration

The main responsibilities of the native administration were to take charge of administration, collect taxes on behalf of government, maintain law and order, and ensure stability in the local communities. Other duties were to provide judicial functions of adjudication and settlement of disputes, and the legislation of customary laws and mediation between the local communities and the British colonial administration in Northern Nigeria.[33]

The above objectives of the Native Authority administration were effectively pursued under a dual system of administration: the traditional institution and the elite bureaucratic system. The establishment of the traditional institution of chieftaincy in 1947[34] altered the socio-political system and broke it down to minute units.

---

[28] John Atagher Adzege, *Blaming the Victim: The Tiv and Ethnicity in Nigeria* (Makurdi: Benue Printing and Publishing Company, 1997), 81.
[29] Evidence in scripture also shows that indigenous kingship promotes a people's identity. The people of Israel came to Samuel and requested for a king in the same way other nations had their kings (1Sam 8:4-5).
[30] Dzurgba, *On the Tiv of Central Nigeria*, 39.
[31] Dzurgba, *On the Tiv of Central Nigeria*, 43.
[32] Dzurgba, *On the Tiv of Central Nigeria*, 46.
[33] Dzurgba, *On the Tiv of Central Nigeria*, 57.
[34] Atel, *Dynamics of Tiv Religion and Culture*, 18.

The paramount ruler is the *Tor Tiv*. The next category of chiefs are the *uter* (plural of Ter), (fathers) of the Tiv whose authority is limited within a Local Government Area. Closely following the *uter* are the district heads *utyombaiorov* (men of the head). *Mbatarev,* (men of the land) rule as kindred heads within districts.[35] Last on the hierarchy are the *ator a kpande,* (Chief tax-collectors) whose duty at the compound unit is to ensure that people pay their taxes for onward remittance to the appropriate authority. The Tiv hierarchical structure of traditional chieftaincy provides an analogical relationship with the hierarchical structure of the Catholic Church.

The paramount ruler and the various categories of chiefs administer Tiv society in an order that is similar to the church's structure. The Roman Pontiff who is the successor of Peter, and the bishops, the successors of the Apostles, administer the Catholic Church in a collegial spirit.[36] The Pontiff, the bishops, and the various collaborators on the hierarchical ladder safeguard, and transmit the deposit of faith handed down by the apostles. While the church's hierarchy is sacred, Tiv traditional chieftaincy is worldly.[37] Both hierarchies are mutually enriching.

The British colonial authorities sidelined Tiv elders, preferring to work with young people.[38] They recognized the value of young people and recruited some of them as tax collectors. However, the age range of those young people is not clear, but it is certain they selected those who were courageous and could influence people to subscribe to the colonial ideology. The colonial administration believed that courageous younger men would be more active in enforcing their demands for tax.[39] Those who were incorporated in the administration contributed greatly to the development of the colonial era economy.

---

[35] Atel, *Dynamics of Tiv Religion and Culture,* 18.

[36] Code of Canon Law, c. 1055, § 1, in the 1983 *Code of Canon Law,* http://www.vatican.va/archive/ENG1104/_INDEX.HTM.

[37] See Tracy, *The Analogical Imagination.* This analogy meets Tracy's criteria of adequacy. The Catholic hierarchical structure can be interpreted in an analogical style with the contemporary situation of the Tiv chieftaincy hierarchy.

[38] Wegh, *Between Continuity and Change,* 54.

[39] Wegh, *Between Continuity and Change,* 54.

Colonizing nations were sometimes concerned with promoting their economic interests. Their departure left the economy of the subaltern countries in precarious imbalance. That notwithstanding, the colonizers need to be praised because their skills and technical know-how brought benefits to many untamed lands. Their work survives to this day. The structural machinery they introduced was not fully developed or perfected, but it did help to reduce ignorance and disease, promoted communication, and improved living conditions.[40]

From an African perspective, colonialism introduced new cultural ideas, beliefs, styles, ethics, occupations, religion, institutions, relationships, settlements, goods and services.[41]

The contact of the Tiv with the British can be assessed at two levels. Positively, young people left the rural areas and were exposed to urban cultures thereby elevating their standard of living. Negatively, it broke down the close-knitted ties enjoyed by individuals in rural communities.[42] Tiv elders had a singular view of this development. They accused the British of *vihin tar* (spoiling the land) as they viewed that some of the British policies opposed Tiv traditional customs and values.[43]

Recreation of Wealth

In pre-colonial Tiv society, the most common form of exchange for goods and services was trade by barter. During the colonial era, the introduction of money in the economy, the imposition of taxation, and abolition of *yamshe* (exchange marriage) brought tremendous changes to Tiv society.

Yamshe was a system of marriage whereby, two different families exchanged their daughters in marriage. A man who did not have a daughter or sister was loaned one by his brother. The beneficiary

---

[40] Paul VI, *Populorum Progressio* [The Development of Peoples], sec 7, http://www.vatican.va/holy_father/paul_vi/encyclicals/documents/hf_p-vi_enc_26031967_populorum_en.html
[41] Dzurgba, *The Tiv and Their Culture* (Ibadan: John Archers, 2011), 53.
[42] Atel, *Dynamics of Tiv Religion and Culture*, 94.
[43] Atel, *Dynamics of Tiv Religion and Culture*, 21.

exchanged his niece for a wife. He was expected to payback when he eventually had a female child. The problem with such marriages was that when the couple was incompatible, another woman had to be replaced. In a situation where there was none for replacement, the other family too withdrew their daughter. This kind of marriage did not offer an opportunity for one to marry a spouse of his or her choice. The introduction of money in the economy significantly transformed trade, marriage institution, and agriculture.

The introduction of money boosted agricultural production, especially the production of benniseed. More people went into commercial agriculture to explore economic opportunities. Young people were at the center of economic activities in Tivland that focused mainly on the production, distribution, and consumption of goods and services. They formed cooperative societies that constituted the labor force on which the elders in Tiv society depended. [44]

Through these associations, they embarked on both subsistence and commercial agriculture. Products that were set aside for sale were conveyed to the market by foot. Young men and women contributed to the economic development of Tiv society. The male labor was complemented by the female labor force which explains why polygamy was economically profitable.[45] The economy in the pre-colonial and colonial periods had revolved around agriculture, taxation and commercial labor. The constitution of cooperative associations was largely responsible for the success of agriculture.

But farm work can be drudgery and painful. Farming in Tivland today has inherent difficulties.[46] Poor harvest, the cost involved in

---

[44] Wegh, *Between Continuity and Change,* 132. Beniseed is a tiny Nigerian sesame that was produced mainly for export. As an export commodity, it dominated the agricultural landscape. Farmers made a lot of money from this trade.

[45] Dzurgba, *On the Tiv of Central Nigeria,* 128. A man that married many wives had more hands to work on his large farm. Many wives worked on the farm, produced more wealth, and raised his economic status.

[46] Kathleen Cahalan, *Introducing the Practice of Ministry* (Minnesota: Liturgical Press, 2010), 40. Their experience in Taraba and Nasarawa States corroborates the experience of the Hebrews in Egypt (Exodus 1:9-10). Also see, Ioannes Paulus PP. II, *Laborem Exercens* [On Human Work], sec. 21, http://www.vatican.va/holy_father/john_paul_ii/encyclicals/documents/hf_jp-ii_enc_14091981_laborem-exercens_en.html. The Pontiff says, agricultural work

58

hiring labor, lack of fertilizer, and the most painful of all, working under harsh weather condition, make farming less attractive. Typically, Tiv farmers are non-mechanized farmers. With the growing population of the Tiv, land in most parts of Tivland is either over utilized or grossly insufficient. Farmers have to trek long distances to acquire farmlands on rent. Some leave their localities entirely to other parts of Tivland or other states in sojourn for farm work. In recent times, many have moved to the neighboring state of Taraba where they have repeatedly suffered losses as a consequence of communal clashes with the indigenous peoples who see them as intruders and a potential threat.

In Tivland today, young people may be unaware that some of the activities they carry out for survival, deplete the environment. Tied majorly to economic factors, such activities include, pollution of rivers by using chemicals for fishing, random burning of bushes for hunting, and deforestation. These have negative consequences such as potential water crisis and increased global warming. Economic factors play a major role in the current ecological crisis. Environmental degradation is often due to the lack of far-sighted official policies or to the pursuit of myopic economic interests, which then, tragically, become a serious threat to creation. To combat this phenomenon, economic activity needs to consider the fact that "every economic decision has a moral consequence."[47]

Physical consequences are apparent in the contemporary world, witnessing ecological crisis of all kinds. In the cities, people are experiencing air pollution and acid rain. Rural areas are seeing a depletion of the once rich soil. Most people are aware of the dwindling

---

involves considerable difficulties, including unremitting and sometimes exhausting physical effort and a lack of appreciation on the part of society. This situation makes agricultural people to feel they are social outcasts and consequently speeds up the phenomenon of their mass exodus from the countryside to the cities. Unfortunately, they encounter still more dehumanizing living conditions in the cities. In addition, they lack adequate professional training and proper equipment. They also suffer unjust situations.

[47] Benedict XVI, "Message of His Holiness Pope Benedict XVI for the Celebration of World Day of Peace," Vatican, 2010, sec.7, http://www.vatican.va/holy_father/benedict_xvi/messages/peace/documents/hf_ben-xvi_mes_20091208_xliii-world-day-peace.html.

natural resources. Experts predict that by the end of the century, humanity will face catastrophic famine and epidemic disease because of what people have done to the environment.[48] As stewards of creation, the challenge is to act responsibly. Otherwise, if current trends continue, our current form of human activity could be the primary cause of extinction of a quarter of the species of plants and animals on the land by mid-century. Further, we could lose as many as half the species of plant and animals on earth by the end of the century.[49]

The attack on the natural world by young people in Tiv society is a sin. It can cause species to become extinct and destroy the biological diversity of God's creation. To degrade the integrity of the earth by stripping it of its natural forests, or by destroying its wetlands constitute sin against nature.[50] Just as young people were at the center of agriculture in the pre-colonial times, they also played a significant role, enforcing the colonial era taxation.

Colonial Era Taxation &
Commercial Labor

In his ministry, Jesus objectively resolved the controversial issue of payment of taxes when he told his Jewish listeners to pay to Caesar what belongs to Caesar and to God what belongs to God (Mark 12:17).[51] But the issue of payment of taxes was alien in Tiv society. The Tiv were not rich yet they were compelled to pay taxes during the colonial regime. The introduction of taxation in the economy brought with it unpleasant experiences.

---

[48] Jack Rogers, *Presbyterian Creeds* (Louisville, London: Westminster John Knox Press, 1991), 112.

[49] Joe Holland, *Pacem in Terris Global Leadership Initiative* (Unpublished, 2012), 14.

[50] See John Chryssavgis, *Cosmic Grace Humble Prayer: The Ecological Vision of the Green Patriarch Bartholomew 1*(William B. Eerdmans, 2003), 221.

[51] See notes on Matthew 22:21 in the New American Bible. The question of payment of taxes was controversial in the time of Jesus. Jesus does not take side in the lawfulness of taxes. Since the Jews were subject to Caesar whose image of the coin they presented, Jesus simply told them to give Caesar his due and to God what belongs to God. Jesus raises the debate to a new level admonishing his disciples that in respect to the law of God, they should be concerned with repaying God with the good deeds that are his due.

Scholars disagree on the disposition of the Tiv toward payment of taxes.[52] Young Tiv who supported the colonial policy of taxation were elevated as *ator a kpande* (tax collectors) to ensure that those who were eligible, paid their taxes unfailingly. These tax collectors entered compounds to collect taxes and mistreated those who failed to pay their taxes. They taunted and humiliated family heads who were responsible for the taxes for their family members. Young people who evaded taxes were severely beaten and exposed to suffer the heat of the scorching sun.[53] The torture was unbearable, and so young people explored avenues to raise money to take care of themselves and fulfill their civil responsibilities. One opportunity was to offer themselves as commercial workers.

In 1920, the construction of a rail line began in eastern Nigeria to connect the northern part of the country. Young Tiv laborers were hired to create an access road along the proposed rail line. By 1922, over four thousand Tiv were employed in a wide range of jobs, from earthwork to track-laying and bridge-building.[54] They earned a lot of money and consequently influenced the abolition of exchange marriage.[55]

The abolition of exchange marriage was spearheaded by the Dutch Reformed Church Mission (DRCM) whose missionaries were working in Tivland at the time.[56] The DRC missionaries penetrated Tivland in 1911. By 1927, the DRC mission spread to other parts of Tivland. The issue of exchange marriage was a huge concern to the missionaries because it often led to complicated family problems. It can be argued that young people who supported the abolition of exchange marriage were influenced by Christianity to advance the teaching that marriage is a free and voluntary engagement. The

---

[52] Wegh, *Between Continuity and Change* (134) disagrees that Tiv were not happy paying taxes. Justin Iyorbee Tseayo, *Conflict and Incorporation in Nigeria: The Integration of the Tiv* (Zaria: Gaskiya Corporation Limited, 1975), on the other hand, argues that the Tiv were not averse to taxes. The fact that they were forced to pay taxes presupposes that they opposed the payment of taxes, which was a strange practice to them.

[53] Wegh, *Between Continuity and Change*, 134-135.

[54] Wegh, *Between Continuity and Change*, 135.

[55] See Wegh, *Between Continuity and Change*, 138.

[56] Dzurgba, *On the Tiv of Central Nigeria*, 80.

abolition of exchange marriage gave them the liberty to marry women of their choice, and conveniently pay the bride-price for their wives.

The rise in economic status also made young people to challenge the unrivaled authority of the elders.[57] They no longer relied on the support of elders and the community.[58] They were financially independent, could accept responsibility for their actions, and make independent decisions.[59] The discovery of crude oil further increased the degree of independence. Young people started leaving the rural areas for the cities in search for better opportunities because the discovery of oil improved the general condition of living.

Exploration of Crude Oil

Crude oil was discovered in Nigeria in 1955 shortly before colonial rule came to an end. It provided opportunities that empowered many young people. Revenue derivation from oil was used in building cities in Nigeria which have made rural life less attractive. Consequently, many young Nigerians abandoned agriculture and moved to the cities to take up jobs in the mines, factory, and households or offices leaving behind their land, homes and relatives.[60] This resulted in the decline of community practices that were visible in rural communities.

Faith & Culture
Challenges for Today

Today, the situation seems to degenerate. Young people who remain in the rural areas do not receive sufficient incentives to carry out farm work. Fertilizer that is subsidized annually for the benefit of farmers has often been diverted by self-serving politicians and corrupt government officials. The phenomenon of political corruption raises the question of injustice that greatly affects Tiv society.

---

[57] Wegh, *Between Continuity and Change,* 137.
[58] Wegh, *Between Continuity and Change,* 139.
[59] See Arnett, *Emerging Adulthood,* vi.
[60] Atel, *Dynamics of Tiv Religion and Culture,* 94.

To challenge these problems, the Catholic hierarchy can illuminate traditional systems. Traditional chieftaincy on the other hand, can facilitate the growth, and spread of the Catholic Church as was the case in the fifteenth century when the great King of the Congo, Nzinga-a-Nkuwu invited missionaries to proclaim the gospel in his land. The degree of honor and respect the Tiv accord their chiefs, and for the most part, adhere to their instructions can enrich Catholicism in Tivland too. (The institution of traditional chiefdom in Tivland also favored some young people who were later elevated to the position of tax-collectors to assist in administering the Tiv.)

Also, theology as a public discourse must address the concerns of injustice and poverty. These challenges have caused young people who carried out organized cooperative farm work to leave the rural agrarian areas for the cities in search of better opportunities, including formal education. Sadly enough, they encounter still more dehumanizing living conditions in the cities.[61] The formal education they receive in the cities supplements the traditional education that taught children to garner the skills and attitudes necessary for integration into Tiv society.

Today, educated Tiv emerging adults can bring positive impact not only in the socio-political structure of Tiv society, but also in the rooting of Catholicism in Tiv culture. One way of doing this is to retrieve the concept of community life that eschews violence and upholds the value of peace, particularly as Tiv society is continually engulfed in land disputes and political violence. For instance, the violent attack on colonial sappers in resistance to the colonial administration led to a series of reprisals.

Against this background, the next chapter will explore the central issue of education, first as seen within the role of Protestant and Catholic missionaries of bringing Western education to Tivland, and second as seen within the present experience of higher education in Tivland today.

---

[61] Ioannes Paulus PP. II, *Laborem Exercens* [On Human Work], sec. 21, http://www.vatican.va/holy_father/john_paul_ii/encyclicals/documents/hf_jp-ii_enc_14091981_laborem-exercens_en.html.

4

YOUNG PEOPLE & EDUCATION
IN TIVLAND

T his chapter discusses the involvement of young people in educational institutions, including religious ones, within Tivland, as a prelude to examining the religious experiences of emerging adults in the contemporary Tiv society. In this connection, the chapter dialogues with the academic community.

Tiv society is generally an oral culture. The most effective method of educating the younger generation was through stories, riddles, myths, and folklores found in Tiv culture. Such cultural texts are sources of theology. The teaching and learning process typically took place at night around the fireplace as children, young people, and adults gathered to keep themselves warm. Children were particularly educated under a bright moonlight. They learned lessons from stories, myths and legends about clever animals such as the rabbit, from significant events, and heroic personalities in Tiv culture.

The story of the green snake *ikyaren* (test)[1] has several lessons including, religious lessons for the Tiv. Tiv Christians connect the story with the story of the crossing of the Red Sea by the Israelites

---

[1] See Dzurgba, *On the Tiv of Central Nigeria,* 13. The snake is generally identified by most Tiv scholars as *ikyaren,* which means "test." Etymologically, *ikyar* means friend, but when used as a possessive noun it becomes *ikyarem* "my friend." When used in the context of *ikyaren,* it could mean that the encounter of the Tiv with a water barrier while fleeing from their enemies was a test of their faith in *Aondo* the God of the Tiv. Most scholars refer to the green snake as *ikyaren,* but the meaning most commonly attached to the concept is *Ikyarem* (friend) of the Tiv that saved the Tiv race from total annihilation. In this context, test as the meaning of *ikyaren* is most appropriate.

and see themselves too as a chosen people. The story of *ikyaren* depicts the experience of the Tiv who were saved from being annihilated by their enemies. They were running away from their enemies but encountered a water barrier. *Ikyaren* appeared and formed a bridge that enabled them to cross. After they all crossed, *ikyaren* reversed to its original state, making the enemies unable to cross.[2] The Tiv were saved. Such stories had moral and ethical lessons for the young.

Apart from imparting moral lessons, the young were also taught skills such as weaving. The weaving industry was relatively developed in pre-colonial Tivland. Tiv people obtained their clothes from this industry. Apart from the skills young people derived from it, the industry also promoted trade in Tivland.[3] In some parts of Tivland today, cloth weaving that was mostly done by elderly people is now done by the young. Cloth weaving is very common in Ushongo, and Adikpo Local Government Areas. The trade offers some of them the opportunity to raise money for the payment of their tuition. Their proficiency in weaving different types and styles of Tiv traditional clothes is a sign that such skills will continue to be handed over to future generations, and the art of weaving in Tiv culture will not die.

The overall goal of education in pre-colonial Tiv society was chiefly for socialization whose primary objectives were; (a) to mold the character of a child into a trustworthy personality within the community with a focus on truth, honesty, and transparency; (b) to teach the child to gain knowledge and skills in farming, craftsmanship, hunting and fishing; (c) to teach the child to gain knowledge and skill in personal cleanliness and environmental sanitation; (d) to teach the child how to live a community life and to share in its religious, social, economic, political, scientific and technological activi-

---

[2] Dzurgba, *On the Tiv of Central Nigeria,* 12-13.

[3] Dzeremo, *Colonialism and the Transformation of Authority in Central Tivland,* 20. Also it is important to note that the weaving industry produces assorted Tiv traditional clothes. These clothes are used during ceremonies in Tivland, such as marriage, funeral, and other cultural festivities. In the Catholic Church, they are also used in making vestments for the clergy. Consequently, these clothes are always in high demand among the Tiv.

ties; (e) to teach the child skills in medicine, sculpture, painting or pottery; (f) to socialize the child on how to think and make independent decisions, and how to relate with others and behave in acceptable ways in the society.[4]

The goal was to ensure that Tiv children grew up as responsible citizens. The Christian missionaries who brought formal education consolidated these gains and broadened the nature of education in Tivland.

Introduction of
Formal Education in Tivland

Formal education was introduced in Tivland through the untiring work of both Protestant and Catholic missionaries. Christian missionaries brought formal education to Tivland to teach the heathens the faith, and also how to read and write. This section introduces the work of those protestant and Catholic missionaries.

Protestant Missionaries

Missionary activities in Tivland was started in 1911 by protestant missionaries from London under the name "Sudan United Mission" (SUM) who in that same year handed over the work to the Dutch Reformed Church Mission (DRCM). During this period, the South African branch of SUM, dominated by volunteers from DRCM, worked among the Tiv.[5] SUM was not a church, but an interdenominational and international organization.[6] The missionaries established mission stations and primary schools. The first primary school was established in 1911.[7]

In 1950, SUM took over the evangelization of Tivland from the DRC, and in 1956, the church was officially named *Nongo u Kristu u Ken Sudan Hen Tiv* (the Church of Christ in the Sudan Among the

---

[4] Dzurgba, *On the Tiv of Central Nigeria,* 132-133.

[5] Dzurgba, *On the Tiv of Central Nigeria,* 71.

[6] Dzurgba, *On the Tiv of Central Nigeria,* 66.

[7] Dzurgba, *On the Tiv of Central Nigeria,* 68. The school was established in *Saai,* a village in the north eastern part of Tivland. Today, *Saai* remains one of the strongholds of the indigenous Tiv traditional Christian church called *Nongo U Kristu U Sudan Hen Tiv*- N.K.S.T (The church of Sudan among the Tiv).

Tiv).[8] The church is commonly identified as N.K.S.T. It is concentrated in Tivland, and evangelization is carried out in Tiv language. As an indigenous church, it is self-supporting, self-governing, and self-propagating.[9]

It was after about twenty years of their missionary work in Tivland that Catholicism appeared on the scene. Today, with the migration of the members of N.K.S.T, the faith tradition is spreading beyond the frontiers of Tivland, and Nigeria gradually becoming a global church in the missionary spirit of the Catholic Church.

Catholic Missionaries

In 1930, the first group of Catholic missionaries arrived in Tivland from Germany and started missionary work among Tiv people. The gospel message was preached in English and interpreted in Tiv. Children were recruited into the Sunday school where they learned how to sing, and to read and write.[10]

This strategy was insufficient to make the faith sink into Tiv culture. However, Catholic missionaries are remembered for their contribution to the teaching of Christian ethics through congregational preaching, introducing the people to ecclesiastical discipline, and the establishment of schools. Holy Ghost Primary School, Makurdi was established the same year the missionaries arrived.[11] Through education and other evangelization approaches, they taught honesty, truthfulness and integrity, emphasizing that obedience to ethical principles and honesty are commands from God.[12]

The missionaries saw education and religion as two sides of the same coin. Both the protestant and Catholic missionaries created great impact in most parts of Tivland by establishing mission stations and schools. Today, Catholicism has permeated Tivland as a whole, but the degree to which Catholicism and Tiv culture are in

---

[8] Dzurgba, *On the Tiv of Central Nigeria,* 83.

[9] Dzurgba, *On the Tiv of Central Nigeria,* 83.

[10] Clement Mato, "The Catholic Church in Tivland," 41.

[11] Godwin Udaa, "The History of Education in the Catholic Diocese of Makurdi," in *Catholic Diocese of Makurdi at 50: A Celebration of Service to Humanity,* ed. Shagbaor F. Wegh (Makurd: Selfers Academic Press, 2010), 95.

[12] Dzurgba, *On The Tiv of Central Nigeria,* 89.

dialogue needs to be explored. The encounter of the Catholic faith with the existing Tiv religion was also an encounter of dual practices. Ways that Tiv religion provides primal religious systems for the rooting of Catholicism in Tiv culture is the subject of the next section.

Tiv Religion

Before the coming of Catholicism, Tiv already had their religion. Tiv religion as part of African religion is a unified worldview in which the human person, nature, and the supernatural constitute a continuum.

The arrival of Catholicism brought some beliefs and practices of the two religions into a dialectical relationship. Some foreigners saw this relationship as conflicting, and so referred to Tiv religion as pagan religion, ancestor worship, animism, superstition, magic, heathenism, fetishism and the like.[13] Drawing from this understanding, Catholic missionaries failed to identify aspects of Tiv religion that resonate with Catholicism. The failure of Catholicism to dialogue with Tiv religion perhaps, accounts for the reason why in the present context of Tiv society, Catholicism still appears to be a foreign religion in need of contextual models of evangelization.

Contextual approaches draw insights from the culture of a people and their beliefs and practices. Tiv religion recognizes the existence of a Supreme Being called Aondo (God), who is the creator of the universe. The human person in Tiv cosmology is the crown of creation with a responsibility to ensure goodness and harmony in the world. Harmony and goodness are achieved through Akombo (a collection of cosmic forces), that God has given to the human person.

The Tiv also believe in *tsav* (witchcraft). Those endowed with *tsav* receive extraordinary powers to manipulate the universe and even unleash misfortune on other human beings. *Adzov* (spirits) are supersensible beings who share a common cosmos with human beings

---

[13] Moses Orshio Adasu, *Understanding African Traditional Religion*, Part One (Sherborne, England: Dorset, 1985), 7 and 9.

and contribute toward the ordering of Tiv society.[14] These belief systems provide a point through which Catholicism can enter into dialogue with Tiv religion. A reciprocal dialogue is a spirit of give and take. In the course of dialogue, Catholicism can give and take some of the beliefs and practices of the indigenous religion, and vice versa.

In regard to Tiv religious beliefs that promote fear, Catholicism reenacts the supreme belief in Jesus who overcomes all evil no matter the length of time the evil prevails. For instance, within the Tiv religious cosmology, witchcraft-practitioners manifest different evil signs.

When an owl appears and hoots[15] in a particular compound, it is a sign of the imminent death of a member of that family. Such signs threaten communal life, and provoke fear, insecurity, and danger in the entire neighborhood. The fear is grave to the extent that parents discourage their children from entering into marriage relationships with communities in Tiv culture known for perpetrating evil signs. Consequently, married women who bore children in those communities were likely to divorce their husbands when the evil signs consequently led to the death of any of their children.

It is only God who has absolute power to take the life of another person. However, in Tiv religion, it is believed that witches are responsible for the death of another human being. Those who hold this belief justify it by saying that the death of Jesus too came through the hands of Roman soldiers. In some instances, daughters who are married in communities that are peaceful refuse to visit their parents for fear that their parents might sacrifice them through witchcraft. Many unpleasant consequences are associated with these evil signs. [16]

---

[14] See *Wegh, Between Continuity and Change,* 60-61.

[15] See Dzurgba, *The Tiv and Their Culture,* 175-176. Other animals such as wild cats, foxes, crabs, chameleons, toads, and big rats are associated with evil signs in Tiv religion. Particular circumstances where people come in contact with these animals determine whether or not is an evil sign.

[16] Dzurgba, *The Tiv and Their Culture,* 178. Tiv people believe that human beings can be used as victims of sacrifice. Such sacrifices are particularly carried out in the ritual of *imborvungu,* explored in chapter four.

The evil signs have often led to isolation, divisions, conflicts and crises in communities and families. Community members, who felt their lives were threatened, took refuge in other places. The phenomenon of the multiplicity of small compound settlements all over Tivland has in part arisen from the religious quarrels among families and communities.[17]

When the religious crisis occurred and the authority of the council of elders was unresponsive, the people experienced widespread diseases, pests, and frequent occurrence of death. Consequently, a massive protest by young people called for a restoration of security of life and property.[18]

The *Namakaa* (anti-witchcraft movement) between 1926 and 1927 was organized by youth who brutally attacked the elders suspected of possessing *tsav*. It has been alleged that *Namakaa* movement was encouraged by the British colonial administration to weaken the authority of the elders and dislodge their political control of the Tiv tribe.[19]

Catholicism offers powerful insights that resonate with the *Namakaa* movement. The belief in exorcism and the practice of crusades, organized for the liberation and deliverance of those who suffer different kinds of problems in Tiv society provides a spiritual panacea to those in distress situations.

Young people played a significant role not only in the religious life of Tiv people, but also in the socio-political, economic, and cultural life in the precolonial and colonial periods. Their engagement in Tiv society lays the background toward understanding how emerging

---

[17] Dzurgba, *The Tiv and Their Culture*, 179. This in part has led to the decline of community life practices.
[18] See Dzurgba, *The Tiv and Their Culture*, 179. The women organized a religious group that went round the whole community singing religious songs and appealing for the return of peace in the community. The women went from house to house, expressing, in their songs their indignation against the current disasters, and at the same time, appealing to *ingbianjov* (their female deity) to come to the aid of the community in the face of the failure of male deities and the collapse of the council's authority. The role of women was significant because it could set in motion a series of council meetings for the restoration of peace in the community.
[19] Moti, *The Early Jerusalem Christian Community*, 96-97.

adults can impact the Catholic Church today. Theology offers reflection on the post-colonial, post-modern context of educated emerging adult Catholics in institutions of higher education in Tivland.

The context of higher education institutions in Tivland is important because if "there is not established ever more profoundly a bond between the Church and the university, it is the human person who will be harmed as a result; ... nor will the culture be fully humanized."[20] In addition, focusing attention on university and college students is important because [t]hese are the human persons who will be shaping the world, nation, culture, and the Church - perhaps, the universe. These are the people who will search out cures for AIDS and cancer, strive for peace among nations, and wrestle with environmental issues and new technologies."[21] Higher education contexts provide the environment to engage faith and culture in a reciprocal dialogue.

Higher Education Context & Catholicism in Dialogue

Higher education institutions have their unique culture. Cultures are constitutive vehicles of revelation. A faith that does not become a culture is no faith at all. In our time, to be able to understand other cultures is to be open to revelation.[22] This discussion is situated in the context of where young people are (the university), who they are (Catholic), and consequently what ministers are supposed to be doing (pastoral ministry).[23]

---

[20] George M. Schroeder, "The Quest for Wisdom: Reflections on Campus Ministry and the Relationship Between the Church and Higher Education," in *The Gospel on Campus: A Handbook of Campus Ministry Programs and Resources, Second Edition,* ed.Michael Galligan-Stierle (Dayton: Catholic Campus Ministry Association, 1996), 11. These are the words of John Paul II as cited by James J. Bacik, "The Making of a Pastoral Letter: The Quest for Wisdom Revisited," in *The Journal of the CCMA*

[21] Schroeder, "The Quest for Wisdom," 12.

[22] Edward B. Branch, "Multiculturalism and Campus Ministry in a Changing University Culture," in *The Gospel on Campus: A Handbook of Campus Ministry Programs and Resources,* 2nd Edition, ed. Michael Galligan-Stierle (Dayton: Catholic Campus Ministry Association, 1996), 22.

[23] Branch, "Multiculturalism and Campus Ministry in a Changing University Culture," 21.

In using the worship experiences of educated emerging adults for contextual Catholicism, higher education contexts are the ideal places to initiate the dialogue between faith and culture. The richness and variety in the university shows that "[t]he university is a freeze-frame, a microcosm of the culture. If the Church enters into a true dialogue with the university, it will be a dialogue between faith and culture."[24] This dialogue will shape not only Catholicism in Tiv culture, but also, the global community.

Ultimately, the world will be a better place because of this dialogue. Without it, faith makes no contribution to culture, and culture tends to overlook the depth dimensions of human life and the realms of ultimate meanings. Without such a dialogue, culture makes no contribution to religion, and such a religion becomes alien and alienating to the new generations who are growing up in a new culture, different from the one in which the religious tradition was shaped and given expression.[25]

Higher education students are heirs of a digital culture with instant telecasting, transmission of message through modern means of communication. Catholicism can dialogue with higher education contexts recognizing that, who people are is very much a product of where they are socially located, of what social and relational forces have formed their lives. And who people are usually does not randomly and unaccountably change over time. What people have been in the past is generally the best indicator of why they are what they are in the present and what they will likely be in the future. That is a fact that needs to condition the understanding of emerging adult religion.[26]

These and other factors influence emerging adult religion. In Tivland, many are affiliated to Catholicism.[27] However, the trend

[24] Schroeder, "The Quest for Wisdom," 13.

[25] Schroeder, "The Quest for Wisdom," 14.

[26] Christian Smith and Patricia Snell, *Souls in Transition: The Religious and Spiritual Lives of Emerging Adults* (New York: Oxford University Press, 2009), 256.

[27] See Pius T. T. Ajiki, "The Good Shepherd Chaplaincy Benue State University," in *Benue State University at 20: Achievements, Challenges and Prospects*, ed.Oga Ajene, Mathieu Armstrong Adejo (Makurdi: SAP Publishing House, 2012), 333. The author is the chaplain of The Good Shepherd Catholic Chaplaincy who recognizes that

sweeping across the world is one that affirms the general disaffiliation of young people to religion. Studies have shown the religious
disaffiliation of young people in some societies.

In the United States, for instance, there is a general trend towards
disaffiliation from religious traditions and a significant growth in
the proportion of American emerging adults who identify as not
religious.[28] However, this does not mean they are not spiritual because "most people grow spiritually without being religious."[29]
Young people are increasingly disconnected from religion, with one
in three Americans aged 18-29 describing themselves as religiously
unaffiliated.[30]

One of the reasons that account for the religious disaffiliation of
young people is unappealing worship.[31] Others include disruptions
such as divorce, death of a family member, leaving home, and job
loss. These factors correlate negatively with religious practice. College students can experience such moments of crisis in their undergraduate years. For example, people who move residences are significantly less likely to attend religious services than people who do
not move.[32] This is a problem of instability that describes emerging
adults as people who are unstable and frequently move from one
residence to another.[33]

Such issues of faith and culture affect Tiv students in various ways.
Traces of religious disaffiliation from Catholicism are becoming

---

Catholic population in the institution is on the steady rise. At inception, the university had few staff and students, majority of the pioneer staff and students were Catholics (335-336).

[28] Smith and Snell, *Souls in Transition*, 141.

[29] Alexander W. Astin, Helen S. Astin, and Jennifer A. Lindholm, *Cultivating the
Spirit: How College Can Enhance Students' Inner Lives* (San Francisco: Jossey-Bass,
2011), 3.

[30] Alessandro Speciale, "Vatican Admits it Doesn't Fully Understand Youth Culture," *Religion News Service* January 31, 2013,
http://www.religionnews.com/2013/01/31/vatican-admits-it-doesnt-fully-understand-
youth-culture/.

[31] Keith F. Pecklers, *Worship: A Primer in Christian Ritual*, 196.

[32] Smith and Snell, *Souls in Transition*, 75. See also Alexander W. Astin, Helen S. Astin,
Jennifer A. Lindholm, *Cultivating the Spirit: How College Can Enhance Students' Inner
Lives* (San Francisco: Jossey-Bass, 2011), 58.

[33] Arnett, *Emerging Adulthood*, 11.

visible among Tiv students. Some of them say the Catholic Church is an old-fashioned church. Such people are leaving the Catholic Church because Catholic doctrines and practices do not connect with them. They accuse the Catholic Church of being too strict on dress code particularly at worship. They refer to the Catholic Church as having a holier than thou attitude.[34]

Others who vow to remain Catholics recount that their peers complain the Catholic Church does not move their spirit. They do not feel the presence of the Holy Spirit when they worship in the Catholic Church, and that they do not experience miracles in the Catholic Church. Other churches move their spirit through deafening praise and worship songs, accompanied by musical instruments, and dancing. On the contrary, worship in the Catholic Church is solemn, but animating.[35] The rapid spread of Pentecostal movement is drawing many away from the Catholic Church into the Pentecostal congregations.[36] Catholic Theology needs to explore emerging youth cultures,[37] and initiate a reciprocal dialogue between the two.

Religious disaffiliation of young people is not very pronounced in present day Tiv society. Tiv people are predominantly Christian.[38] However, the postmodern age with its digital culture, dominant on campus, presents a challenge in engaging young people today in the global Christianity including Tiv society.

The digital culture gives emerging adults a distinct identity and must be taken seriously. Young people are moved by what is hap-

---

[34] Aondongu Kpako (a twenty-five-years old student of Benue State University), in a one-on-one interview on May 15, 2014 at Makurdi.

[35] Awuese Tongov (a twenty-three years old student of Benue State University), in a one-on-one interview on May 17, 2014 at Makurdi.

[36] Victor Igbum, "Charismatic/Pentecostalism: Its Impact on Christianity in Tivland," *Ate: Journal of African Religion and Culture* 1 (December 2010): 57.

[37] See "Emerging Youth Cultures: Preparatory Document for the Plenary Assembly of the Pontifical Council for Culture, 2013," http://www.cultura.va/content/dam/cultura/documenti/pdf/Incontri/Plenary2013/pre paratorydocument.pdf for principal characteristics of emerging youth cultures, which include affective, self-centric, and consumer cultures. Others are culture of social indifference, digital culture, a flattened culture of fast humanism, performative culture, and new religious cultures of youth, aggregated in new communities and new movements.

[38] Wegh, *Between Continuity and Change*, 146.

pening today in the digital and communication worlds. The internet and related phenomena are more than just media; they are a total environment of living. The digital world can insulate one from the community. Facebook for instance, provides an avenue for reaching friends. The problem arises when one is completely immersed in the digital world and forgets moments of prayer, contemplation, and engagement with the community of faith and church. The digital world, if not carefully used, can affect community life, and the practice of faith.

The challenge is to draw young people using the positive aspects of the media, and also to show that relationship with actual persons in the church is important. The media context, if properly used can enrich Catholicism by transmitting the beliefs, and practices of the Catholic faith.[39] The use of media is an effective way of engaging emerging adults because many of them are interested in religion. Despite assumptions one might make about young people's disengagement from faith and community life, religion remains a core component of their identity.[40]

This is particularly true of most educated Tiv emerging adults who have vowed to remain Catholics. Such people have a distinctive worldview and approach to life. They have higher self-esteem and a sense of self, and they hold more traditional views about family, sex, and marriage.[41] They are more connected to family and community. A sense of community on campus too must be vigorously pursued for students to recognize that, although every human being is autonomous, they are deeply dependent upon one another.[42]

As Catholics, the Eucharist as the source and summit of the life of the church is the central symbol of community. In human cultures, community often happens around the table and in the kitchen. Coming together over a meal is a natural setting for students, facul-

---

[39] See Ann Schneible, "Cardinal Dinardo on Youth and the Digital World: Plenary Assembly for Young People Continues in Vatican City," *Zenit News*, February 8, 2013, http://www.zenit.org/en/articles/cardinal-dinardo-on-youth-and-the-digital-world.

[40] Greenberg, "OMG! How Generation Y Is Redefining Faith In the iPod Era," 15.

[41] Greenberg, "OMG! How Generation Y Is Redefining Faith In the iPod Era," 15.

[42] See Schroeder, "The Quest for Wisdom," 13.

ty, and staff to mingle with one another."[43] Resonating with the Eucharist, the image of a common meal offers a means to the campus minister to synthesize faith and culture. The people who come to the Eucharist are vital to the Eucharist, and the Eucharist is vital to a community of faith. All who assemble for the Eucharist must strive to be part of a welcoming community, offering hospitality to all peoples.[44] Community includes, but is not limited to the symbol of the Eucharist.

Other forms of worship such as liturgy of the hours, scripture services, communion services, thematic prayer services add another dimension to a faith community.[45] All these constitute part of emerging adults' worship experiences. The goal of this theology is for community theologians to emerge from communities of worship. Their task is to articulate and explain the faith to others through natural networks of interaction. This community works toward bringing the Catholic faith and Tiv culture in a reciprocal dialogue.

Conclusion

The ritual practices of young people in the pre-colonial and colonial periods in Tiv society lay the background toward understanding the impact educated emerging adults can bring to Catholicism in the present day Tiv society. This chapter explored their ritual practices in socio-political, economic, educational, and religious life of Tiv society, and concludes that Catholic presence in higher education contexts can raise community theologians who will promote the dialogue of faith and culture.

To raise community theologians requires making contact with the context of emerging adults in institutions of higher education chaplaincies by using the circle method that explores the possibility of

---

[43] Kathleen Dorney, CND, "Aspects of Campus Ministry: Forming Faith Communities," in *The Gospel on Campus: A Handbook of Campus Ministry Programs and Resources*, 2nd Edition, ed.Michael Galligan-Stierle (Dayton: Catholic Campus Ministry Association, 1996), 129.

[44] Dorney, CND, "Aspects of Campus Ministry: Forming Faith Communities," 127.

[45] Dorney, CND, "Aspects of Campus Ministry: Forming Faith Communities," 128.

linking faith and life. The next chapter describes the framework helpful in achieving the set goals.

5

DESCRIPTIVE THEOLOGY
OF WORSHIP

A nalogies provide the connection between faith and culture, and worship and life. This link leads to a development of a local theology that uses emerging adults to explore ways of rooting Catholicism in Tivland, including the grassroots level. Young people have their idiosyncrasies with a distinctive social, religious, and cultural worldview.

In this postmodern age, educated emerging adults are buying into the global culture and neglecting the local culture. Understanding their worship experiences and practices, and what these mean to them, is helpful in constructing a local theology.

This book uses three interrelated praxis-oriented methods, but stresses the circle method, to describe the methodology used in addressing the specific questions laid down in Chapter One. By exploring the context of emerging adults, this chapter coincides with the first movement of the circle method. The cycle method, most often used in pastoral situations, is used to explore the problem of the split of faith and culture, which is a pastoral problem for Catholicism in Tiv culture.

The Circle Method

A helpful approach to offer solution to the problem of the split of faith and culture in Tiv culture is to embark on a descriptive theology[1] that uses the framework of practical theological spiral also called the pastoral circle as a roadmap to achieve the goals. The description of situations is not just a task only for psychology, sociology, economics, and anthropology, but one for theology as well.[2] The theological task then, is not to discern the question of worship in some simple, logical way but rather to describe the question in its situated richness.[3]

The practical theological spiral used in describing the question is a modified form of the Holland and Henriot model of the pastoral circle that explores the possibilities of linking faith and justice in global and local situations. [4] It is rooted in the "see, judge, act" method.[5] The pastoral circle is helpful in studying pastoral situations and offers the most appropriate means to respond to the issue of contextualizing the Catholic faith in Tiv culture.

The method recognizes that to address, to communicate with, to support, or to transform situations is to make contact with them in their fullness. The best churches, ministers, lay leaders, and religious actors are not only those with the best answers, but also those with the best grasp of the questions in their richness.[6] Having a full grasp of the situation entails having contact with the context, this naturally leads to ways of finding a solution to the problem.

---

[1] Don S. Browning, *A Fundamental Practical Theology: Descriptive and Strategic Proposals* (Minneapolis: Fortress, 1991), 77.

[2] Browning, *A Fundamental Practical Theology*, 77.

[3] See Browning, *A Fundamental Practical Theology*, 94.

[4] The model begins with insertion, and moves to the stages of social analysis, theological reflection, and ends with pastoral planning. Joe Holland, and Peter Henriot, *Social Analysis: Linking Faith and Justice* (New York: Orbis Books, 1983).

[5] Joe Holland, "Roots of the Pastoral Circle in Personal Experiences and Catholic Social Tradition," in *The Pastoral Circle Revisited: A Critical Quest for Truth and Transformation*, ed. Frans Wijsen, Peter Henriot, and Rodrigo Mejia (New York: Orbis Books, 2005), 10.

[6] Browning, *A Fundamental Practical Theology*, 94-95.

Observing, analyzing, and evaluating, helps to identify strategic actions that will improve the pastoral situation in Tivland. This design is divided into four stages corresponding with the four movements of the circle method. The first movement discusses the context of the study, and the protocol used in gathering information.

First Movement:
The Context of Tiv Society

The general context of this book is Tiv society of Benue State, in central Nigeria. To explore the context is a helpful approach because a people's worldview is a starting point for contextual theology.[7]

Various historical traditions agree that Tiv people descended from a common ancestor called Tiv.[8] However the story of his ancestry has several versions that are sometimes confusing.[9]

Tiv had two sons, *Ipusu* (uncircumcised) and *Ichongo* (circumcised).[10] The two sons combined, gave birth to twenty-eight children. These have become clans in Tivland named after each of the sons. The progenies of *Ipusu* include *Nanev, Shangev-Ya, Ikyurav-Ya, Kunav, Ikyurav-Tiev, Mbagba, Ishangev-Tiev, Ukan, Ukum, Mbayion,* and *Gaav*. Others are, *Mbagen, Ikov, Shitile, Ishorov, Kusuv, Mbatyav, Tombo, Utange, Maer, Mbakor,* and *Ipav*. *Ichongo* had six children.

---

[7] See Schreiter, *Constructing Local Theologies*.

[8] See Atel, *Dynamics of Tiv Religion and Culture,* 8. Also Dzurgba, *On the Tiv of Central Nigeria,* 13.

[9] See Atel, *Dynamics of Tiv Religion and Culture,* 8. He observes that of the three ancestors of Tiv, *Takuluku, Awange, and Shon,* scholars have not agreed on who is the actual father of Tiv. Dzurgba, *On the Tiv of Central Nigeria,* 13-16, analyses two of the ancestors, *Awange* and *Takuluku,* mostly favored by scholars. He concludes that the question of Tiv's father, mother and wife are historically irrelevant. He observes that history focuses on the religious, social, economic, political, scientific and technological successes or achievements and failures of one great person in a biographical narrative.

[10] Dzurgba, *The Tiv and Their Culture,* 87. The Tiv name their children based on the situation surrounding the birth of the particular child. In Tiv society, most names recognize the sovereignty of God as opposed to names such as *Mbatsavwua* (witches have killed.) For instance, names such as *Terseer* (the Lord has added), *Aondofa* (God knows), *Aondongu* (God exists), are given in recognition of the role of God in the life of the family at the time the child was born. It is not clear why Tiv chose to name his children *Ipusu* and *Ichongo*.

These are *Iharev, Isherev, Masev, Nongov, Ugondo,* and *Turan.*[11] These progenies in-turn multiplied and have become a large ethnic group. Today, the Tiv tribe is the fifth largest in Nigeria with over five million people.[12] The Tiv are found in the Benue region.

The original home of Tiv people is not clear. The general assumption is that they are of Bantu origin somewhere in central Africa.[13] They migrated from the south east of the Republic of the Cameroon, and later to the present territory called Tivland[14] likely in flight from their neighbors. Tiv people live in Benue State, and are also found in neighboring states such as Nasarawa, Plateau, Cross River, Adamawa, and Taraba.

Benue State has cultural diversity with Tiv as the major tribe, followed by *Idoma,* and *Igede.* Tiv is a monolithic ethnic group united under a common ancestor called Tiv, but with a variety of clans or districts. Each clan is divided into several *uipaven* kin units.[15] Tiv as an ethnic group is homogeneous, yet diversified, thanks to its twenty-eight clans. Several clans or districts form a Local Government Area. Benue State consists of twenty-three Local Government Areas, fourteen occupied by Tiv people.[16] Other minority languages like Agatu and Akpa combine with Idoma and Igede to make up the other nine Local Government Areas in the state. Benue State is predominantly a Christian state. Christianity has spread to the hinter-

---

[11] Dzurgba, *The Tiv and Their Culture,* 87-88. Out of the 23 local government areas in Benue State, these clans fall within fourteen local government divisions as follows; *Kwande, Vandeikya, Konshisha, Ushongo, Katsina-Ala, Gboko, Buruku, Ukum, Logo,* and *Tarkaa.* Others are *Guma, Gwer, Gwer West,* and *Makurdi.*

[12] Daniel Ude Asue, *Catholic Sexual Ethics and Tiv Women: A Case-study of Pastoral Practice in Regard to HIV/AIDS* (PhD dissertation, St Thomas University, Miami, 2012), 75.

[13] Wegh, *Between Continuity and Change,* 36. Other scholars who opine that Tiv people originate from the Congo, base their argument on the similarity between Tiv language and language of the Bantu Nyaza who live in the present-day Malawi.

[14] Wegh, *Between Continuity and Change,* 37.

[15] Dzurgba, *On the Tiv of Central Nigeria,* 21.

[16] Dzurgba, *On the Tiv of Central Nigeria,* 22. A small tribe called Etulo migrated in the seventeenth century and settled in Buruku, and Katsina-Ala local government areas in Tivland. The Nyifon or Iordaa, Jukum, Hausa, and Abakpa are other minority tribes found among the Tiv.

lands of the state. This has consequently diminished the impact of traditional religions.

Africans are notoriously religious.[17] This is also true of the Tiv. Africans do not talk of a formal distinction between the spiritual and the material areas of life. They take their religion wherever they go. They carry it with them to the field when sowing seeds or harvesting new crops. They take it to public drinking places or to a funeral ceremony, and if they are educated, they take their religion with them to the examination room at school or in the university. If they are politicians, they take it to the parliament.[18] Emerging adults in institutions of higher education also bring their faith to campus.[19] The next section describes three higher education contexts, but what follows immediately is a description of the setting.

Focus on Local Contexts

The context of this book is narrowed down to three institutions of higher education in Tivland. These include, the College of Education (COE), plus Katsina-Ala, Federal University of Agriculture (Uniagric), and Benue State University (BSU), with the last two located in Makurdi, the state capital. The College of Education is a three-year teacher training college that offers a Nigeria Certificate in Education (NCE), an equivalent of an associate degree. It is located about one hundred and twenty-nine kilometers or 80 miles away from Makurdi. The two universities have accredited undergraduate and graduate programs.

Each of the three institutions has a strong Catholic ministerial presence. With the recent creation of Gboko and Katsina-Ala dioceses out of Makurdi Diocese, College of Education chaplaincy falls under Katsina-Ala Diocese, while the two universities fall under Makurdi Diocese.

---

[17]John S. Mbiti, *African Religions and Philosophy* (London: Heinemann, 1985), 1.
[18]Mbiti, *African Religions and Philosophy*, 1-2.
[19] Other Christian denominations too are present on campus. See John Agaba, and Ezekiel A. Hanior, "The Goodnews Chapel, Origin, Growth and Development 1993-2012," in *Benue State University at 20: Achievements, Challenges and Prospects,* eds., Oga Ajene, Mathieu A. Adejo, and Member George-Genyi (Makurdi: SAP Publishing House, 2012).

Chaplaincies are diocesan establishments whose structure is not the same as a parish. These include schools, hospitals, and pious societies. A priest is specially assigned to give spiritual and pastoral care to the people who belong to such institutions or organizations. Students admitted in these institutions come from different states of the federation, but the majority is from Benue State. This suggests that the institutions have a heterogeneous cultural setting. The setting provides an appropriate context for the study of the worship experiences and practices of Catholic students of Tiv extraction.

College of Education, Katsina-Ala.

Established in September 1976, the College of Education is the first higher education in Benue State. It was first called Advanced Teachers College with Mr. Idah D.O. as the first principal. The first set of students arrived at the college campus on November 15th, 1976.

At the inception of the college, the local ordinary of the Catholic Diocese of Makurdi, Most Reverend Donald Murray CSSp, ensured the inclusion of Reverend Father Gottery on the faculty team to lead the Catholic community. In 1988, the St Augustine Catholic Chaplaincy was established. The letter establishing the chaplaincy was endorsed by Bishop Athanasius Atule Usuh, who was the Coadjutor bishop of Makurdi diocese at the time. At present, Most Reverend Wilfred Chikpa Anagbe of the Claretian congregation is the bishop of Makurdi diocese. He was ordained Coadjutor bishop of Makurdi on October 4, 2014. Following the retirement of bishop Usuh on grounds of ill-health, bishop Anagbe was installed bishop of Makurdi diocese on July 25, 2015. Reverend Father Moses Orshio Adasu was the first substantive chaplain of the college.

A brief History of St Augustine Catholic Chaplaincy, written by Francis Asor KSM to mark the pastoral visit of Bishop William A. Avenya on October 2-3, 2010 shows that Father Adasu left the priesthood temporary for politics. He was elected member of the defunct Constituent Assembly in 1989. He later joined partisan politics and was elected the second civilian Governor of Benue State in 1992. He laid a solid foundation for the sustenance of the chaplaincy. Catholic population of both staff and students at inception constituted 60 percent of the entire college population. The population has continued to grow during the ministerial work of succeeding chaplains like Fathers Bennet Owasomba, Didacus Kajo, Clement Iorliam, Moses Igba, and Michael Ikyem.

As of September 2013, faculty members numbered 297. Of this, 242 are male, while 55 are female. Non-faculty members total 409, of which 285 are men, and 125 are women. Gender disparity in this figure is very striking: 526 men and 180 women. The population of students in the 2012-2013 session was 9,712. Male students number 5,392, and female students 4,320.[20] These figures give useful statistical information about the college but fail to identify the number of Catholics, Protestants, and other religions. Since this was the first higher education chaplaincy to be established, population figures were very important in determining its sustainability. The staff population is significant because the chaplaincy relies on their financial contribution for its sustenance.

College of Education management under the leadership of the Provost Hans Senwua allowed students to practice their faith on campus without hindrance. The present Provost, Mr Orze Kor too supports the practice of faith on campus. Students are predominantly Christians. Catholics and members of NKST are the dominant religious groups in the college. Other Christian denominations are also a part of the school population. Moslems are very few, and do not worship on campus. People of other faith traditions have not publicly identified themselves on campus. It is not clear if they are a part of the college community.

Members of the NKST were the first to build a church on campus, located at the north eastern side of the college. The college management allows other Christian traditions to conduct worship in lecture rooms. As the population of Catholics continued to grow, the college management allocated bigger facilities that would conveniently accommodate worshippers at those particular times.

---

[20] Emmanuel Torna (a staff in the office of Records and Statistics, College of Education Katsina-Ala), in a one-on-one interview on June 8, 2014.

At present, Catholics perform their worship in the church located on the school campus, currently undergoing construction through the financial contributions of students, faculty, staff, and others. A few men and women in business are also a part of the congregation. These too make substantial financial contributions to the overall sustenance of the chaplaincy, including support for whatever project the chaplaincy sets out to execute. From time to time, individuals from other places are invited to make donations that would enhance the work of the chaplaincy.

The church building shares a boundary with the boys' dormitory at the extreme of the eastern side of the college. It is a serene environment fitting for worship with mango trees providing comfortable shade at both ends of the church. It is a rectangular building with multiple windows and a door on every side. The four doors have been fitted with shutters, but windows have been barricaded with iron rod design until such a time when the special v-shape windows would be constructed and fixed. Built with cement bricks and roofed with iron rods and corrugated aluminium roofing sheets, the facility is apparently durable and sizeable enough to accommodate about two thousand worshippers. The outside wall of the building is yet to be plastered, but the inside wall has been plastered, and the floor is yet to be smoothened.

Yet, the community has commenced worship in the building. When the college is in session, two Masses are offered every Sunday at 7:00 am and 8:30 am. The first is in English and the second is offered in Tiv to accommodate the surrounding population that is predominantly illiterate. Many Tiv students prefer to attend the second Mass celebrated in Tiv.

The Chaplaincy is in the process of making seats for the Church. The few pews that have been made so far occupy about half of the worship space. While the project is ongoing, some worshippers bring seats from their homes. Many, mostly students, stand as long as worship lasts. Drawing from Tiv culture that has high regard for seniority, the few pews are reserved for staff, faculty members, and other elders who worship in the chaplaincy.

Solomon Sesugh a student of the college who hails from Vandeikya Local Government area stated that he was inspired worshipping in a learned environment because it was different from what he experiences in his village. However, he was "dissatisfied with the gross insufficiency of seats. The few that are available are reserved for lecturers."[21] This is in line with the Tiv practice that gives preference to elders where seats are insufficient. Usually, people come to worship in large numbers. This particular day I observed worship at the chaplaincy was a Pentecost Sunday, and the church was filled to capacity. Many worshippers were seen standing throughout the duration of worship.

The Chaplain Father Michael Ikyem gave me the privilege as a participant observer to celebrate the 7:00 am Mass. The general mood of worship was exciting. The choir sang traditional hymns such as "Come Holy Ghost," and the "The comforter has come." Many worshippers sang with the choir. During offertory, people came in procession dancing and singing familiar choruses to offer their gifts to God in a collection box placed in front of the sanctuary. They sang songs such as:

> *What shall I say unto the Lord*
> *All I have to say is thank you Lord*
> *Thank you Lord, thank you Lord*
> *All I have to say is thank you Lord.*

After the post communion prayer, the commentator came forward and announced that "you already know our tradition in this chaplaincy. I now invite the choir to give us a song so that you can come forward joyfully and respond as we usually do." The announcement was shrouded in codes unintelligible to outsiders. People started coming in procession again with closed palms, singing, dancing, and dropping something in the box.

After the Mass, I withdrew to the Chaplain's residence located about a quarter mile outside the college campus. The chaplain handed over an envelope to me containing money with a comment

---

[21] Solomon Sesugh (a nineteen years old student of College of Education, Katsina-Ala), in a one-on-one interview on June 8, 2014 at Katsina-Ala.

that it was a gift from the worship community. It immediately dawned on me that the announcement was for this purpose. The Tiv offer gifts to visitors as an expression of a happy privilege to host them. This practice was transposed into the church on campus, providing an excellent symbol to contextualize Catholicism.

The freedom to carry out religious activities on campus, attending Mass, and carrying out devotional activities through pious societies is not peculiar to College of Education. The most vibrant societies in COE include the Catholic Biblical Movement of Nigeria, English and Tiv choirs, and Altar Boys' Association. Other colleges and universities within the state also enjoy this level of religious freedom.

Federal University of Agriculture, Makurdi

The Catholic community in the Federal University of Agriculture is one such institution. The university was established on January 1, 1988, and it is the first autonomous university in the state. The overall goal was to train people to improve agriculture in Nigeria. Benue State was chosen as a site to enhance its agricultural performance as the food basket of the nation.[22] Several attempts to gain access to the detail statistics of staff and students based on gender affiliation proved unsuccessful.

As a federal establishment, it has a federal character as students are admitted from all over the country. As of 2013/2014 session, 4,361 undergraduate students were admitted into various programs of the university.[23] Many of the students practice either Christianity or Islam, with the majority being Christians.[24] Admission is given to

---

[22] See Dzurgba, *The Tiv and their Culture*, 65.
[23] University of Agriculture, Makurdi, "2013/2014 Admission List,"
http://uam.edu.ng/Resources/Downloads/2013-2014-Admission-List.
[24] Didacus Kajo (the Chaplain, Pope John Paul II Catholic Chaplaincy, University of Agriculture, Makurdi), in a one-on-one interview on June 3, 2014 at Makurdi. He observed that the Catholic and Protestant traditions are strong on campus. He also noted that Chaplains before him that helped to consolidate the chaplaincy include, Reverend Fathers William Avenya (now Bishop of Gboko Diocese), Kenneth Agede, Peter Gbulum (deceased), and Godwin Udaa.

all, including Benue indigenes on merit. Candidates from various Local Government areas are given equal opportunities to ensure that no area has more representation than another.

The school community is heterogeneous, which implies that the worshipping community, under the umbrella of the Saint John Paul II Catholic Chaplaincy, consists of Catholic students from different parts of the country, and indeed different parts of Tivland.

The Saint John Paul II Catholic Chaplaincy has over two thousand worshippers at two Masses every Sunday. The worship is currently conducted in the Professor J. O. Ayatse Convocation Square located at the south core of the university. The north core houses the main administrative unit of the university, while the south core houses mainly the lecture rooms and student accommodation.

As the name implies, the square was built primarily for the university commencement ceremonies, but several activities take place here, including religious activities. It is a large roofed open-air arena, not very conducive for worship. Located very close to the main access into the south core, worshippers are often distracted by moving vehicles, and other distracting noises. Every Saturday, student volunteers clean and arrange the square for the celebration of the Eucharist on Sunday. The former Vice Chancellor, E. I. Kucha is a Catholic, and sometimes worshipped on campus with students, staff and faculty. The Chaplain Reverend Father Didacus Kajo lives on campus in the accommodation reserved for the senior faculty members of the university.

Society meetings also take place within the convocation square. The Chaplaincy has several societies that bring students in close relationships.[25] The Catholic community is currently undertaking a

---

[25] These include the Catholic Charismatic Renewal of Nigeria (CCRN), Legion of Mary, Precious Blood, St. Cecelia's English Choir and Queen of all Hearts. Others are the Communities of *Tiv, Idoma* and *Igbo* students, Lectors' Society, Mass Servers' Association, Block Rosary Crusade, St. Rita Society, Marian Movement for Priests and Laity, Association of Artists, Divine Mercy Society, Young Catholic Students of Nigeria (YCSN) and the Sacred Heart of Jesus/Immaculate Heart of Mary. See I. N. Itodo (a faculty member, and Chair, Church Council of Pope John Paul II Chaplaincy, University of Agriculture, Makurdi), in an unpublished history of the chaplaincy, 2014.

church building project on campus. Unlike the Saint John Paul II Catholic Chaplaincy, The Good Shepherd Catholic Chaplaincy, Benue State University has consolidated chaplaincy services with a completed church project.

Benue State University, Makurdi

Benue State University was established in 1992 to offer academic opportunities to the hundreds of qualified candidates of Benue State origin who were unable to gain admission into the Federal University of Agriculture and other universities within the catchment area.[26] At inception, the student population was 306 with 149 faculty members. As of 2014, out of 1,991 staff, 677 of them are faculty members. The overall student population for 2011/2012 session was 21,448. Out of this number 18,383 were undergraduates predominantly consisting of emerging adults. As of 2015 under Professor Msugh Moses Kembe, student population was 32000. [27]

The above statistical information does not identify male and female categories, and demographic issues of religious affiliation of the staff and students. However, the data does not render the discourse on the contextualization of the Catholic faith in Tiv culture ineffective. What is crucial to the discussion is the BSU setting.

The university has seven faculties, a College of Health Sciences, as well as a center for Continuing Education, and 22 Departments. Graduate programs have grown from nineteen to fifty, spread across the faculties. One of the objectives of the university is to "provide ready access for Benue State Citizens to higher education for self-reliance."[28] The university is a microcosm of Benue State

---

[26] Nguemo Adi and Ngove Peter Pever, "Student Enrolment at Benue State University, Makurdi," in *Benue State University at 20: Achievements, Challenges and Prospects,* ed. Oga Ajene, Mathieu A. Adejo, and Member-George Genyi (Makurdi: SAP Publishing House, 2012), 102.

[27] "History of Benue State University," http://bsum.edu.ng/downloads/BSU_Brief_History.pdf.

[28] See "Benue State University," http://www.campusflava.blogspot.com/2009/11/benue-state-university.html. This suggests that the majority of the students are indigenes of Benue State, who come from the three major tribes. Tiv students are the majority and Tiv language is commonly spoken on campus.

implying that the goal to admit Benue indigenes has been realized to a large extent. The institution focuses on the holistic development of the human person.

In this regard, Benue State University has a well-organized Catholic ministerial presence that pays particular attention to the spiritual formation of emerging adults. Their chapel, built in isolation at the southern part of the institution and half way between the first and second campuses, is of modern architectural design. The choice of location seems to have been calculated to ensure easy access for people who live on both sides of the campus.

In an interview, the chaplain stated that the building can conveniently accommodate two thousand worshippers. Constructed in a rectangular shape, it has two layers of windows on the lower and upper walls. The rectangular shaped windows are numerous, perhaps to ensure abundant in-flow of fresh air to tackle the naturally hot Makurdi city weather. Ceiling fans are also installed to enhance a cooling atmosphere. The church has six doors, two on both sides of the building, one at the end of the church facing the sanctuary, and the other behind the sanctuary as an entrance for ministers. Usually, when the first Mass is over and people rush to leave the church, one of the side doors serves as exit and the other as entrance for those attending the second Mass.

Churches in Makudi diocese are typically furnished with long pews. On the contrary, the BSU church was furnished with plastic chairs arranged in rolls between five aisles. The chaplain stated that the use of chairs is a tentative arrangement. Ultimately, pews will replace the chairs. The left side of the sanctuary area is reserved for the choir, whose singing is accompanied by musical instruments such as keyboard, drums, and a set of bands.

Nigeria, Vatican, and the USA flags are installed on the same side occupied by the choir. As far as Catholicism in Nigeria is concerned, the reasons for installing the Nigerian and Vatican flags are taken for granted. Moved by curiosity to know the purpose of a US flag in a local church in Nigeria, I was told the chaplain enjoys dual citizenship of Nigeria and the USA. This is a wonderful symbol of identifying with one's roots. In particular, the Vatican flag representing the universal Roman Catholic Church with headquarters in the Vatican City symbolizes the foreignness of Catholicism. This supports the view that Catholicism is foreign to Tivland. The Nigerian flag on the other hand is a symbol of rooting Catholicism in the local culture.

The statues of Jesus and Mary are raised on a platform on both sides of the altar. A huge cross is hung on the upper part of the wall in the middle of the sanctuary area. Images of the Stations of the Cross are hung around the church. Fou speakers meant to boost the communication system are hung on the top four corners of the church, all securely locked in an iron cage. All visible images in the church reflect the identity of a Catholic Church except that the tabernacle could not be identified. When asked about the location of the tabernacle in the church, the chaplain stated that the church is built in an isolated area, and therefore, no security is guaranteed for the Eucharist if left in the tabernacle. He prefers taking the remnants to his residence in the senior staff quarters within the university campus. His explanation reflects the high regard Catholics attach to the Eucharist.

The church is located in an area that appears to be designated for religious buildings. The rectory that is under construction is closely located to the chapel. It is designed to offer accommodation conveniently to seven priests, including priests on the faculty, and also, those who may come for graduate studies will stay on temporary basis. This strategy enhances community life among priests on campus, which again offers a rich symbol of contextualizing Catholicism in Tiv culture.

A few meters away from the rectory is a chapel for the separated brethren that is almost completed. No evidence of a mosque was visible. This raises the question of the absence of a mosque in an area that appears to be mapped out for religious buildings. In response, the chaplain said the mosque was deliberately eliminated to control Muslim extremism such as Boko Haram[29] insurgency on the BSU campus.

---

[29] See Agbonikhianmeghe E. Orobator, "Why is Boko Haram Succeeding?" *Commonweal*, March 3, 2015,

Generally, the area is a tranquil environment good for worship activities. Most societies hold their meetings in the environment outside the church. Students are strongly warned not to read around the chapel area. A security was employed to guard the property of the church, and to enforce the law that forbids students from reading inside the church or around the corridors of the church building. In the course of observing the environment, students occasionally came into the chapel either as individuals or small groups, prayed and left after a few minutes. My perception of their practice of faith challenged me to participate at worship with them to know more about their worship experiences.

Students at Worship

I participated at worship with the members of the BSU community as with COE. Participating at a Eucharistic celebration as a minister offered an opportunity to observe the actual worship experiences of emerging adults, who constituted the major part of the three selected worshipping communities. It is helpful to participate and observe the worship ritual because people enter into worship first through their bodies. Though words determine the significance of the rite, they can be interpreted only within the ritual context.[30]

Observation focused on the various dispositions people brought into worship and the degree to which individual members of the congregation brought their bodies into worship. The way people arrived, interacted with each other, and left were observed as important dynamics in worship.[31]

---

https://www.commonwealmagazine.org/why-boko-haram-succeeding?utm_source=Main+Reader+List&utm_campaign=53dc39f726 July+18_The_Week_at_Commonweal&utm_medium=email&utm_term=0_407bf353a 253dc39f726-91226109.

Boko Haram is an Islamic insurgent group that says "Western education is an abomination." Their goal is to establish "true Islam" in Nigeria. They fight and kill people perceived to be against their ideology. It has been declared a terrorist group by the Nigerian government.

[30] David N. Power, *Sacrament: The Language of God's Giving* (New York: Crossroad, 1999), 149.

[31] See James F. White, "Moving Christian Worship Toward Social Justice," *Christian Century* 104, no. 19 (1987): 559.

No formal time was allowed for participants to greet themselves before the commencement of worship. Those who arrived before Mass exchanged greetings before worship commenced. Others were seen coming late. After the celebration, many stood in groups and exchanged greetings. This "process of observation examines whether the community does what it means."[32] Where practices or expressions were not clear, I sought for clarification.

In the course of participating and observing worship, clarification was sought on certain aspects of worship that appeared particularly symbolic. For example, the Mass offered at the Good Shepherd Chaplaincy was an inaugural Mass for the session. The Vice Chancellor of the university at the time, Mrs Charity Angya, key university officials, staff, faculty, and many students were in attendance. When inquired about the significance of the inaugural Mass, Judith Utoo, a student and member of the chaplaincy said, it is the day their chaplain prays for the university management, and the entire university community for the success of the academic session.[33]

Typically, Sunday Masses are scheduled at 7:00 am and 9:00 am. On the Sunday of the inaugural Mass, a combined Mass was celebrated at 9:00 am. After the liturgy of the Eucharist, the Vice Chancellor donated money on behalf of the university management toward the construction of permanent seats for the church. The whole church went jubilant with students shouting, and making joyful noises accompanied by a standing ovation as a sign of approval of the Vice Chancellor.

The joyful spirit continued after Mass as students shared a common meal. This symbol is important to BSU because the meal is open to all members of the academic community, Catholics and non-Catholics alike. Students ate their meal under canopies that were erected temporarily outside the church, while the chaplain and his assistant, staff, faculty and other invited guests went to the university club house for their refreshment. The image of common meal advances the work of the church in the local Catholic community.

---

[32] White, "Moving Christian Worship Toward Social Justice," 559.
[33] Judith Utoo (a twenty-two years old student of Benue State University, Makurdi), in a one-on -one interview on May 18, 2014 at Makurdi.

Participant observation of this kind has been widely used in practical theological work.[34] Cartledge argues in favor of this approach asserting that "when I conducted case study research, I joined in the worship of the churches I was studying and therefore participated with them."[35] Such participation allows for an assessment of the analogical relationship between the worship experiences and practices of emerging adults and Catholic worship at this particular time in Tiv society.

Observation also leads to analysis as the observer looks at the actions of emerging adult Catholics, including roles and words observed in terms of faith, as well as any hidden message. This process involves checking how actions conform to words. However, participant observation has its limitations. These include interviewing people in an ad hoc manner, and the inaccessibility to certain locations that are "out of bound"[36] To deepen my theological work, I created time to ask some students questions concerning their experience of worship.

One-on-one interviews particularly brought much information about emerging adults. There is simply no substitute for sitting face to face with people and talking to them about what they have experienced and what the experience means to them.[37] Interviews focused primarily on emerging adults' demographics, their experience of the Catholic Church and worship and the meaning they derive from the Eucharist as the climax of worship in the Catholic Church.

I asked them questions that focused on, (1) demographics and family background, including how emerging adults perceive themselves and how they want others to see them; (2) what emerging adults say about the Catholic Church; (3) how they see worship in the Catholic Church, and; (4) gave them room to make other remarks to conclude the discussion. Questions sought to identify how these topic areas can help to contextualize worship in Tiv culture. (For exam-

---

[34]See Mark J. Cartledge, *Practical Theology: Charismatic and Empirical Perspective* (London: Paternoster, 2007), 70.

[35] Cartledge, *Practical Theology*, 71.

[36] Cartledge, *Practical Theology*, 70.

[37] Arnett, *Emerging Adulthood*, vii.

ple, could you tell me how you see yourself as an educated emerging adult from your particular clan of Tiv society?).

This simple protocol was used in the sites I participated at worship with students, thus producing similar interview transcripts each time.[38] Of course, new questions emerged to deepen the conversation.[39] Such questions were taken up with appropriate probes such as "can you tell me more about that" and "what does what you have said mean to you." I analyzed the information I got using social and cultural perspectives.

Second Movement:
Social & Cultural Analysis of Symbols

The second movement of the circle method moves from the context toward insight into the social and cultural world of educated Tiv emerging adult Catholics. Social and cultural analysis helps to identify the root causes of the problem of why Catholicism has yet to be contextualized in Tiv culture. This includes exploring social and cultural symbols, the role of social context, and demographic issues.

This movement of the circle method is primarily concerned with social analysis, which is broadened and deepened by combining it with cultural analysis.[40] The central issue is to determine social and cultural factors in the worship experiences of emerging adults. Education as a social symbol, and the family as a cultural symbol have either enhanced or plummeted the worship experiences of emerging adults. Such symbols are analyzed and interpreted using Tracy's analogical framework. The framework recognizes a three-pronged criterion: a criterion of adequacy, a criterion of appropriateness, and a criterion of internal coherence.

Hermeneutics is an essential tool in analyzing the family and education as symbols. Analysis of these symbols helps to establish an

---

[38] Cartledge, *Practical Theology*, 72.

[39] Cartledge, *Practical Theology*, 72.

[40] Frans Wijsen, "The Practical Theological Spiral: Bridging Theology in the West and the Rest of the World," in *The Pastoral Circle Revisited: A Critical Quest for Truth and Transformation,* ed.Frans Wijsen, Peter Henriot, and Rodrigo Mejia (New York: Orbis Books, 2005), 117.

analogical relationship with Catholic worship. It is important to pay attention to these symbols because symbols give rise to thought.[41] This is particularly true of young people as education and family have a variety of influences on them. The hermeneutical perspective[42] in social and cultural analysis enhances theological reflection as it unravels every situation that appears symbolic. Education and family are public symbols that are expressed in and through everyday life because these symbols sustain intersubjectivity and express different meanings that are sometimes taken for granted.[43]

For example, when a Tiv parent says, my child attends Queen of the Rosary Girls Secondary School, Gboko, the parent is communicating the importance of educating the girl-child as the school is a bit expensive, and is a top ranking girls' school in the state. The Tiv commonly express many other symbols in their thinking, speech, and everyday life.

As the family and education are symbols that influence the worship experiences and practices of emerging adults, the contribution of the social sciences is important in analyzing these symbols.[44] The intradisciplinary approaches of sociology, anthropology, and psychology are helpful in exploring a broad base analysis. Social science analysis identifies and explores the impact of the family and education on emerging adults. It identifies the degree to which their worship experiences in particular, are influenced by these symbols. This movement of the circle challenges the Catholic Church to take the world of Tiv emerging adults seriously, thus getting to know more about them. A serious commitment to emerging adults ex-

---

[41] Veling, *Practical Theology*, xviii.

[42] Many practical theologians integrate the hermeneutical perspective in their theological work. These include, Gerben Heitink, *Practical Theology: History, Theory, Action Domain*, Trans. Reinder Bruinsma(Grand Rapids: William B. Eerdmans, 1993); Terry A. Veling, *Practical Theology: On Earth As It Is in Heaven* (New York: Orbis Books, 2005); Edward Farley, "Interpreting Situations: An Inquiry into the nature of Practical Theology," in *The Blackwell Reader in Pastoral and Practical Theology*, ed. James Woodward and Stephen Pattison (Malsen: Blackwell Publishers, 2000).

[43] See Manuel A. Vasquez, *More Than Belief: A Materialist Theory of Religion* (New York: Oxford University Press, 2011), 213.

[44] Holland, "Roots of the Pastoral Circle in Personal Experiences and Catholic Social Tradition," 6.

plores ways that make them truly Tiv and truly Catholic. This movement integrates the hermeneutical perspective bearing in mind that symbols and concepts need to be interpreted.

Third Movement:
Mutual Enrichment of Catholic Worship Symbols & Tiv Cultural Symbols

The third movement in the circle method is theological reflection. This movement evaluates the link between the symbols of worship in the Catholic Church and those of Tiv culture, observed and analyzed in light of education and family factors. Devoting this stage to theological reflection does not make the first two stages pre-theological, for theology is not limited to a particular movement of the circle.[45] Rather, theological reflection specifically evaluates worship as experienced by emerging adults in Tiv culture in the light of Christian tradition establishing the connection between faith and culture.

Questions that evaluate such practices are at the heart of theological reflection. For example, "when you think of the Eucharist, what comes to your mind?" Asking the interviewee appropriate questions helps to connect theological discourse about culture and the practice of faith.

In response to this question, interviewees expressed the meaning they derived from the Eucharist, and even connected the Eucharist with *imborvungu*, and other symbols in Tiv culture. The analogy of the Eucharist and *imborvungu* has been used to mutually enrich emerging adults in the practice of faith, and their expression of Tiv culture. Such analogies explored the similarities and differences that led to theological reflection.

The exercise of theological reflection is one in which pastoral experience serves as a context for critical development of basic theological understanding of Catholic worship symbols and cultural sym-

---

[45] Wijsen, "The practical Theological Spiral: Bridging Theology in the West and the Rest of the World,"118.

bols.[46] Drawing from the Catholic tradition, theological reflection on faith and culture advances the identity of emerging adults as truly Tiv and truly Catholic. Theological reflection draws from appropriate sources of the Catholic tradition such as the Bible, papal documents, and magisterial documents of both universal and local churches.

After diagnosing the problem affecting the contextualization of Catholicism in Tivland, this movement retrieves from the faith tradition, appropriate biblical and theological wisdom to evaluate it.[47] Talk about God emerges from emerging adults' experience of worship, and what those experiences mean to them. In reflecting theologically, the Catholic tradition challenges emerging adults to defend the church's position concerning doctrinal issues or issues of practice that are most often misunderstood.

This is important because most emerging adults displayed their ignorance of Catholic doctrines such as sacramentals, the use of sacred images in worship, and the role of Mary in the church often challenged by their separated brethren. Practical theological reflection is rooted in the experiences of emerging adults that require practical responses from them as people of faith. Those responses emanating from the link between faith and culture, worship and life propose a grounding symbolically of Tiv Catholics.

Fourth Movement:
Community, Catechesis, & Service
as Hallmarks of Contextualization

The final movement of the circle is oriented toward planning[48] and active response; it also proposes pastoral lines of strategy.[49] Educated Tiv emerging adults at this point take up the challenge to devel-

---

[46] See Elaine Graham, Heather Walton, and Frances Ward. *Theological Reflection* (London: SCM, 2005), 6.

[47] See Holland, "Roots of the Pastoral Circle in Personal Experiences and Catholic Social Tradition," 10.

[48] Wijsen, "The practical Theological Spiral: Bridging Theology in the West and the Rest of the World," 120.

[49] Holland, "Roots of the Pastoral Circle in Personal Experiences and Catholic Social Tradition," 10.

op and express this local theology. As community theologians, they are animators who can interpret and pass on the faith in diverse and planned or unplanned ways through natural networks of relationships with local communities.

Every emerging adult hails from a local community of district, clan, and clan unit. Typically, Tiv people who live in urban areas go back to their local communities during festive periods of Christmas and New Year celebrations. They also return home for funeral and marriage ceremonies. Such occasions provide the opportunity to reunite with people in the local communities.

As enlightened people, rural communities look up to them for guidance. They are the educated people who decide political alliances for those in local communities. The local dwellers expect them to provide solutions to the many unanswered questions confronting them. They can also make critically important contributions in local communities and can also interpret the faith as the need arises. These practical strategies are taken in the light of appropriate biblical and theological wisdom. This stage is a faith-filled refection on the need to make worship contextual in regard to Tiv emerging adults' experiences.[50] The goal is to ensure a praxis-oriented action.

Catholicism is contextualized both at the micro and macro levels. At the micro level, chaplaincies in institutions of higher education facilitate the creation of community theologians on academic campuses who support this local theology. These community theologians spring from the pious organizations present on campus. They receive adequate catechesis within the group meetings that prepares them to be effective interpreters of the faith. At the macro level, their unprogrammed pedagogical work at grassroots level helps to contextualize the Catholic faith in the wider Tiv society. Generally, this strategy is a mutually enriching model aimed at contextualizing Catholicism in Tiv culture.

---

[50] Holland, "Roots of the Pastoral Circle in Personal Experiences and Catholic Social Tradition," 8.

A Contextual Model

The figure below is a mutually re-enforcing model that demonstrates an understanding of what most connects emerging adults with Catholic worship and what the Catholic Church needs to know about them. The figure also illustrates educated young people as community theologians who will interpret the faith to others including, those in rural communities through natural networks. Their task is to theologize between Tiv culture and Catholic worship to contextualize the Catholic faith in Tiv culture.

Emerging Adults/Catholic Worship ⟷**Understanding**⟷ Catholic Church/Emerging Adults

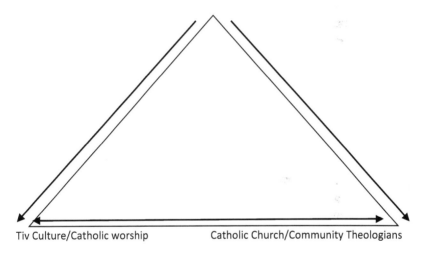

Tiv Culture/Catholic worship   Catholic Church/Community Theologians

Figure 1. The above drawing shows how emerging adult Catholics can theologize between Tiv culture, and Catholic worship.

Conclusion

The goal of every investigation is to answer basic questions. This chapter has described the method to solve the issue of the separation of faith and culture that is critical in rooting Catholicism in Tiv culture. Central to the chapter is the exploration of the context of the investigation, and a map of how to answer the questions using praxis-oriented methods including, the circle method. To effectively address the split of faith and culture, the chapter utilized the main sources of practical theology; human experience, culture, and Christian tradition. Using information provided by the social sciences, the next chapter analyzes the experiences of emerging adults from social and cultural perspectives. In particular, it identifies the family and education as symbols that influence the worship experiences of emerging adults.

6

SOCIAL & CULTURAL ANALYSIS
OF SYMBOLS

S ocial and cultural factors contribute majorly to the situation that prevails in any given context. Such factors can affect the practice of faith too. This chapter argues that social and cultural factors influence the ritual experiences of educated emerging adult Catholics. Social and cultural analysis identifies issues that influence the understanding of Catholic ritual in a Tiv context. In this context, the family and education are symbols that play a major role in emerging adults' expression of Catholicism in Tiv culture. These factors affect emerging adults first, in rural contexts, and later in urban cities where they pursue higher education.

This chapter coincides with the second movement of the circle method, and it explores symbols that affect the worship experiences of emerging adults. The chapter discusses the family unit as the primal context of emerging adults' encounter with culture and the Catholic faith, and views education as a multivalent symbol that socializes, and integrates emerging adults in Tiv culture.

The Family as a Cultural Symbol

The Family is the basic unit of society.[1] It is the point of entry into Tiv culture and it is a symbol of cultural identity. To say one is a legitimate Tiv person means tracing the person's genealogy to several generations.[2] The traditional life of Africans in particular is centered around the family. The family is where life is generated, and the values of the clan, the tribe, and generally those of Africa are consciously or unconsciously transmitted.[3] The family comprises of parents, children, and extended relations. Marriage is a necessary component of family life.

The Apostolic Exhortation of Pope Francis, *Amoris Laetitia* (The Joy of Love) underscores the importance of marriage and the family.[4] Children are legitimately born through a marriage union. Marriage is a critical institution in Africa in general, and Tiv society in particular. It is a symbol of discipline. A man who marries is seen as shielding himself from a promiscuous life. A woman who is over thirty years old and is still unmarried has to answer many questions from family and acquaintances why she is still unmarried. The parents of a young woman who marries immediately after graduating from college are credited for raising their daughter in the most ac-

---

[1] Shagbaor F. Wegh, *Marriage, Family and the Church in Tivland* (Makurdi: Dekon Computer Services, 1994), 15.

[2] For instance, *Tyover* grew up in his maternal home. People who knew him at that time identified him as the son of *Ayom*, who was the biological father of his mother. In Tiv society, this implies that *Tyover's* mother gave birth to him out of wedlock. *Tyover* was a victim of a failed exchange marriage that necessitated his kinsmen to withdraw his mother including, *Tyover* who was then an infant back to her biological family. As he grew up, he was confused as his mother was addressed as the daughter of *Ayom* just as he was addressed as the son of *Ayom*. This raised several questions for him. To establish the legitimacy of his roots meant tracing his paternal home to find answers to the question of his patrilineage. Eventually, he received satisfactory clarification on the issue by his paternal uncles, who told him his genealogical roots. Today, *Tyover* identifies himself with a long genealogy as follow, Abraham, *Ayom, Zeka, Mstaa, Agema, Mngele, Leva, Gbaa, Adigbe, Shan, Kyor, Tiv, Awange.* Genealogies are a way of establishing the biological roots of a person. See the genealogy of Jesus (Matthew 1:1-17; Luke 3:23-38).

[3] See Adasu, *Understanding African Traditional Religion Part One,* 19.

[4] Pope Francis, *Amoris Laetitia* [Apostolic Exhortation on the Joy of Love], sec 2, http://w2.vatican.va/content/dam/francesco/pdf/apost_exhortations/documents/papa -francesco_esortazione-ap_20160319_amoris-laetitia_en.pdf .

ceptable practices and norms of Tiv culture. Above all, marriage is a symbol of life.

Experience of Marriage
in Tiv Cosmology

Marriage is a symbol of life, and life is generated exclusively within the context of the matrimonial union between a man and woman. In Tiv culture, monogamy and polygamy are the most popular and common types of marriage. Polygamy is an acceptable form of marriage in most African societies. However, Catholicism is gradually diffusing this understanding, and the Tiv are beginning to see it as an economic burden.[5] In spite of the influence of Catholicism, most families are still practicing polygamy.[6]

The majority of the subjects who participated in the theological investigation acknowledged they come from polygamous families. Such parents are Catholics who may or may not be baptized. They do not have access to the Eucharistic meal because they are incapable of a sacramental marriage. The practice of faith by Catholics in Tivland requires full communion with the Catholic Church, and participation in the Eucharist. Under no circumstance is permission given to baptized men/women in polygamous marriages to receive Holy Communion.[7] Concession is given only to the first un-baptized wife to an un-baptized man to be admitted to baptism and Holy Communion after the required catechumenate program or preparatory period.[8]

---

[5] Justice Utsaha (a retired Justice of the Customary Court, Nigeria in a presentation on marriage on the floor of the Makurdi Diocesan Synod), at Makurdi in 2011. Utsaha is an elder statesman who has contributed immensely to the development of Tiv society. He observed that marrying many wives brings a lot of economic hardships not just on the husband, but on the entire family. With many offsprings, it increases the number of dependants with limited resources for sustenance. Similarly, Wegh, *Between Continuity and Change*, 95, says polygamy is a great burden on the polygynist. He must all the time try to be fair with every wife, ensuring an equitable distribution of love, and material things.

[6] See Pope Francis, *Amoris Laetitia*, sec 53.

[7]*Guidelines on Pastoral Ministry in the Catholic Diocese of Makurdi*, "Holy Matrimony" (Makurdi: Office of the Chancellor, 2012), 21

[8]*Guidelines on Pastoral ministry in the Catholic Diocese of Makurdi*, 21.

A few of the interview subjects stated that their parents are wedded members of the Catholic Church. Emerging adults who are born into such families were proud of the sacramental status of their parents' matrimonial union. Those whose marriages are blessed by a priest are perceived as courageous and committed Catholics. Most Tiv couples have not taken advantage of the sacrament of marriage for frivolous reasons. Instead of seeing marriage as a free and voluntary engagement, they view it as a burden. In some cases, after the marriage is ratified, both spouses begin to exhibit wanton behaviors. This distorted notion of sacramental marriage explains why couples live a life of infidelity, and exhibit physical, psychological, and other kinds of abuse, recognizing that the nuptial knot cannot be loosened.

Many Tiv couples are scared that after the ratification and consummation of marriage, a spouse may be unfaithful and abusive, or may decide to withdraw from the marriage leaving the other single for the rest of his or her life. This can lead to intense feelings of regret by the other. Felicity Anger, a student of Benue State University was vehement that her father is a bad example on her Catholic faith. After entering into a marriage covenant with her mother, he further took a second wife. "He eventually left us with our mother in the family house and lived elsewhere with his new wife.[9] Abandonment of this kind is a violation of the marriage covenant of love and life that can affect the worship experiences of children of such parents, and ultimately leave the Catholic faith on the surface of Tiv culture.

Couples are made to understand that in the Catholic Church, marriage is a union of love and life. The way marriage was celebrated under Tiv native law and custom, and the different emotions that were expressed on the day of marriage resonate with the biblical understanding that marriage is a lifelong affair (Genesis 3:24; Matthew 19:3-6). Such emotions help to understand Catholic marriage ritual.

---

[9] Felicity Anger (a twenty-two years old student of Benue State University, Makurdi), in a one-on-one interview on May 14, 2014 at Makurdi.

Before the bride formally left for her matrimonial home, young people created artificial road-blocks anticipating money from the groom as a token of remembrance for their sister who was leaving them finally. Mothers wept bitterly on the day their daughters were given out in marriage. These emotions were expressed uncontrollably when mothers realized that their daughters would no longer be available to assist them in fixing domestic chores. The official handing over of the bride to the groom automatically made her a wife to every man in the groom's family. It is her duty to feed and care for all, except sexual contact that was the exclusive reserve of the husband. She consolidated the marriage by giving birth to a male child, and she was ultimately rooted in the groom's family.

The image of the bride as one who takes root in the family by producing a male offspring is representative of the Church, the bride of Christ that must necessarily take root in Tiv culture. The capacity of the bride to produce a male child also helps to understand the ritual of marriage and baptism. The preface of the revised rite for the celebration of marriage in the Roman Missal conveys the truth that the birth of children through marriage gives beauty to the world, and their rebirth in baptism gives increase to the church. In Tiv culture, when a bride is incapable of giving birth to a male child, she is not fully grounded in the family leading to the husband's craving to marry more wives. A Tiv person who is yet to have a male child in his family thinks he has not established a family and hence, no one to inherit his property. The male child is valued as he continues the family lineage through procreation.[10] This is why an average Tiv

---

[10] Wegh, *Between Continuity and Change,* 93. Tiv cultural practices in regard to property inheritance exclude female children from the right of inheritance. A female child is expected to be married to someone else ultimately belonging to that family with the privileges of a married woman. Educated people in Tiv society today ensure that their female children have as equal opportunities of property inheritance as their male children. Matthew Icheen, a pharmacist, and Knight of St Mulumba resident in Adikpo town of Kwande Local Government Area before his death in 2010, willed his property to his local church community, extended family members, his wife, and his male and female children alike. The will was declared publicly at his funeral ceremony.

man in his search for a male child continues to procreate or marry as many wives as can produce a male child.[11]

A female child is expected to marry at some point in her life. From birth, she is a potential member of someone else's family. When husbands begin to develop lukewarm attitudes and strange behaviors toward women who are incapable of giving birth to a male child, it is apparent that they are fed up with the marriage. Women, who are unable to contain such pressure, and can no longer bear the ploys of the husband, withdraw from marriages contracted under Tiv native law and custom.

In Tiv society, instances of people withdrawing from sacramental marriages are rare. Men or women who withdraw from a sacramental marriage have given others satisfactory evidence to be skeptical of the sacrament. As a result, men in the patriarchal Tiv society who anticipate the reception of the sacrament keep procrastinating. Since the decision to enter into a sacramental marriage is mostly the prerogative of the man, most men now say, *saa me nenge inja i kwase wam a kumam man me er ivese ken chôôchi ye* (I must be satisfied with my wife's behavior before I will go into church marriage).

This situation scares many couples away from sacramental marriage particularly as Catholics in Tivland are made to understand that in the Catholic Church, no divorce is entertained after marriage is ratified and consummated. It is even more worrisome as people who sought for nullity never received such judgment until recently that one case was nullified after several years of litigation in the Makurdi diocesan marriage tribunal.

Hardly will Catholicism take root in Tiv culture if the distorted notion of sacramental marriage among Tiv Catholics does not change. Emerging adults who have critically observed the practices of marriage today have decided to pay particular attention to their educational career. Giving priority to education and postponing marriage is often motivated by fear. Having witnessed the failed marriages, and consequent divorce of their parents, acquaintances, and other

---

[11] Gowon Ama Doki, "Images of Womanhood in Tiv Society: A Critical Appraisal," in Review *of Gender Studies in Nigeria,* Vol. 2,ed. C. Angya (Makurdi: Black Heritage Publications, 2003), 8.

spouses, they desperately want to avoid making the same mistakes.[12]

Despite all that scare people away from marriage in the Catholic Church, some emerging adults are gradually accepting sacramental marriage as the norm. They anticipate a time to prepare for the sacrament soon after the cerebration of their traditional marriage to avoid breaking their participation in the Eucharistic meal in the Catholic Church. This makes some young people do their traditional marriage and church wedding in the same week.

Emerging adult females have come to realize that most people who seek their hand in marriage are not actually committed to the marriage proposal. The proposal they make is a mere subterfuge to lure the females into sex. Realizing the contrived stratagems of emerging adult males, most females who are influenced by the doctrines of the Catholic Church, and the exemplary lives of their Catholic parents insist on sex after marriage.

The Catholic Family

A Catholic family springs from the idea of marriage between a Catholic and a Catholic in the Catholic Church.[13] The bond of sacramental marriage for Tiv Catholics is a manifestation of love by the couple and a commitment to begin a family, and live together till death. Some wedded couples take their practice of Catholicism to the next level of engagement. They enroll either as members of the Knights of St John International or St Mulumba. Families of Knights and those that have priests as close or extended family relations demonstrated a sound knowledge of Catholicism. Young members of such families are properly educated in the faith of the Catholic Church.

---

[12] Setran and Christ A. Kiesling, *Spiritual Formation in Emerging Adulthood*, 168. Also see Pope Francis, *Amoris Laetitia*, sec. 40.

[13] See Code of Canon Law, c. 1055, § 1, in *The 1983 Code of Canon Law*, http://www.vatican.va/archive/ENG1104/_INDEX.HTM. The Catholic family is intrinsically connected to the notion that marriage binds those who are baptized in the Catholic Church and have agreed to raise their children according to the teaching of the same church.

Terwase Oraya a student and altar server at the Benue State University was particularly proud of his Catholic and royal family background that have influenced him to be a committed Catholic. He acknowledged that his grandfather was a second-class traditional chief who was deeply Catholic, and two of his uncles from the nuclear family are Catholic priests.[14] The traditional chieftaincy and the Catholic priesthood are respectable institutions in Tiv society. Such a family has the synergy of grounding one both in Tiv culture and the Catholic faith.

The influence of the family has been overwhelming in the faith experiences of emerging adults. The family is a school of social virtues that society needs greatly. The right of families to educate their children comes from the mission entrusted to them by God and by society itself. Since parents have given birth to their children, they have to worry about how the children live out their lives in the world.[15] Emerging adults who participated in the interviews were practicing Catholics who attributed their faith to parental upbringing. Such parents act as "priests" to their children.[16] In the course of interview, emerging adults continued to make reference to issues of the practice of faith they learned from their parents. The issues that include, church attendance, prayer, and good moral conduct have become the guiding principles of their lives particularly when confronted by people who offer bad examples.

Jude Tyopev observed that emerging adulthood is a period of struggle to find meaning in life, continuously exploring every opportunity that comes their way. When exposed to bad company and bad leadership patterns either at home, or in other critical institutions, they copy those improper behaviors exposed to them.[17] The

---

[14] Terwase Oraya (a twenty-three years old student of Benue State University, Makurdi), in a one-on-one interview on May 14, 2014 at Makurdi.

[15] Aloys Otieno Ojore, "Helping Young People Identify their Vocation in Life and Service to the Community," *Ministry to Youth and Young Adults* (Nairobi: Paulines Publications Africa, 2001), 32.

[16] See Ojore, "Helping Young People Identify their Vocation in Life and Service to the Community," 33.

[17] Jude Tyopev (a twenty-three years old student of Benue State University, Makurdi), in a focus group discussion on May 17, 2014 at Makurdi.

good examples laid down by the family have influenced them in positive ways.

Aaron Abo, an indigene of Shitile in Katsina-ala Local Government area, while expressing emotions of happiness said, "we accompany our parents to the prayer meetings of the Knights of St John International as members of the junior cadet section. My parents always advise me to carry my Catholic flag wherever I go."[18]

Livinus Agba, a Uniagric student from Tarka local government area said his parents are wedded Catholics. "We all live together as a happy family. Every day we read, meditate and share the word of God."[19] In Tiv culture, the faith of the children is derived from the faith of their parents. The generational conception of faith among young Tiv Catholics associates their faith with that of their parents.

This view is contrary to the findings of a study conducted in the five dioceses of Indiana in the United States. The study revealed among other things that post Vatican II Catholics who were young people at the time of the study have individual conceptions of faith. They were more interested in being a good person than being a good Catholic. "When asked what it takes to be a 'good Catholic' many participants said that participation in the sacraments, Mass attendance, and contributing to the church financially are unimportant. Many said that 'being a good person' makes someone a 'good Catholic.'"[20]

It is helpful for parents to be involved in the faith development of their children. Parents who neglect this duty and abandon their children to the company of the mass media, and juveniles in the society can only imagine the effects of the media, and other forms of violence on their children. Typically, parents who share a common faith tradition have positive influences on the faith expression of

---

[18] Aaron Abo (a nineteen years old student of University of Agriculture, Makurdi), in a one-on-one interview on June 1, 2014 at Makurdi.

[19] Livinus Agba (a twenty-eight years old student of University of Agriculture, Makurdi), in a one-on-one interview on June 3, 2014 at Makurdi.

[20] Andrea S. Williams James D. Davidson, "Catholic Conceptions of Faith: A Generational Analysis," *Sociology of Religion*, 57 no 3 (Fall 1996): 285.

their children. The phenomenon of different faith traditions affects the religious upbringing of children.

Disparity of cult is a common phenomenon among Tiv couples. While the husband worships in one church, the wife attends another. Typically, children follow the faith tradition of the mother. Mixed marriage is an unfamiliar concept in Tiv Catholicism. Most Tiv husbands are overbearing on matters of religious affiliation. As Catholics or NKST members or members of other churches, they compel their wives to renounce their faith tradition and join them to register as members of one church.

This corroborates the saying that *kwase geman nom adua ga, ka nom nan geman kwase adua ye* (the wife does not change the faith tradition of the husband, it is the husband that changes the faith tradition of the wife). In some instances, husbands have complied with the request of their wives to change their religious affiliation or faith tradition. In Tiv society, men who succumb in matters of this nature have been criticized for being too flexible to submit to the pressures of their wives as it is often said *kwase na kighir un* (his wife presses him down).

A spouse who advocates for a common place of worship argues that children benefit more from family upbringing when they share common beliefs and practices with their parents. For the Tiv, religious beliefs define a person in the same way the church talks of *lex orandi, lex credendi* (the rule of prayer is the rule of faith), referring to the relationship between worship and belief. Tiv people are prejudiced in matters of religious affiliation. The lenses through which they see Catholicism, NKST, or Pentecostal churches, is the same lenses they see their respective adherents.

Some marriage proposals have been rejected on the basis of disparity of cult. Experience has shown that some wives reluctantly convert from their original faith tradition to please the husband, but underneath, they are not convinced of the beliefs and practices of their new religious affiliation.

Patricia Kombo observed that her father pressurized her mother to leave the Catholic Church for NKST. After some time, he (father) declined from church attendance. Consequently, her mother re-nounced membership of NKST and raised them in the Catholic tra-dition.[21] Typically, the Tiv are averse to interfaith marriages. Through formal and informal ways of education, they are gradually understanding the religious implications of marriage. The work of interreligious and ecumenical dialogue too is neutralizing senti-ments of prejudice existing among families practicing different faith traditions. The family is an important unit in Tiv culture. It social-izes children in different aspects of life, including religion, culture and education.

Education as a Transforming Symbol

Education is commonly viewed as a vehicle for empowerment, lib-eration and the transformation of the world. Others have used it as an oppressive tool.[22] "An education that transforms the human per-son is one that is complete, engaging the hands and the heart as much as the mind."[23] The aim of education is to form the human person with respect to his or her ultimate goal, and simultaneously with respect to the good of the societies of which he or she is a member.[24] Emerging adults have positive views about education, observing that they have already started reaping the benefits of higher education. In answer to the question of how they see them-selves as educated emerging adults, respondents acknowledged

---

[21] Patricia Kombo (a twenty-three years old student of College of Education, Katsina-Ala), in a one-on-one interview on June 8, 2014 at Katsina-Ala.

[22] Paulo Freire, *Pedagogy of the Oppressed,* trans. Myra Bergman Ramos (New York: Continuum, 2000), 72, 125 and 133. Education is perceived as a transforming tool of the society. Human beings as creatures of the praxis have unique human activity of action and reflection geared toward praxis or transformation of the world. He criti-cizes the banking system of education whereby, teachers are depositors of knowledge, while students are mere receptacles, who are not exposed to tasks that challenge them to think critically. Education can also be used as an oppressive tool when the oppressor ideology is to absolutize ignorance. By this myth, the oppressor is the only person that knows, and every other person does not know.

[23] Jeffrey Labelle, SJ, and Daniel Kendall, SJ, *Catholic Colleges in the 21st Century* (Mahwah: Paulist, 2011), 78.

[24] See George E. Ganss, SJ, *Ignatius of Loyola: Spiritual Exercise and Selected Works* (Mahwah: Paulist, 1991), 281.

that attending higher education was a wonderful privilege they enjoyed.

Terwase Oraya for instance, said, it is simply a privilege because he was not the most endowed or the most brilliant person. His age mates who apparently are more erudite than he is, do not have this opportunity.[25]

The majority of emerging adults stated that higher education has changed their character, attitudes, and way of expressing themselves. In a focus group discussion, Cynthia Terver was particularly grateful observing that "I was very stubborn, and very disrespectful while at home, but now I have changed. My parents are impressed with me because I am focused, and I spend much time for my studies."[26]

They acknowledged too that the exposure they have enjoyed through higher education has aided them to develop better ways of doing things. It has also changed their general perception of life as they view life more positively. Godwin Fatyo sees himself as someone that has changed to be more dedicated to activities in the Catholic Church.[27] Andy disclosed that being in the college saved him from the bad things that were almost engulfing him. He confirmed membership of a gang of restive youth in the village, but he acknowledged that higher education has broadened his horizon to see such activities in a different light.[28]

Educated Emerging adults were optimistic that higher education avails knowledge that potentially transforms the society. They perceive their exposure as an opportunity to move Tiv society forward in the social, religious and educational aspects. Although most of them could not adequately articulate their vision, a few things stood out clearly. Religiously, most respondents stated that they will pro-

---

[25] Terwase Oraya (a twenty-three years old student of Benue State University, Makurdi), in a one-on-one interview on May 15, at Makurdi.

[26] Cynthia Terver (a twenty-one years old student of College of Education, Katsina-Ala), in a focus group discussion on June 8, 2014 at Katsina-Ala.

[27] Godwin Fatyo (a twenty-six years old student of College of Education, Katsina-ala), in a focus group discussion on June 8, 2014 at Katsina-Ala.

[28] Andy Tyolumun (a twenty-five years old student of College of Education, Katsina-Ala), in a focus group discussion on June 8, 2014 at Katsina-Ala.

vide catechetical, organizational, financial and other forms of service to the Catholic Church in their rural communities.

The desire to impact the religious sphere confirms that emerging adults are potential community theologians. Educationally, their goal is to offer counseling services to the young. Socially, emerging adults have high concerns to help rural communities, and to offer financial support to needy members of their respective communities. Emphasis was repeatedly laid on financial aid with the understanding that one who benefits from such support should extend it to others as well.

At present, not many Tiv people are prepared to help needy members of the community. Those who have the capacity to help are not willing to do so. The unwillingness to offer financial assistance to needy members of the community has resulted to a lack of opinion leaders, and continuous recycling of poverty. People are prone to listen to members who are generous in using their resources for the good of the community.[29]

Daniel Mfa's vision for Tiv society springs from his study of political science, observing that the core value of a political scientist is to act as an administrator to the society. He identifies majority of the problems in Tiv society today as political problems.[30] Educated emerging adult females also spoke of transforming their communities in positive ways.

In the past, very few women had access to formal education. It was not common to have women with a vision to represent their rural communities due to cultural factors that made women inferior to men. Today, economic fortunes derived from education have positively shaped the change of attitude toward the education of women. Parents who want to boost the dignity of their daughters in marriage, enjoy good bride price, and attract respect for themselves, invest in the education of their female children.

---

[29] Patrick Hol (a thirty years old student of Benue State University, Makurdi), in a one-on-one interview on May 16, 2014 at Makurdi.
[30] Daniel Mfa, (a twenty-six years old student of Benue State University, Makurdi), in a one-on-one interview on May 18, 2014 at Makurdi.

An educated Tiv woman is now seen as an asset because she attracts high economic value both for her parents and her husband. Parents who were responsible for the formal education of their daughters are already reaping the dividends of their investment.[31] From the perspective of the women too, education is an essential tool in their personal development,[32] and empowerment for the ultimate good of the society.

Seen as a symbol of empowerment, education is broadening the horizon of women as they begin to see the evils of patriarchy in Tiv society. They support the church's position that challenges Tiv culture's inhuman treatment of women. Apart from the reality of poverty and other forms of evil women suffer by virtue of gender, they undergo other forms of trauma. The failure of most marriages is blamed on the woman. If the woman does not give birth to a male child, she is blamed. Worst still, if she is incapable of bearing children, she is asked to quit the marriage.

In most African societies as in Tiv society, a female child has no right to inherit her late father's property. The right is reserved for male children. Similarly, a widow has no right to inherit her late husband's property and, in some societies, she is even accused of his death. After the burial of the deceased husband, she is confined indoors observing a mandatory period of mourning for a specified period of time with a particular dress code meant for the mourning period.

---

[31] See Wegh, *Between Continuity and Change,* 181-182. Investment in this context does not mean a business intended to maximize profit, but using money wisely and consciously to better the future of the other. In Tiv society today, successful educated women who are married in other places often visit their parents, and provide their basic needs. Some have even bought vehicles and built better houses for their parents. Most commonly, those who are not buoyant enough to provide a vehicle or build a house try to give a befitting burial to their deceased parents. Almost all Tiv people aspire to the privilege of a befitting burial. Some women who are not educated end up marrying their kind as the saying goes *hanma anjondo ngu a kughul na* (every calabash has its cover). They spend most of their life in rural areas with unpleasant conditions of living. In some instances, such women run to their parents and family from time to time to receive material and other forms of assistance.

[32] Wegh, *Between Continuity and Change,* 182.

These issues do not apply to men. A man may marry as many wives as he wishes and even keep concubines outside the matrimonial home in order to satisfy his sexual urge. This is viewed as a normal way of life. In contrast, if a woman has sexual relations with somebody other than her husband, it is viewed as adultery. The action of a bereaved husband who marries as soon as his deceased wife is buried is not perceived as an abnormality, but the wife who does a similar thing is looked upon as a reprobate woman.

Emerging adult females were particularly concerned with creating awareness on the issues mentioned above, and other related issues. Their goal is for women to assert themselves and claim their dignity. In furtherance of this agenda, they envision counseling as an effective means of creating awareness.

Mwuese Agan, who hails from Kwande area, said a girl should be thoroughly informed concerning basic issues that affect women. She should be given sex education when she turns a teenager to avoid common mistakes girls usually make. The respondent decried a situation where she was not told what she needed to know and do. As a result, she was tricked, and put into family way, and jilted afterward. "I am making personal efforts to develop myself. I do not blame others for my mistakes. Rather, I am struggling to correct my past and redefine myself. I will try the best I can to help other girls not to fall into a similar situation."[33] Such an approach helps a person to fully actualize him or herself. Corroborating the idea of self-actualization,

Agatha Terlumun from Katsina-ala area said, as one who did not enjoy much of paternal support, she is determined to attain greater heights, so that her story could be a source of inspiration and encouragement to others in a similar situation.[34]

Education can also be seen as a symbol of exposure that provides the rudiments needed in social relationships. Mimidoo Isha, who originates from Ushongo area observed:

---

[33] Mwuese Agan (a twenty-two years old student of Benue State University, Makurdi), in a one-on-one interview on May 15, 2014 at Makurdi.
[34] Agatha Terlumun (a twenty-two years old student of Benue State University, Makurdi), in a one-on-one interview on May 19, 2014 at Makurdi.

Education has provided me the basic etiquette in my social inter-actions with other people. Ultimately, my goal is to be a shining example of good behavior for the young to emulate. With a trans-parent character, I can impact positively on my local community. Typically, I spend quality time with my family, and give the rest of my time to church activities.[35]

Education has helped to define what educated emerging adults are today, and what they shall be in future. Education has close ties to family and should be provided to nurture the gifts of every young man and woman. Priority should be given to education and family as settings where individual's talents are able to thrive.[36] "Young people today are asking for a suitable and complete education which can enable them to look to the future with hope instead of disenchantment."[37] In Tiv society, the low economic status of most families is impeding the full realization of emerging adults' vision of a better future.

Economic Status
& Formal Education

Tiv parents attach great importance to formal education. They rec-ognize that education as a multivalent symbol is capable of provid-ing their children alternative opportunities to life, other than the painful experiences of strenuous work on the farm.

Kenneth Tyav, from Guma Local Government area captured his father's passion for formal education. "My father encourages all his children to pay particular attention to formal education so, they will

---

[35] Mimidoo Isha (a twenty-three years old student of Benue State University, Makur-di), in a one-on-one interview on May 19, 2014 at Makurdi.

[36] Kimberly Scharfenberger, "Pope Francis Encourages Europe to Invest in Education and Family," *The Cardinal Newman Society,* December 3, 2014, http://www.cardinalnewmansociety.org/CatholicEducationDaily/DetailsPage/tabid/1 02/ArticleID/3759/Pope-Francis-Encourages-Europe-to-Invest-in-Education-and-Family.aspx#. This was part of the speech Pope Francis delivered to the European parliament.

[37] Scharfenberger, "Pope Francis Encourages Europe to Invest in Education and Family."

not depend solely on farming that comes with painful experiences as he is currently experiencing."[38]

Formal education is a symbol of wealth and exposure in Tiv society. When a Tiv parent publicly declares that his/her child is resident in an urban city in any part of the world, such a parent is saying the child is either a student or an educated person engaged in a public sector employment.[39] Formal education provides access to upward social mobility. Unfortunately, not many parents are buoyant enough to ensure their children receive quality education.

The low economic status of most parents accounts for the reason why they send their children to schools with low academic standards. Typically, children in polygamous families do not have access to qualitative education.[40] Most parents of the interview subjects were peasant farmers who lived in rural areas and carry out subsistence agriculture. In the past, female children did not enjoy equal opportunities with boys as far as formal education was concerned. Today, most parents insist on formal education for their male and female children alike. In the midst of scarce resources, families with low income earnings give preference to the male child.[41]

The Tiv are predominantly an agrarian people. The few parents who are civil servants work with government organizations particularly at local, state, and federal levels either as janitors, clerks, teachers, nurses, or as administrative officers. Some are interested in politics, and either combine civil service jobs or business with political activities. Others engage in different kinds of businesses and retail trading. Grace Gwaza from Kwande Local Government area said, "my mother does petty trading, she sells cooked rice and *Akpekpa*" (home-made pie).[42]

---

[38] Kenneth Tyav (a twenty-two years old student of Benue State University, Makurdi), in a one-on-one interview on May 18, 2014 at Makurdi.

[39] See Wegh, *Between Continuity and Change,* 192.

[40] Wegh, *Between Continuity and Change,* 99.

[41] Charity Angya, "Early Marriage in Tivland and its Social Consequences," in *Review of Gender Studies in Nigeria Vol. 2,* ed. C. Angya (Makurdi: Black Heritage Publications, 2003), 175.

[42] Grace Gwaza, (a twenty-four years old student of University of Agriculture, Makurdi), in a one-on-one interview on June 3, 2014 at Makurdi. *Akpukpa* is aTiv delica-

From these low-income earnings, parents struggle to cope with the financial responsibilities of formal education. Some students acknowledge the hardships of their parents and are determined to justify the money spent on them by avoiding irresponsible acts capable of bringing shame and disappointment to their parents. Parents have to struggle to raise money to upset their children's tuition fees because Benue State government offers very few scholarship opportunities at very meager amount to deserving students who are indigenes of the state. Even the meager amount is sometimes delayed or never paid at all. The low economic status of parents forces them to enroll their children in schools they can afford.

Some schools in Benue State are affordable, but due to poor management, and inadequate funding,[43] they are known for poor academic standard and indiscipline. At the time of this investigation, government hired elementary school teachers in the State embarked on strike action that commenced on October 24, 2013 and eventually ended on July 7, 2014. In a text message on September 15, 2014, Rosemary revealed that the teachers were agitating for better working conditions, including staff promotion, payment of leave bonus and the implementation of minimum wage. The strike action brought painful economic hardship to parents who are elementary school teachers.

Bernie Shua, a student of BSU, confirmed that she was greatly affected by the strike action because her mother, an elementary school teacher, who provides most of her needs was not paid for several months. "As a girl, there are a few things I am most comfortable asking my mother to provide. Unfortunately, my mom is going through serious economic challenges that make her incapable of

---

cy made mostly from beans and bambaranuts eaten at breakfast and in some cases at dinner. It is not baked, but cooked in a pie-like size sometimes with eggs and vegetables. Children particularly love to eat *Akpukpa* in the morning and they cry if their parents fail to provide this delicacy.

[43] See Unongo, OFR, "The Imperative of Youth Leadership Development in the Current Millenium," 13. Politicians and heads of civil institutions are most often not fully prepared to adequately fund education, health and social infrastructure. Their choices have affected the actualization of most young people in Tivland.

responding promptly to my needs."[44] Poverty can be a major constraint to religious practice and academic excellence by emerging adults. In addition, incessant strike creates restive youths and gangsterism as students roam the streets aimlessly. Strike actions, very common among government hired academic staff can also contribute to the lowering of standards and facilitation of indiscipline particularly in government owned schools.

Some informers stated that they attended government owned schools, while others said they attended mission and private sector schools both at elementary and high school levels. Most of the standard high schools in Benue State are owned by the Roman Catholic, the NKST, Anglican, and Methodist missions. These schools offer better academic opportunities as well as discipline, faith and character formation to students.

Solomon Agbatar, a student of Uniagric from Kwande area acknowledged the influence of Catholic education on his faith formation. He said, his father is a member of the NKST church, but sent him to a Catholic school, where he received Catholic education, and voluntarily changed to Catholic faith.[45] The strict enforcement of discipline in the mission and private sector schools does not completely eradicate cases of indiscipline. Typically, such cases are recorded in some schools within Tivland.

Tarlumun Orngu of Benue State University testified:

While in junior high school, I was involved with bad companions that exerted tremendous peer pressure on me. Some of my peers were members of secret societies. Their influence pushed me to smoke marijuana and drink alcohol in excessive quantity. I smoke till 2014. These brought challenges and set-backs to my life. I was rejected by my family and people connected to me. I had no peace of mind, no peace with my family and with the neighboring environment. I always needed money to buy drugs. I frequently made

[44] Bernie Shua (a twenty-three years old student of Benue State University, Makurdi), in a one-on-one interview on May 18, 2014 at Makurdi.

[45] Solomon Agbatar (a twenty-five years old student of University of Agriculture, Makurdi), in a one-on-one interview on May 18, 2014 at Makurdi.

away with domestic items I could sell and get money to enable me
smoke and drink.[46]

He acknowledged that the life of drugs and deviancy did not help him in anyway, but rather brought set back to him, including his academic carrier as his entry into the university was delayed. Other informants confirmed that their entry into the university was delayed not because of deviant behavior. They were simply unfortunate at different times Nigerian universities recruited candidates for university programs.

Admission Challenges

The desire to attend higher education institutions particularly the university burns strongly in the minds of Tiv emerging adults. Higher education is seen as a symbol of liberation, transformation, exposure, prestige and wealth among others. After high school education, most emerging adults struggle before they finally gain entrance into institutions of higher education in Benue State. To admit the teeming population of emerging adults who apply to Benue State University presents serious challenges to the admission committee, and indeed the university management.

The Nigerian Universities Commission (NUC)[47] approves a specific number of students to be admitted every year to avoid overstretching the existing structures in Nigerian universities. In many instances, including the 2011/2012 session, BSU flouted this policy as a result of high demand. In that session, 17,681 candidates applied, but the university was mandated to admit only 3224, which reflected the university carrying capacity. Instead, 5,201 students were admitted that particular session.[48] Compliance with this policy be-

---

[46] Tarlumun Orngu (a twenty-seven years old student of Benue State University, Makurdi), in a one-on-one interview on May 17, 2014 at Makurdi.

[47] See Adi and Pever, "Student Enrolment at Benue State University, Makurdi," 92. Among other things the NUC is a regulatory body that ensures Nigerian universities maintain an acceptable academic standard. The approval of admission quota for universities is one method the body employs to ensure that universities recruit students within the limit of their facilities and personnel.

[48] Adi and Pever, "Student Enrolment at Benue State University, Makurdi," 102. The University admission commission did not set out to deliberately defile NUC approv-

comes near impossible due to immense pressure exerted on the university by teeming applicants.[49] This administrative policy may account for the reason why emerging adults who graduate from senior high school with excellent results fail to gain admission after successfully passing the universities matriculation examinations. This again delays their attainment of adulthood.

Terna Nyom recounted the experience of his repeated attempt before he finally got admitted:

> *After high school, I applied several times for entrance into the university, but was unsuccessful. I made another attempt at Ibrahim Badamasi Babangida University Lapai in Niger State where I was accepted. However, I could not attend the university because of the attack by Boko Haram insurgents on a Catholic Church in Suleja, a city in Niger State at the time. At a point, I contemplated going to the seminary to train for the Catholic priesthood, but upon the advice of my parents, I applied again to go to the university and was finally accepted in BSU.[50]*

His decision to change his direction to the seminary may have arisen when he was increasingly frustrated after several unsuccessful attempts to be admitted into the university. Those recruited for academic programs in Nigerian universities undergo several challenges of sustenance before completing four years of university education. The crave for success in the midst of these challenges pushes some students into activities of all kinds, including prostitution, cultism, and robbery.

Seminarians on the other hand, go through eight years of philosophy and theology without interruption and problem of sustenance as those responsible for their training ensure that they are well cared for.[51] Emerging adults may decide to go to the seminary to

---

al quota for that year. However, the policy was violated based on genuine need to strike a balance between NUC and admission pressure.

[49] Adi and Ngove Peter Pever, "Student Enrolment at Benue State University, Makurdi," 92.

[50] Terna Nyom (a twenty-three years old student of Benue State University, Makurdi), in a one-on-one interview on May 17, 2014 at Makurd.

[51] See Elochukwu E. Uzukwu, *A Listening Church: Autonomy and Communion in African Churches* (Eugene, Oregon: Wipf and Stock, 2006), 95.

escape recruitment challenges in Nigerian universities, and the unfavorable economic conditions that affect university students. Dioceses and religious houses in Nigeria recruit seminarians and send them to the seminaries.

In the Diocese of Gboko, for instance, hundreds of students apply every year, but in the end only about twenty-five are admitted. This shows that many emerging adults are interested in receiving higher education and are flexible in making career choices. This raises the question of the genuineness of their vocation not disregarding the fact that God calls people in different circumstances. Those who miss admission, and who are not patient to try again, misdirect their energies to political thuggery.

Osmond Guda shared this experience:

> *From my experience of campus unionism, students reciprocate the little favors they receive from us by giving us optimal support during campus political campaigns and subsequent elections. In the macro society they are ready to do anything to the extent of sacrificing their lives for politicians who conscript them as thugs and occasionally give them tips.*[52]

The majority of Nigerian youth,[53] including Tiv youth do not have access to higher education. Those who are neither admitted nor employed and are determined to succeed through legitimate means endure excruciating pains on the farm and other challenging ventures. Young people who want cheap means of survival find themselves on the street in crime and anti-social activities. They fall prey to drugs, prostitution, political thuggery, or join rebel groups of all kinds.[54]

A few informants said, they did not encounter any difficulty in entering the university. Through the grace of God, some got admitted

---

[52] Osmond Guda (a Nineteen years old student of College of Education, Katsina-Ala), in a one-on-one interview on June 8, 2014 at Katsina-Ala.

[53] Unongo, OFR, "The Imperative of Youth Leadership Development in the Current Millenium," 13. In the context of his discussion, he uses the term youth in line with the universal idea that it is the period of life between six and twenty four years old.

[54] Unongo, "The Imperative of Youth Leadership Development in the Current Millenium," 21.

at the very first application attempt. For instance, Kenneth Tyav said, "I did my elementary school and high school education in Makurdi. I completed my high school education and proceeded straight to the university after passing the university matriculation examination."[55]

The challenge to acquire higher education does not end when the problem of admission is solved. Most students begin to encounter the problem of who bears the financial burden of their university education particularly where parents are not in good economic standing. Some are fortunate to benefit from the generosity of extended family relations. Mimidoo Isha, who hails from Mbavyende in Ushongo local government, saw God deeply involved in the process of her enrollment in the university.

> *My mother is alive, but my father is no more. I graduated from high school with good grades with all the requirements to enroll into the university, but unfortunately I was not admitted the three consecutive times I applied until now. Now that I am admitted, I consider it a privilege that has come at God's appointed time. Good enough, I am being sponsored by my uncle (dad's brother) whom I least expected will take up this responsibility.[56]*

A feature of Tiv families is the strong ties shared by extended family members. This gives meaning to the concept of ecclesiology where community and family form the basis of identity and relation to God. It is through this prism that this local theology is seen. This makes sense in Tiv area where extended family is important and permeates every aspect of Tiv life.[57] Many testified that extended family relations were responsible for their tuition. The support offered by relations reduces the financial burden on parents who in most cases are in polygamous unions, and give birth to numerous children without adequate means of sustenance. Where external help is lacking, most emerging adults encounter economic hardships in school.

---

[55] Kenneth Tyav (a twenty-one years old student of Benue State University, Makurdi), in a one-on-one Interview on May 15, 2014 at Makurdi.

[56] Mimidoo Isha (a twenty-three years old student of Benue State University, Makurdi), in a one-on-one interview on May 19, 2014 at Makurdi.

[57] Schreiter, *Constructing Local Theologies*, 30.

Polygamy is one effect of cultural practices on the academic attainment of emerging adults. The birth of many children from numerous wives becomes the problem of others who have to bear the brunt of their training. Most women who are caught up in polygamous situations bear the greater responsibility for their children's sustenance with little or no support from their husbands. Some students experience economic hardship in school as a consequence of polygamy, and they depend solely on their mothers. The former Governor of Benue State suffered a similar situation:

> *My father had more than 15 wives. You know in a polygamous family, if your mother does not struggle, you end up in the village. I was lucky my mother was a struggling woman. I grew up basically with her picking up the bills. We were six but two have died and I am third in line of the boys.*[58]

Children of divorced and remarried parents, on the other hand, are left to survive strictly on the charity of their stepmothers. The husband pays attention to the children of his current wife and neglects those of the divorced wife.

A majority of the informants acknowledged they were sponsored in school either by parents or relations. Recognizing that most of their sponsors are of low economic status, some students resort to business or farming activities to supplement their income. In a text message on August 20, 2014, Simon Ayila who is solely responsible for his tuition solicited for assistance. He had a tuition of #34,450.00 (thirty-four thousand, four hundred and fifty naira) an equivalent of $212 to pay for the semester. He stated, "I made #19,000.00 (nineteen thousand naira) or $117 from the sale of groundnut from my farm. I am still looking for the remaining balance to complete my tuition fee."[59]

---

[58]Yusuf Alli, and Sanni Onogu, "I Joined Politics out of Circumstances"—Suswam at 50,"*The Nation*,http://thenationonlineng.net/new/i-joined-politics-out-of-circumstances-suswam-at-50. This interview was conducted on the fiftieth birthday of Governor Gabriel Suswam.

[59] Simon Ayila (a twenty-four years old student of College of Education, Katsina-Ala), in a one-on-one interview on June 10, 2014 at Katsina-Ala. The exchange rate for Naira/dollar at the time of data gathering was $1 to #163.

Wuese Aga acknowledged that her parents provide 50% to 60% of her financial needs. She stated:

I work hard to augment their efforts by providing the rest of what I need. I do this by engaging in retail trading, buying and selling bed covers, used shoes and clothes. I go to Wadata market in Makurdi town, pick stuff sold at lower prices such as #200.00 (two hundred naira) or $1.23. Even when I sell at #300.00 (three hundred naira), or $1.85, I make a gain of #100.00 (one hundred naira) or 0.62. This is what I do to keep myself going.[60]

As an emerging adult, she sees herself as one who has to struggle in the midst of harsh economic challenges. Most parents cannot provide all the needs of their children due to economic hardships. "As a result, I am determined with strong will, courage, and hard work to succeed in life. Above all, I believe with prayer, God can make things work for me."[61]

Conclusion

This chapter is linked to the second movement of the circle method. It analyzed the family as a cultural symbol, and education as a social symbol. These symbols impact the worship experiences of emerging adults, influencing them in both positive and negative ways. The family integrates emerging adults both in Catholicism, and Tiv culture. Polygamy as an aspect of family life has unpleasant effects on both the practice of faith and the educational attainment of emerging adults.

That notwithstanding, education has raised their social status, and has brought new experiences of self- perception and social transformation. Factors such as poverty, unpleasant marriage experiences of parents, and academic challenges including, overwhelming admission challenges negatively impact their worship experiences.

These factors, and many others have affected the rooting of the Catholic Church in Tiv culture. What does Catholic theology say

---

[60] Wuese Aga (a twenty-three years old student of Benue State University, Makurdi), in a one-on-one interview on May 15, 2014 at Makurdi.

[61] Wuese Aga, one-on-one interview, Makurdi.

regarding these issues? Reflecting theologically on these issues offers an opportunity for the grounding of Catholicism in Tiv culture.
The task of theological reflection is reserved for the next chapter.

7

ANALOGY OF SYMBOLS

T he previous chapter analyzed the family and education as
symbols that affect the worship experiences of emerging
adults. The family integrates emerging adults into Tiv culture. Pursuit of higher education in urban cities on the other hand, has insu-
lated them from cultural practices that are mostly carried out in the
rural communities. Consequently, the younger generation of Tiv is
not grounded in many aspects of Tiv culture and Catholicism.

This chapter coincides with the third movement of the circle method, and argues that Tiv ritual practices or symbols such as *imborvungu* (a ritual practice that uses unblemished human beings for
sacrifice for the prosperity of Tivland) provide an analogical way of
enriching both the Catholic faith and Tiv culture. The chapter elucidates the analogical framework used in interpreting symbols, followed by a description of *imborvungu* ritual. It further explores the
views emerging adults hold about the Catholic Church, and analogically explores Catholic worship symbols in relation to selected cultural symbols, and it concludes with a theological synthesis supported by appropriate theological wisdom that is authentically
Catholic.

Criteria for Interpreting Symbols

Tracy's analogical framework is used in the analogical interpretation of Catholic worship symbols and cultural symbols. A theological discourse on analogies entails the language of similarities and differences. This framework recognizes a three-pronged criterion namely; a criterion of adequacy, a criterion of appropriateness, and a criterion of internal coherence. In this context, the interpretation of each symbol is subsumed into the three mentioned criteria.

First, in the criterion of appropriateness the symbol must represent the tradition of which it speaks. For instance, in drawing an analogy between *imborvungu* and the sacrificial death of Jesus, this criterion is used to bring out a theological synthesis between the Catholic tradition and Tiv culture. In Tiv culture, the ritual practice of *imborvungu* represents the act of repairing the land, while in the Catholic tradition, the cross and the Eucharist represent the historic event of the sacrificial dead of Jesus. The Christian tradition through the earliest witness of the Jesus-kerygma of the New Testament, and the affirmations of Nicaea and Chalcedon, and contemporary Christological affirmations whether from below or from above attest to the Jesus' event.[1] This criteria determines that the dual symbols are appropriate to the traditions of which they speak.

Second, the criterion of adequacy opens another perspective to the interpretation. In the earliest Christian communities, the scriptures were relatively adequate expression of the Jesus event. In contemporary times, a fully adequate criteria of interpretation must be open to new experiences, new questions, new and even more adequate responses for later generations who experience the same event in ever different situations.[2] In contextualizing worship in Tiv culture, such an interpretation of symbols focuses on the contemporary experiences of emerging adults, and the questions they often raise concerning Catholicism, and its failure to connect their experiences. Interpreting the symbols in the light of new questions, and

---

[1] Tracy, *The Analogical Imagination,* 235.
[2] Tracy, *The Analogical Imagination,* 249.

contemporary experiences is a sure way of rooting the Catholic faith in Tiv culture.

The third criterion is that of internal coherence that is closely linked to the criteria of intelligibility. It deals with the tradition's present self-understanding. In this context, the interpretation of symbols is from the perspective of the meaningfulness or truth of the tradition. This understanding raises the question of the meaningfulness of cultural symbols in relation to the event of Jesus the Christ. This criterion asks questions such as, how is *imborvungu* with its repeated ritual of human sacrifice meaningful to the contemporary Tiv person?

Analogical interpretation of this nature touches the heart and soul of the doctrinal life of the Catholic Church. As a dual theological engagement (Tiv culture and worship symbols), it is crafted in creative fidelity[3] with the church's teaching. In this regard, it is important to make a fundamental distinction between the logical and ontic rule of this interpretation. Logical interpretation does not appeal to matters distinct from the matter to be interpreted. The logical interpretation interprets by giving precisions, but it does not affirm anything else in the interpretation of the matter at hand. Ontic interpretation on the other hand asserts something other than the matter in question. What is asserted is capable of rendering it intelligible and preserves the matter from misunderstandings by indicating the cause, precision and concrete ways in which it came about.[4]

For instance, the dogma of transubstantiation is a logical explanation because it relies on the words of Christ, which are to be explained and guarded against all misunderstanding that would weaken or deny their sense.[5] This theological exploration favors the ontic rule of the interpretation that makes appeal to matter. In other words, it uses materials from Tiv culture to explain symbols of worship.

---

[3] See Francis A. Sullivan, SJ., *Creative Fidelity: Weighing and interpreting Documents of the Magisterium* (Eugene, Oregon: Wipf and Stock, 2003).
[4] Sullivan, SJ., *Creative Fidelity*, 124.
[5] Sullivan, SJ., *Creative Fidelity*, 124.

Using the ontic approach, analogical interpretation can most effectively link faith and culture, and provide the resources that ground emerging adults both in Tiv culture and in Catholicism. This particular link between faith and culture has a pedagogical import to educate emerging adults to understand and appreciate Catholic symbols and practices, as well as Tiv cultural symbols.

In the course of oral interviews, emerging adults were asked to mention what comes to mind when they think of the Eucharist. All of them acknowledged it as the real presence of Jesus in the symbols of bread and wine and connected it with Tiv ritual practices such as *imborvungu, igbe* and *poor.* In Tiv culture, these practices are carried out by *mbatsav* (witches and wizards) for protection and advancement of community living, and they are exclusively for initiates. With appropriate probes, the respondents further observed that just as the Eucharist is open only to the initiates, so are these cultural practices. Those who are not initiated in the rituals violate the ritual practices either by merely seeing or touching the emblems. As a result, such people are compelled to pay a ransom, either with own blood or someone else's for the purpose of purifying and strengthening the emblem they have violated.

The ability of emerging adults to link the Eucharist with Tiv ritual practices actually inspired the interest to build on their limited knowledge by developing a practical theological synthesis of Catholic worship symbols and cultural symbols. Exploring the connection between cultural practices and Catholic ritual creates an informed knowledge on the harmony between the two to equip emerging adults in articulating the faith of the Catholic Church using cultural resources. On the other hand, these community theologians can use Catholic symbols and practices as potent tools to insert themselves in Tiv culture. This approach explores mutually enhancing symbols.

The use of symbols and images in worship is an aspect that needs elucidation. Most of the symbols and images used in Catholic worship are not intelligible to emerging adults. For instance, the use of incense at worship is increasingly confusing to most worshippers when viewed with the lens of traditional healers in Tiv culture. The use of fire and smoke for the treatment of sickness and misfortune is a superstitious act. Catholics who come to worship hardly connect with Catholic worship because of its symbolic nature as it manifests itself in a variety of images and practices that convey a negative meaning in Tiv culture. This discussion is germane as it situates the analogical interpretation of worship symbols, and Tiv ritual practices in the context of educated emerging adults, who are a symbol of the future of Catholicism in Tiv culture. *Imborvungu* ritual described below can be linked with the heart and soul of Catholic worship symbols namely, the Eucharist and the cross.

Imborvungu:
A Ritual Practice

The term *imborvungu* has an incomprehensible rendering in English. Even in Tiv, its meaning is not clear. One can only attempt to explain the concept by splitting the word into *imbor* (spring as of water), and *ivungu* (owl). When the two words are combined, the concept does not render any specific meaning either. The function of *Imborvungu* is better explained or described rather than defined. However, a grasp of its operational background leads to a fuller understanding that *Imborvungu* ritual is intrinsically connected with the prosperity of the land.

The concept of *tar* (land) among the Tiv is not limited to the physical composition of the land, but it encompasses all the beliefs of the people's worldview. An idea of *tar* binds the human person and the land. The land is not just seen as a piece of the earth on which the Tiv live. It is the land of their fathers, which they conceive as sacred. Recognizing that life springs from the *tar* (land) and is rejuvenated by it, the Tiv are obliged to relate to the land with religious reverence and good moral conduct.[6]

Human acts, of omission or commission affect the land in both positive and negative ways. Negative acts may cause infertility to the land, sickness and misfortune in the society. A situation of this kind is highly lamentable by Tiv elders who say *tar vihi* (the land has

---

[6] Atel, *Dynamics of Tiv Religion and Culture*, 69-70.

spoiled) as opposed to *tar doo* (the land is good) when things are normal.[7]

One way of repairing the land, enhancing its prosperity, restoring the fecundity of women, and ensuring health for all, is through the use of *akombo* (magic) rituals that relate to different aspects of human life from birth, fertility, hunting, and death.[8] One of the *akombo* used in repairing the land is *imborvungu*.

In Tiv religion, *imborvungu* is considered a sacred image. The *mbatsav* (witches and wizards) who belong to the cult have high regard for it. It is used for setting right the land. Those who do not belong to the cult are so scared of it due to its blood sapping nature. Ironically, it has a great value not commensurate with its insignificant appearance. Its main composition is a human bone. Some say it is a shin-bone, others maintain, it is taken from the arm. "It looks more like an arm-bone, as it is hardly big enough for a shin-bone, unless possibly that of a small child."[9] The human bone, which is an essential component of *imborvungu* is taken from a dead person by those who practice *tsav* (witchcraft).

The person whose organ is used must have been a noble person in the society who was an initiate of all types of *akombo* (magic) and mastered all *akombo* rites. He was *orbeen akombo* (one who experienced all magic). Such a person must have been *Cighan Or* (a consecrated person) or *Or kpôghkpôgh* (real man), or *Or u akum kwagh yô* (a man of capability).[10] The human organ is embellished with basic human features such as eyes, ears, nose and mouth. The upper end

---

[7] Atel, *Dynamics of Tiv Religion and Culture*, 70.

[8] Atel, *Dynamics of Tiv Religion and Culture*, 70.

[9] Rupert East, trans., *Akiga's Story: The Tiv Tribe as Seen by One of Its members* (London: Oxford University Press, 1965),225.

[10] See Atel, *Dynamics of Tiv Religion and Culture*, 71. An ancestor, whose organ is used as a component of *imborvungu*, must have been a good person. In this connection, the definition of ancestor resonates with Jesus Christ the proto ancestor, who was without sin, and gave his life as a ransom for many. Scholars have argued that African ancestors are deemed inappropriate for analogous relationship with Jesus, on the grounds of contrasting definitions, qualifications, and characteristics of ancestors. Consequently, to portray Jesus as ancestor or even "Proto-Ancestor" is to compromise his divinity. See Diane B. Stinton, "African Christianity," in *Jesus the Complete Guide*, ed. Leslie Houlden (London: Continuum, 2003), 9.

of the bone is firmly fixed into the base of the skull of an ancestor that is decorated with human hair.[11] It is believed that today *imborvungu* is also made of brass with similar features as that made of a human organ. In recognition of the noble role some women have played in Tiv culture, some *amboravungu* (plural of *imborvungu*) are embellished with female heads.[12]

Imborvungu can be owned by an individual and by a group. The individual or his family may have purchased it for the purpose of acquiring honor, wealth, fortune, and good harvest. In the case of private ownership, it is the blood of the house-mouse that is used to make it efficacious.[13] One who owns an *imborvungu* for private use performs its rites secretly in such a way that no member of the community knows about it. If his ownership of *imborvungu* is no longer covert, he is persuaded to submit it to the custodian of group *imborvungu* appointed by the community. This suggests that *imborvungu* must be directed toward community use.

An *imborvungu* that is owned by a lineage group is used for the common good of the community. Contrary to the private one that is sustained by the blood of the mouse, the group one feeds on human blood to continuously render it effective. An elder generally referred to as *orsoruntar* (the man who sets right or repairs the land) is appointed the custodian of community *imborvungu* or *amboravungu* (plural). His task is to ensure that the ritual is duly carried out for the prosperity of Tivland.

The Tiv believe that such rituals must be renewed repeatedly so they can be effective in repairing the land.[14] The ritual practice of *imborvungu* has positive and negative elements. The positive elements synthesize Catholic symbols, while the negative ones speak to a perspective of human torture opposed by the Catholic tradition.

---

[11] Godfrey Tor Geri, *A History of Tiv Religious Practices and Changes: A Focus on Imborvungu, Poor and Ibiamegh* (Makurdi: Aboki Publishers, 2012), 43.

[12] Geri, *A History of Tiv Religious Practices and Changes,* 44.

[13] Geri, *A History of Tiv Religious Practices and Changes,* 45.

[14] Wegh, *Between Continuity and Change,* 65-66.

Synthesizing *Imborvungu*
with Catholic Symbols

Sacrifice is the offering of something valuable or precious for something that is more important.[15] This is the context in which the Tiv perform a ritual sacrifice of human blood to purify *imborvungu*. The Tiv idea of sacrifice as a community act is often connected with the interpretation of the Eucharist as sacrifice.[16] Catholic worship has several forms, and the Eucharist is the climax. The liturgy of the word and the liturgy of the Eucharist constitute two major components of the Mass. The Church has always venerated the divine Scriptures just as she venerates the body of the Lord. In the sacred liturgy, the church unceasingly receives and offers to the faithful the bread of life from the table both of God's word and of Christ's body.[17]

Emerging adults experience these sacred mysteries in diverse ways. Their overall experience of the Catholic Church in Tiv culture influences their experience of worship particularly of the Eucharistic celebration. Their views of the church lay the background for an effective analogical interpretation of symbols.

Views about
the Catholic Church

Emerging adults in Tiv society have both positive and negative views of the Catholic Church. Those who come from very strong Catholic backgrounds have positive views of the Catholic Church. They love the Catholic Church for its well organized and orderly liturgy. They say the solemn nature of worship is animating, and they believe the Catholic Church was established by Jesus Christ (Matthew 16:18-19; Acts 2:1-41). They prefer the Catholic style of

---

[15] See Dzurgba, *On the Tiv of Central Nigeria,* 170.

[16] See Adasu, *Understanding African Traditional Religion Part One*, 30.

[17] Vatican Council II, "Dei Verbum [Dogmatic Constitution on Devine Revelation]," sec 21,

http://www.vatican.va/archive/hist_councils/ii_vatican_council/documents/vat-ii_const_19651118_dei-verbum_en.html.

worship in comparison with the Pentecostal style that has no definite format or structure.

Pentecostal mode of worship is spontaneous, unstructured, uninhibited, and lasts for several hours with joyful shouting, swaying and singing, clapping of hands , dancing and moving round the church.[18] Emerging adults criticize this style of worship and argue that God can be encountered in a still small voice (1Kings 19:11, Psalm 46: 11).

On the opposite side, the majority of the emerging adults were very critical of the Catholic Church, observing that it is too traditional, holding onto the past, and not being in tune with the post-modern context. Their view correlates with the concept of traditionalism, which is the dead faith of the living as opposed to tradition, the living faith of the dead.[19] They criticize the Catholic Church that it overemphasizes the need for members to donate money, promotes the worship of images, and worships Mary the mother of Jesus.

They also say the Catholic Church is too strict on dress and moral codes and has too many embodied practices. Worship is dull and not spirit moving, and they condemn the rote teaching and learning of catechism. They are also concerned that the reception of the Eucharist is too frequent, and that the Catholic Church does not insist on the study and reading of the Bible. Furthermore, people who expect miracles in their lives do not experience them in the Catholic Church, homilies are too scholastic, and typically, Catholic priests do not lead with good examples, and that they do not preach well.

These criticisms demonstrate that emerging adults in Tiv culture are not well grounded in the faith of the Catholic Church. Those who raised these issues indicated they are still hanging in as members of the Catholic Church because they were initiated into the Catholic Church as infants. Their concerns about the Bible and homilies open the discussion on the celebration of the Word that constitutes an important aspect of the Eucharistic celebration.

---

[18] Victor Igbum, "Charismatic/Pentecostalism: Its Impact on Christianity in Tivland," *Ate: Journal of African Religion and Culture* 1 (December 2010): 57.

[19] Mary C. Boys, *Educating in Faith: Maps and Visions* (San Francisco: Harper & Row, 1989), 193.

The Word of God
as Symbol of Wisdom

The priest who presides at a Catholic worship acts in *Persona Christi* (the person of Christ). In Tiv culture, one who occupies an esteemed position is automatically looked upon as an "elder" who communicates to the people and anticipates positive changes from them. An elder's words are taken seriously for the Tiv say *imo i organden ka imo ivungu* (the voice of an elder is the voice of an owl). The hoot of an Owl in this context is a symbol of wisdom. Thus, the phrase is often interpreted, "the voice of an elder is the voice of wisdom."

An elder in Tiv culture is expected to be gentle in speech, not talking down on people. In times of community feuds, the elder considers the various opinions of the disagreeing parties and draws an objective conclusion. Elders spontaneously integrate Tiv traditional wisdom enshrined in myths, proverbs, idioms, and stories in their speech to add value to the discussion, and to bring out the message in a profound way. Anyone who heeds an elder's word is said to *war shom* (escapes being hacked with a machete or escapes danger). The Bassa people of Liberia see old age as a symbol of wisdom.[20] The proverb that says, "it is on an old mat that one sits to make a new mat," demonstrates the necessity of younger people to rely on older members of the community to learn wisdom.

The image of old age associated with wisdom leads to the understanding that the position of a preacher is an exulted position of one who is called to communicate divine wisdom, exhorting listeners to heed the commands of Yahweh and reform their lives.[21] He may be young but the clerical office challenges him to act maturely. In Catholic worship, the word of God occupies an important position.

People come to worship with different experiences and expect the word of God to give meaning to their experiences. Catholic priests must acknowledge the transforming effects of the word of God en-

---

[20] Pinnapue Early (a Ph.D. student in the School of Theology and Ministry, St Thomas University, Miami Florida) in a seminar presentation on Cultural and Ritual, 2013.
[21] Kathleen A. Cahalan, *Introducing the Practice of Ministry* (Collegeville: Liturgical Press, 2010), 75.

suring that their homilies connect the experiences of the people. Emerging adults criticize some homilies preached by Catholic priests for being out of touch with the realities confronting the people. Even when homilies are down to earth, they are not supported with appropriate biblical passages. This critique supports the claim that the culture of reading or studying the Bible is not deeply ingrained in the life of Catholics.

Dorothy Mayange of Benue State University said, in the Catholic Church today, Sunday readings are printed on the bulletin. The bulletin has replaced the Bible. The introduction of the bulletin has diminished the practice of going to church with Bibles. Worse still, some Catholic priests do not make reference to biblical passages as they preach. The preacher preaches from experience and does not root the homily in sacred scripture.[22] This approach of preaching without using appropriate biblical texts fails to comply with the church's insistence that all the preaching of the church must be nourished and regulated by Sacred Scripture.[23] The preaching of the word that integrates Scripture and Tiv cultural sources potentially roots Catholicism in context.

The traditional wisdom found in proverbs, myths, stories, idioms correlate effectively with biblical wisdom. For instance, in talking about the concept of community or unity (1 Corinthians 12:12-26), the preacher can correlate the symbolic saying, *ka tema imongo Mbagbera ve fe iwa ye* (it is in sitting together that Mbabgera people have come to know the art of blacksmithing). This saying has a powerful message in Tiv context, but it is most often taken for granted. In Swahili language spoken by some societies in East Africa, they say, *umuja ni nguvu* (unity is strength).[24] The value of keeping a confidential report or the seal of confession correlates positively with the saying that *kwa ua lamen, or man nan ôô iyol ga* (if the bathroom could talk, no one would ever take a shower). This promotes the value of the sacrament as a sealed conversation and helps

---

[22] Dorothy Mayange (a twenty-three years old student of Benue State University, Makurdi), in a one-on-one interview on May 19, 2014 at Makurdi.
[23] Vatican Council II, "Dei Verbum," sec 21.
[24] Joseph Healey, mm and Donald Sybertz, mm, *Toward an African Narrative Theology*, 38.

to build the confidence of the confider (penitent) in the confidant (confessor).

On caution, a popular Swahili proverb says *henri pazia kuliko bendera* (better a curtain hanging motionless than a flag swaying in the wind). This proverb is sometimes used in the context of cautioning young people on the effects of Hiv/Aids, calling them to stay with one partner (the one partner in the house) rather than play around with many partners (like a flag swaying to and fro).[25] The value of equality is effectively enhanced with the Bassa proverb that says, "a trap set in the market square is not for rats alone."[26] What is done with the intent to harm the downtrodden members of the community might affect royals too. Stories also communicate messages in powerful ways.

The story of *Adagba* for instance, is analogous to the Christian belief in the resurrection. *Adagba* was said to have been an excellent entertainer who died but was believed to have been raised through the machinations of witchcraft to entertain an august visitor in Tiv society. In the process of dancing, *Adagba* held spectators spellbound. When he noticed that spectators were carried away by his performance, he took to his heels and disappeared. To this day, Tiv people believe he is alive, but cannot tell where exactly he is. Correlating the scriptures with proverbs and stories found in culture is helpful in making Catholics to grow in the faith as well as in culture, making them effectively integrated in both. The failure to communicate the word in a style that roots it in biblical and traditional wisdom is making emerging adult Catholics to experience an insatiable thirst for the word of God. That thirst is gradually being satisfied by Pentecostal preachers.

Pentecostal preachers are conscious of the realities strangulating people and have taken advantage of the situation. They are alive to the signs of the times and capitalize on situations by providing solutions to the problems of insecurity, loneliness, and stress affecting

---

[25] Joseph Healey, mm and Donald Sybertz, mm, *Toward an African Narrative Theology*, 37.
[26] Early, Culture and Ritual, Miami.

people on a daily basis.[27] Where the proposed solutions are unsuccessful, they blame the devil, and the victim's lack of faith in the Spirit.[28] They reflect the concrete experiences of people in their homilies quoting appropriate biblical passages to support their claims. They also quote scriptures to support their criticisms of some practices in the Catholic Church.

On the contrary, even when Catholics are familiar with the topic, they are unable to quote scriptures to support their argument.[29] They preach prosperity messages that attract many emerging adults who anticipate quick economic prosperity. Preaching is an important aspect of worship. The preaching of a pastor may help the church to grow rapidly or slowly or even lose members.[30] Their style of preaching the word that promises quick prosperity connects well with people.

Preaching is a public act, a dialogical event between the preacher and the listeners. It is a charisma that includes knowledge of and the capacity to interpret the word of God, the ability to speak persuasively to the people, and the virtues of empathy and truth telling.[31] Empathy is the ability to be sensitive to the feelings, thoughts, ideas, and circumstances of the hearer. Truth telling involves what the preacher witnesses in the text as well as in the community.[32]

John Igbana of BSU said, Catholic priests must base their homily on the situation of the people and allow the word to speak to people. Drawing their warrant from Scriptures, they must call a sped a sped, not flattering their listeners, but telling the story as it is.[33] The

[27] Igbum, "Charismatic/Pentecostalism: Its Impact on Christianity in Tivland," 57.

[28] Arbuckle, Culture, Inculturation, Theologians, 135.

[29] Dominic Swande (a twenty-four years old student of College of Education, Katsina-Ala), in a one-on-one interview on June 7, 2014 at Katsina-Ala. The respondent acknowledged the challenges emerging adults face when confronted by their contemporaries in other churches.

[30] Patricia Kombo (a twenty-three years old student of College of Education, Katsina-ala), in a one on one interview on June 8, 2014 at Katsina-Ala. Also see, Godwin I. Akper, "Prosperity Gospel: A Case Study of Benue State in North-Central Nigeria," Journal of Reformed Theology 1 (2007): 47.

[31] Cahalan, Introducing the Practice of Ministry, 76.

[32] Cahalan, Introducing the Practice of Ministry, 77.

[33] John Igbana (a twenty-seven years old student of Benue State university, Makurdi), in a one-on-one interview on May 17, 2014 at Makurdi.

degree to which the preacher is knowledgeable about the Bible is not enough to make him or her an effective preacher. It entails listening to God's voice in the Scripture and bearing witness about this truth for a particular community.[34] To interpret the word for the community requires study and exegesis of the Scripture that includes appreciation for the cultural and social setting of the text as well as the tradition of interpretation about texts.

Educated emerging adults are concerned with the quality of the word proclaimed to them. The failure of the Catholic clergy to connect their experiences using the power of the word is gradually eroding their membership of the Catholic Church. Ministers of the divine word need to pay attention to the duty to preach, to effectively provide the nourishment of the Scriptures for the people of God, to enlighten their minds, strengthen their wills, and set their hearts on fire with the love of God.[35] When the word and Eucharist are celebrated in the context of people's experiences, the celebration roots their faith in culture, and culture also enriches their faith tradition. This leads to the symbol of the Eucharis as the climax of worship in the Catholic tradition.

Symbol of the Eucharist as Common Meal

In Chapter One, the image of sitting round, and sharing a bowl of mean was identified with the Eucharist. Irrespective of the quantity, Tiv people are disposed to share their food with the other person. A Tiv person does not hesitate to give the last lump of food to a stranger, who appears visibly tired and hungry as the saying goes, *ka kyev ruam imom i waren or ye*(it is a single lump of food that saves life). The ordinary food human beings eat provides energy and nutrients to keep the human body healthy and active. It is made of different recipes with a variety of nutrients. Food is very important because it sustains life.

---

[34] Cahalan, *Introducing the Practice of Ministry*, 77.
[35] Vatican Council II, "Dei Verbum," sec 23.

Realizing that Jesus has the power to provide bread, the crowd was moved to follow him wherever he went. Jesus accused the crowd of looking for him not because they saw signs, but because they ate the loaves and were filled (John 6:26). He challenged them to not work for the food that perishes, but the food that endures for eternal life (John 6:27). By this saying, Jesus makes allusion to the Eucharistic meal as food for the soul.

The Eucharist is Jesus' voluntary self-giving of his body and blood for the salvation of the world. The earliest account of the Eucharistic celebration is contained in 1 Corinthians 11: 23-26. Catholics believe that the elements of bread and wine are transformed into the body and blood of Jesus during consecration. This mystery that is at the center of the church's life is familiar to Tiv Catholics at different levels. At the most primary level, it is a symbol of common meal. At a complex level, it resonates with the ritual of *imborvungu* in Tiv culture.

The doctrine of the Eucharist can be compared with the ritual of *imborvungu* by drawing out the similarities and differences of both so that Catholicism can build a home in Tiv culture. The Eucharist is similar to *imborvungu* at four levels. First, both are practices exclusive for initiates. Second, in each, the goal is to uplift humanity and indeed the world to a higher level. Third, both rituals are efficacious because they spring from the sacrifice of human victims. Fourth, they are approached with a high sense of decorum and reverence.

What fundamentally distinguishes these ritual practices is that, while the institution of the Eucharist is of divine origin, the ritual of *imborvungu* is a mundane cultural practice. While the Eucharist was instituted as a result of the free self-giving of Jesus in love for the world, *imborvungu* repeatedly sheds the blood of human victims who are secretly conscripted to make it effective for ritual performance. For the purpose of contextualization, a discussion about Catholicism in Tiv culture with non-believers or believers who are not grounded in culture can begin by appreciating *imborvungu* and similar cultural practices.

Emerging adult Catholics in Tiv society lack the wisdom to articulate a deeper analogical connection between the Eucharist, and other Catholic practices with Tiv cultural practices. However, those who come from solid Catholic backgrounds have acquired a sound understanding of the Eucharist as the real presence of Jesus. They acknowledge that when the preacher fails to use the word of God to uplift listeners, the Eucharist gives them hope of the continuous presence of God in the diverse experiences of God's people.

In an interview with Doo Atume of Uniagric, her facial expression indicated that she was not very satisfied with the quality of homilies delivered by some Catholic priests. "I participate in worship in the Catholic Church merely because of the importance I attach to the Eucharist."[36]

The opportunity to partake of the Eucharist is seen as a privilege by some emerging adults unworthy as they are. Anthony Venda lacked words to adequately express the meaning he derives from the Eucharist, observing that he is overwhelmed by the mystery of the Eucharist.[37] Other students owe their admission into the university to the power of Jesus in the Eucharist.

Terdoo Ikpa observed that he derives a strong meaning from the Eucharist. "The Eucharist gives me hope. I applied several times for admission into the university but was not recruited. The moment I took my problem to Jesus in the Blessed Sacrament, my problem was solved."[38] During exams, they attend Mass regularly, and frequently visit the Blessed Sacrament with the belief that Jesus will grant them success in the exams.

Many emerging adults shared stories of how they received miraculous healing through the Eucharist. Some said, when they are confronted with difficult problems that defile all human solution, they forward the intention to God during consecration, and eventually receive solution.

---

[36] Doo Atume (a twenty-two years old student of University of Agriculture, Makurdi), in a one-on-one interview on June 1, 2014 at Makurdi.

[37] Anthony Venda (a twenty-three years old student of University of Agriculture, Makudi), in a one-on-one interview on June 2, 2014 at Makurdi.

[38] Terdoo Ikpa (a twenty-seven years old student of Benue State University, Makurdi), in a one-on-one interview on May 15, 2014 at Makurdi, Nigeria.

Terfa Asor said, "I was very sick to the degree that every medication I took did not relieve my pains. I took my problem to Mass. During consecration, I aligned my intention, and I received instant relief."[39]

Victoria Sonter prayed before the Blessed Sacrament for solution to a problem she encountered, and immediately experienced a heavy burden taken off her shoulders. This transforming experience made her to fall in love with the hymn: "The comforter has come." When asked if she could sing a part of the song, without hesitation she cheerfully sang the following verse and chorus with an excellent and gifted voice.[40]

> Oh spread the tidings round, where-ever man is found,
> Where-ever human hearts and human woes abound,
> Let every Christian tongue, proclaim the joyful sound,
> The comforter has come.

Chorus:

> The comforter has come,
> The comforter has come,
> The Holy Ghost from heaven,
> The father's promise given,
> Oh spread the tidings round,
> Wherever man is found,
> The comforter has come.

In the Catholic tradition, this hymn is associated with Pentecost Mass or Masses of the Holy Spirit, but drawing from her faith experience, Victoria found a deeper meaning connecting it with the Eucharist. Many emerging adults acknowledged the centrality of the Eucharist in their lives.

The Eucharist is in an outstanding way the sacrament of the paschal mystery. It stands at the center of the Church's life. This is already clear from the earliest images of the Church found in the Acts of the Apostles: "They devoted themselves to the Apostles' teaching and

---

[39] Terfa Asor (a twenty-three years old student of Benue State University, Makurdi), in a one-on-one interview on May 17, 2014 at Makurdi, Nigeria.
[40] Victoria Sonter (a twenty-two years old student of Benue State university, Makurdi), in a one-on-one interview on May 16, 2014 at Makurdi.

fellowship, to the breaking of bread and the prayers" (2:42). The "breaking of the bread" refers to the Eucharist.[41] Eucharist has both a universal and cosmic character. It is cosmic because even when it is celebrated on the humble altar of a country church, the Eucharist is always in some way celebrated *on the altar of the world*.[42] It unites heaven and earth. It embraces and permeates all creation.[43]

The celebration of the Eucharist, however, cannot be the starting point for communion. It presupposes that communion already exists, a communion which it seeks to consolidate and bring to perfection. The sacrament is an expression of this bond of communion both in its *invisible* dimension, which, in Christ and through the working of the Holy Spirit, unites us to the Father and among ourselves.[44] The bond of communion is an expression of solidarity and sharing among Christ's faithful, including Tiv Catholics who are already familiar with these concepts.

For Catholicism to be meaningful to the Tiv, and take root in Tiv culture, Tiv Catholics may retrieve the image of sharing equally of a common meal by all.[45] A central image of the Eucharist is to feed the hungry. The Eucharist continues Jesus' miraculous ministry of feeding the thousands of hungry people.[46] Whenever the Church celebrates the Eucharist, the faithful can in some way relive the experience of the two disciples on the road to Emmaus: "their eyes were opened and they recognized him" (Luke 24:31).[47] Such a luminous experience entails recognizing Christ in the thousands of hungry Tiv people. When the multitudes of hungry people are fed, Christ is not only discovered in the church building and in the tabernacle,

---

[41]John Paul II, *Ecclesia De Eucharistia* [Encyclical Letter on the Eucharist in its Relationship to the Church], sec. 3,
http://www.vatican.va/holy_father/john_paul_ii/encyclicals/documents/hf_jp-ii_enc_20030417_eccl-de-euch_en.html

[42]John Paul II, *Ecclesia De Eucharistia*, sec. 8.

[43]John Paul II, *Ecclesia De Eucharistia*, sec. 8.

[44]John Paul II, *Ecclesia De Eucharistia*, sec. 35.

[45] See Nathan D. Mitchell, "History of the Relationship between Eucharist and Communion." *Liturgical Ministry* 13 (Spring 2004): 62.

[46] Mitchell, "History of the Relationship between Eucharist and Communion," 63.

[47]John Paul II, *Ecclesia De Eucharistia*, sec. 6.

but his presence is recognized in towns and cities as he cries out for food and shelter.[48]

Christian worship includes the periphery, those on the margins who become the center, the place of pilgrimage, for there the cross of Christ is encountered most acutely. In other words, it is the poor and the powerless, the abused and injured, the despondent and the useless who become icons within Christian worship, for it is there that Jesus' preferential option and our mission are discovered most profoundly.[49] In this way, the Eucharist is meaningful, not only as an exclusive reality to eligible Catholics, but more as an inclusive reality. It unites all categories of people, the haves and the have-nots, the hungry and the satisfied. This image expresses the social dimension of worship, thus resonating with *imborvungu* ritual as a transforming symbol in Tiv culture.

Just as *imborvungu* ensures the ordering and prosperity of Tivland, at the end of the Eucharistic celebration, the priest also sends the faithful to go and do the work of transforming the society.[50] Worship needs to continually push outward empowering worshippers to become instruments of restoration in the healing of society's brokenness and despair[51] similar to what *imborvungu* does for the Tiv. Jesus instituted the Eucharistic sacrifice to perpetuate the sacrifice of the Cross throughout time, until his second coming.[52] Through the sacrifice of the cross, Jesus atoned for the sins of the world. This concept of sacrifice is well known to the Sukuma people of Tanzania.

---

[48] Pecklers, *Worship: A Primer in Christian Ritual*, 168.

[49] Pecklers, *Worship: A Primer in Christian Ritual*, 183.

[50] See Pecklers, *Worship: A Primer in Christian Ritual*, 190.

[51] Pecklers, *Worship: A Primer in Christian Ritual*, 181.

[52] See Vatican Council II, "Sacrosanctum Concilium [Constitution on the Sacred Liturgy]," sec. 47, http://www.vatican.va/archive/hist_councils/ii_vatican_council/documents/vat-ii_const_19631204_sacrosanctum-concilium_en.html

Sacrifice Among
the Sukuma People

Jesus gave his life on the cross to reconcile humanity with God. The Sukuma people have a specific sacrifice of reconciliation that resonates with the sacrifice of Christ. Among the Sukuma[53] people of East Africa, when an indigenous diviner-healer or a leader of a *Bagalu* or *Bagika* Dance Societies dies, a ceremony of *Isabigula* (uncovering) is performed to uncover the tools and instruments the healer used in the practice of medicine that were covered soon after his death. In the case of the diviner-healer, the ceremony is performed to determine who takes over the possessions.

The ceremony is performed with a white innocent female goat. A sacrificial goat is killed with a spear, which is slowly driven into the left chest of the goat in such a way that the heart of the goat is not pierced. When the sacrificial goat emits its screaming and piercing cry (an agonized bleating), all the people sorrowfully respond by humming "mmm." This ritual may take half an hour.

After the death of the sacrificial goat, the blood and heart portion is prepared. It is mixed with medicine, which is later used for cleansing the other medicine, the fly-whisk, the calabashes and all the people in the family. The goat's death while screaming is a symbolic act that restores power to the medicine and peace to the family of the deceased person. This is an important example of a Sukuma sacrifice of reconciliation. This type of sacrifice brings special peace and restores a right relationship with the ancestors.[54]

The sacrificial goat in the Sukuma tradition has parallels with Jesus Christ who is the sacrificial lamb in the Christian tradition. Both undergo innocent deaths. These parallels include similarities and contrasts. (i) Both the sacrificial goat and Jesus Christ are brought

---

[53]The Sukuma ethnic group is the largest ethnic group (approximately five million people) in Tanzania. The Sukuma are located mainly in Western Tanzania in the Mwanza Archdiocese and the Geita and Shinyanga Dioceses. See Joseph M. Lupande, Joseph G. Healey, and Donald F. Sybertz, "The Sukuma Sacrificial Goat and Christianity: An Example of Inculturation in Africa," *Worship* 70 no, 6 (1996): 506.

[54] Lupande, Joseph G. Healey, and Donald F. Sybertz, "The Sukuma Sacrificial Goat and Christianity: An Example of Inculturation in Africa," 509.

before the people. The goat is dragged unwillingly and protests. Jesus gives himself willing; (ii) Both are innocent victims who must die so that the rest of the people may live; (iii) Both are sacrificial victims who take on the sin, weakness and death of the people; (iv) Both actually die.

It is not like the story of Abraham and Isaac where the son is saved from physical death. In fact, both the sacrificial goat and Jesus undergo painful, agonizing and violent deaths. They are both slowly tortured and bleed profusely before they die. Before dying the goat cries out for help in a piercing scream. When Jesus feels abandoned on the cross he cries out for help to his Father with a loud voice: "My God! My God! Why have you forsaken me?" (Matt 27:46); (v)

Participants in the Sukuma ceremony are really emotionally involved in this rite of passage when the goat dies in anguish. In particular the Sukuma women actually weep as they sorrowfully hum "mmm" during this part of the ritual. The biblical parallel is the faithful women in the Gospel who accompanied Jesus on his "Way of the Cross." "But Jesus turned to them and said, 'Daughters of Jerusalem, do not weep for me, but weep for yourselves and for your children' " (Luke 23:26). The women wept at Jesus' anguish and were sorrowfully present at the foot of the cross. They actually shared in Christ's suffering and death.[55]

While the Sukuma sacrifice of reconciliation is analogous to Jesus' atoning death on the cross, the ritual of *imborvungu* in Tiv culture resonates with the sacrificial act of Jesus both as a symbol of reparation and a symbol of torture.

Symbol of Reparation

The ritual of *imborvungu* is a cultural symbol that has the aspect of repairing the land through a ritual sacrifice as its goal. The land as already observed is the entire cosmology of the Tiv, encompassing the earth, physical action, and ethical behavior. The Tiv offer sacrifice for the ordering and prosperity of the land. Sacrifice as a way of

---

[55] Lupande, Joseph G. Healey, and Donald F. Sybertz, "The Sukuma Sacrificial Goat and Christianity: An Example of Inculturation in Africa," 510-511.

ensuring a harmonious relationship between the human community and the realm of the divine and mystical power is a regular event in Tiv culture. When the Tiv perform a sacrifice, they anticipate it to achieve the set goals.[56] Such a ritual performance has meaning in Tiv culture as in Christianity.

The Tiv understanding of sacrifice to repair the land corroborates the sacrifice of Jesus, an act of atonement meant to purge human sin and wrong-doing as described in the Letter to the Hebrews. Hebrews states that it was an annual event to use the blood of animals for atonement. The Tiv are also familiar with the use of animal or human blood for some of their ritual sacrifices.[57] Since Israel's use of animals was an ineffective means of taking away human sin, Jesus gave himself freely as a ransom.

In purifying the land through the ritual sacrifice of *imborvungu*, no animal or sub-human victim can be used. It must be a human being that has achieved success in life. The use of human blood underscores the seriousness of what it means for the Tiv to repair the land. While the Tiv and Israel repeatedly undertook the ritual sacrifice using the blood of animals, the sacrificial death of Jesus on the cross was a supreme sacrifice offered once for all (Hebrews 1:3). No number of animals or human victims offered to purify or repair Tivland can equal the one perfect sacrifice Jesus made for all humanity.[58]

When the Tiv offer their sacrifices, they are acknowledging their total dependence on *Aondo* (God) as their creator, sustainer, and provider of all they have. In this regard, they perceive turbulent experiences and ill luck as God's anger for their misdeeds.[59] A befitting sacrifice of human blood must be used to purify *imborvungu*, and that act, ultimately appeases God to reverse God's anger.

---

[56] See Bediako, *Jesus in Africa*, 28.
[57] See Dzurgba, *On the Tiv of Central Nigeria*, 173. Different kinds of animals are required for various sacrifices. Animals may include snakes, birds, chickens, ducks, goats, dogs, sheep, pigs, and cows.
[58] Bediako, *Jesus in Africa*, 28-29.
[59] See Geri, *A History of Tiv Religious Practices and Changes*, 47.

Opinions are divided on whether it was an adult or a baby or a fetus' blood that was used as victim for the ritual purification of *imborvungu*. Some argue that the Tiv prefer fetal blood obtained from the termination of a pregnancy by the *mbatsav* (witches or wizards) as the purest substance for purification. Others observe that the blood of young people who are perceived to be successful in life is preferred.

The sudden death of a young person from a brief illness like headache, raises serious questions for old people in the village. They are also blamed when someone dies of tangible causes such as snakebite, drowning in the water, falling from a tree, eating or drinking poison, and being attacked with a dangerous weapon. It was believed that these material causes in themselves are incapable of killing because they lack spiritual efficacy, potency and spell.[60] In this sense, a human subject is alleged to employ spiritual machination to cause the death of another human being. On the day of funeral, elders usually gathered to investigate, and ascertain the killer. This suggests that for the Tiv, the death of a human being is caused by another.

Typically, Tiv students in institutions of higher education attribute the death of a young person to witches or wizards as an act of immolation for the sacrificial strengthening of *imborvungu*. Most of those used as victims are educated people. Education, which has been seen as a symbol of empowerment, liberation, and transformation has become a symbol that invites pain and malice. A successful person may suffer the machinations of the witches and wizards, and subsequent death just to bring set back to his or her family. This happens when evidence shows that such a person may bring wealth to his or her family.

The wanton destruction of life through witchcraft is a practical case of bad witchcraft. Within an extended family system, those who are unable to train their children due to poverty or negligence become envious of those whose children have attained higher level of education. This is a fact in Tiv society today that contradicts the concept

---

[60] Dzurgba, *The Tiv and Their Culture*, 168.

of community that was held in the past when the success of one person was shared and celebrated by the whole community.[61]

In an interview, Tardoo Akpur of Benue State University narrated how students who attended the funeral of an enterprising student of their university unleashed violence on the old people in that village. Students accused them of being responsible for the death of their mate.[62] Students react violently to the death of their colleague in view of the painful challenges of economic hardships, admission challenges, and other challenges they experience in school. In the midst of these painful experiences, they anticipate a time of relief when they graduate, pick a job, earn money, and live a comfortable life.

When a student dies suddenly, it brings pain and despair to them with no option than to accuse and react violently to the old people. In Tiv society today, old people in the rural communities are scared of attending the funeral of a student. They blame young people for associating old age with the practice of *tsav* (witchcraft), and argue that as potential old people, young people will suffer a similar fate, that is, they will be accused of witchcraft, and consequently of spilling human blood.

The use of the blood of a credible victim supports the claim that *imborvungu* ritual is very selective on the quality of human victim of the sacrifice. It prefers an offering without blemish[63] to strengthen

---

[61] As a religious belief, the Tiv see witchcraft in two ways. There is *tsav bu bough* (bad witchcraft) used with the intention to destroy or to cause pain, and *tsavbu dedoo* (good witchcraft) used for the good of the community as in the case of *imborvungu* ritual. Also see Elochukwu E. Uzukwu, *A Listening Church*, 106. The author discusses the phenomenon of witchcraft as a way of taking revenge against some members of the society. Jealousy demonstrated toward wealthy members of the community finds expression in sortilege. The author says he is inclined to use the "imaginary" metaphor of witchcraft to interpret social inequalities.

[62] Tardoo Akpur (A twenty-seven years old student of Benue State University, Makurdi), in a one-on-one interview on May 19, 2014 at Makurdi.

[63] See Dzurgba, *On the Tiv of Central Nigeria,* 172. The author sees blemish as a mark on someone's body that disfigures his appearance. In the case of *imborvungu,* a blemish victim is one that is not sound in moral character and has no economic success. Also, a Tiv greeting can help to understand the notion of blemish. The usual greeting *u pande nena* (how are you?), is followed by a spontaneous response, *kwagh eren ibume or ga* (nothing happens to a fool). This symbolically suggests that the respondent is a

its effectiveness in appeasing God. The human sacrifice as an element of *imborvungu* has a connection with Jesus' sacrificial death on the cross for the reconciliation of the world. The cross is a unique symbol for Christians. It is a symbol of the triumph of Christ and the election of Christians (Rev 7:3; 9:4; 14:1; 22:4).[64]

The analogical link between *imborvungu* as a symbol of reparation, and the cross as a symbol of triumph provides a mutual enrichment for both Catholicism and Tiv culture. By using human blood to repair the land, the Tiv have indirectly accepted Christianity, which is the event of Jesus Christ, ransomed with his blood. Christianity on the other hand is not proclaiming a strange religion to the Tiv, but proclaiming what is already familiar to them that only need an articulation. Such an articulation exposes and discards negative elements of the symbol for it to be fully integrated in Catholicism. In this regard, the aspects of *imborvungu* that promote torture are explored.

Symbol of Torture

In the Roman Empire the cross was a symbol of torture and it has become in many cultures and various Christian traditions a symbol that brings together different evils or suffering.[65] In this connection, the analogical relationship between *imborvungu* and the Christian cross can be deciphered. The main component of *imborvungu* is the bone of a deceased good person. The use of the bone of a good person symbolizes the usage of the best quality materials in repairing the land.

This again calls to mind the delivering up of the sinless Jesus for the salvation of the world. It can also be argued that the life of virtue, total self-giving, and the willingness to die for the community is the path to setting the land right. The repeated human sacrificial offering to strengthen its effectiveness suggests the extent to which the

---

fool that is why he is still alive. On the contrary, if he were a morally upright person, and enjoyed some measure of material success, he would be a potential victim of ritual sacrifice. This does not mean that every community in Tiv society practices *imborvungu* cult.

[64] Uzukwu, *Worship as Body Language Introduction to Christian Worship*, 22.
[65] Gebara, *Out of the Depths*, 112.

Tiv are committed to using human victims to reduce pain and bring comfort to the community.

Any successful young man, and pregnant woman can be subjected to pain in trying to reduce the community's pain. The manipulation and the ritual act of aborting women's pregnancy by the *mbatsav* (witches and wizards) to use the fetal blood to strengthen *imborvungu* comes to mind. This is just one of the agonizing plights Tiv women encounter, and a higher level of showing how women are worthless in Tiv society. In most societies, women can speak of such trouble as "my cross."[66] To speak in this manner is to speak of something that weighs one's life down, a burden, something heavy to carry. It is something someone has not chosen.

The cross is commonly understood as something negative.[67] This understanding is also true of Tiv society manifesting itself in different ways, including the unbalanced relationship between men and women. The presence of evil, pain and social imbalance are sometimes sanctioned by culture, but most importantly they are consequences of the event in the Garden of Eden. The desire to pursue self-interest against the divine command resulted to a rupture in creation, disharmony between women and men, an imbalance in social relations, and the subjugation of women.[68] In the context of *imborvungu,* women do not stand alone in suffering violence.

Successful young people's blood also provides the means for the effectiveness of *imborvungu,* and the prosperity of Tiv society. As potential victims of the sacrificial offering, the fear of death believed to be caused by *mbatsav,* who are mostly found in rural communities has made some young people to have little or no contact with their local communities. University students who shared this opinion stated that their parents are conscious of this reality and discourage them from arbitrary visiting the village.

Iortyom Igbadoo of COE said, his father has cautioned them (children) to visit the village only when there is good reason to do so.

---

[66] Gebara, *Out of the Depths,* 112.

[67] Gebara, *Out of the Depths,* 112.

[68] See Renita J. Weems, *The Women's Bible Commentary,* eds. Carol A. Newson and Sharon H. Ringe(Louisville: John Knox, 1992), 160.

"We live in Makurdi and visit the village when there is an important occasion such as the funeral of a close family member."[69]

Angbiandoo Uma of Uniagric said, she was born and raised in Makurdi. She does not go to the village. As a Catholic, she does not believe the superstitious stories she hears about people in the village, noting that the stories are true for some people.[70] The overall goal of *imborvungu* as a practice of repairing the land has a positive value. However, the means to achieving the goal cannot be devoid of the shedding of human blood, hence the means does not justify the end. Catholic theology considers the protection of human life as an imperative and absolute norm.

Theological Synthesis:
Respect for Human Life

To apply the criteria of adequacy to this interpretation means addressing the questions that affect human life in the context of young men and women in the contemporary Tiv society, and to draw lessons from the wisdom of the Catholic tradition. Catholic theology supports the dialogue between faith and culture. However, for pregnant women, unborn children, and young people to suffer violence as a result of a nefarious cultural practice contradicts the divine will.

In the case of women particularly, both the Hebrew and Christian scriptures have sometimes been interpreted from a subjective point of view to support violence against women. The account of creation where Eve the woman was created out of the bone from the rib of Adam the man (Genesis 2:22), is often cited as evidence of divine sanction of woman inferiority. St Paul in his letter to the Ephesians 5:22 addressed women thus: "wives should be submissive to their husbands...as the perfect will of God."[71]

---

[69] Iortyom Igbadoo (a twenty-two years old student of College of Education, Katsina-Ala), in a one-on-one interview on June 10, 2014 at Katsina-Ala.

[70] Angbiadoo Uma (a twenty-two years old student of University of Agriculture, Makurdi), in a one-on-one interview on June 1, 2014 at Makurdi.

[71] Mary Dorothy Eze, "A Christian Response to Gender Inequality Against Women," in *Religion, Violence and Conflict Resolution in Nigeria*, ed. Cyril Obanure (Makurdi: Aboki Publishers, 2008), 106.

However, one must not disregard the fact that other biblical periscopes uphold the dignity of women. In particular, the Song of Songs is a critique both of culture and of scripture concerning women issues. The book can be seen as a commentary on certain portions of scripture that undermine human sexuality in general and female sexuality in particular. An obvious story that the Song counterbalances is the creation story in Genesis 2-3. The Song of Songs advocates balance in male and female relationships urging mutuality not domination.[72]

When a woman is not fecund in Tiv culture, she is degraded in a marital relationship, and is subsequently compelled to quit the marriage. When she is an expectant mother, she is celebrated only to be used as a blood donor for the ritual purification of *imborvungu* in some cases. Women are already victims of intermittent blood lose. To use them as objects or tools to produce fetal blood for the good of the community directly opposes the divine plan.

The discussion on *imborvungu,* and its violence on pregnant women and young people expands to other critical issues affecting human life. These issues include, direct abortion, contraceptives, and other artificial means of birth control, and indeed all forms of violent attack on human life identified with young people today.

Patricia Kombo of College of Education observed that love of material things has made emerging adult females to buy into a promiscuous culture that offers financial gains, and other forms of material benefits. The search for material things through illicit sex has resulted to a massive irruption of victims of sexually transmitted infections including, HIV/AIDS, and perpetrators of abortion, endangering their lives and harming the life of the unborn.[73] Sexual related problems have led to the death of many in Tivland.

---

72 See Weems, *The Women's Bible Commentary,* 160.
73 Patricia Kombo (a twenty-three years old student of College of Education, Katsina-ala), in a one-on-one interview on June 8, 2014 at Katsina-Ala. Also see, Magesa, *Anatomy of Inculturation,* 28. The author says, poverty among unemployed girls and women tends to make sexual promiscuity appear the only way of acquiring money for their needs.

Emerging adult males on the other hand are often involved in heinous crimes that cause death such as rape, armed robbery, political thuggery, and rivalry between secret cult groups. The rivalry between cult groups results from the struggle for supremacy that often leads to the brutal death of members of both rival esoteric groups as well as innocent students. These acts are increasingly debasing human life both on campus and in the wider Tiv society. Educated emerging adults who associate the death of a young person with the ritual of *imborvungu,* orchestrated by the old people cannot be justified when they are also accused of glaring acts of murder. In a situation such as this, they can also be accused of destroying human life.

Observing the numerous cases of abuse of human life in Tiv culture, the need arises to draw lessons from the Catholic tradition on the most acceptable ways of handling life. Beginning with scripture, the fifth commandment of the Decalogue categorically forbids killing (Exodus 20:13). The Old Testament considers blood as a sacred sign of life (Lev 17:14). This teaching remains necessary for all time. Human life must be respected and protected absolutely from the moment of conception. Direct abortion, that is, abortion willed either as an end or a means, is gravely contrary to the moral law.[74] Human life is sacred. No one has right to life, but God.

As the author of life, God allowed God's Son to be delivered up for the reconciliation of the world communicated to us in the Eucharist in the form of bread and wine.[75] The dialogue between the Eucharist, the Cross, and *imborvungu* mutually enriches the Catholic faith and Tiv culture. This discussion will be deepened with catechesis, a critical too in rooting Catholicism in Tiv culture.

---

[74]*Catechism of the Catholic Church,* sec. 2260, http://www.vatican.va/archive/ENG0015/__P7Z.HTM. Also see sections 2270 and 2271.

[75] Jürgen Moltmann, *The Trinity and the Kingdom: The Doctrine of God* (San Francisco: Harper and Row, 1981), 21.

Conclusion

This chapter coincides with the third movement of the circle method. It reflected theologically on the issues analyzed from the perspective of social and cultural factors. In particular, it analogously evaluated *imborvungu* ritual, and other cultural practices with the symbols of the Eucharist, and the cross that constitute core beliefs of the Catholic tradition.

The chapter evaluated the dual symbols in the light of biblical sources and Catholic theological foundation and concludes that some symbols in Tiv culture are analogous to Catholicism. This link mutually enriches both traditions in a way that makes emerging adults truly Tiv and truly Catholics. Most importantly, it is a link that proposes a grounding of Catholicism in Tiv culture.

The goal of fully contextualizing the faith in Tiv culture can effectively be achieved with the adoption of practical strategies. The next chapter discusses the appropriate pastoral lines of action.

8

CONTEXTUALIZATION IN
COMMUNITY, CATECHESIS, & SERVICE

T he fourth and final movement of the circle method centers on pastoral planning, oriented toward achieving the goal of contextualizing the Catholic faith in Tiv culture. The question at the center of this movement is, what shall we do?

The answer to this question proposes three practical lines of action. As the designated community theologians, the task of emerging adults is to articulate a theological synthesis between Catholic worship and Tiv culture. This can be done by adopting a variety of strategic actions including:

1. *The need to create communities.* These communities facilitate an understanding of what most connects emerging adults with Catholic worship and what the Catholic Church needs to know about them. From this community of Catholic students emerges a mutually re-enforcing movement of community theologians who theologize between Tiv culture and Catholic worship leading to an articulate interpretation of the faith in rural communities.

2. *The need to give the community theologians catechetical training.* This is done through seminars, conferences, and workshops that grounds them in the faith, and empowers them to be effective interpreters of the faith;

3. *The need to identify the charisms or gifts of emerging adults.*
    They can bring these to worship to make the Catholic Church
    alive and active in Tivland.

These approaches are necessary because in the past, the church adopted inadequate pastoral plans in addressing the needs of young people. There seems to be a general lack of strategy at the administrative and organizational levels of church planning. If they are there, they are not documented, if documented, they are not taken note of, if noted, they are not implemented.[1]

Recognizing the alleged failure that characterized the church in the past, this chapter discusses the above practical approaches as well as implementation strategies beginning with the first strategic action that proposes the creation of communities among emerging adults.

Community Life
Among Emerging Adults

This section retrieves the notion of community from the perspective of African societies, and Tiv society in particular. It builds on the reality of cultism on campus, and its pervasive influence in Nigerian society, and maps out a strategy for emerging adult Catholics to impact local faith communities in concrete ways.

In most African societies, secret societies or cult groups were instituted for the purpose of self-preservation and for the preservation of the community. The main functions of the cult groups in traditional African societies were to enforce and maintain traditions, customs and beliefs as well as determine ritual behavior and regulate social attitudes.[2] Since the groups operated secretly, their practices were covert as is the case with the practice of *imborvungu* in Tiv culture.

---

[1] Paulino Tuesigye Mondo, mccj, "Youth in the Heart of the Church: Steps in a Journey of loving Family [The Approach of the African Church to Youth from *Gaudium et Spes* to the Third Millennium]," *Bringing the Church to Youth or Youth to the Church* (Makuyu: Paulines Publications Africa, 2006), 26-27.
[2] Abdulrazaq Kilani, "The Changing Faces of the Terror of Cultism in Nigerian Society, 99.

Both covert and overt practices of community life are present in Tiv culture. Community is sustained by many overt practices seen from various perspectives. From the perspective of theological ethics,[3] when one commits a crime, it affects the community as a whole, and when one accomplishes a major achievement, the whole community shares in the honor. Community is also seen as a practice that encompasses and emphasizes cohesion, solidarity, stability, security and survival against the pursuit of an individual's aspirations.[4]

In some African societies, community life is gradually declining. In many African urban centers, some Africans have embraced individualistic tendencies that exclude other members.[5] Reclaiming the lost centrality of community living in the context of emerging adults provides a good foundation not only for theological ethics, but also for other areas of theology such as interreligious dialogue, ecumenism, ecclesiology, sacraments, and pastoral ministry, among others. In Tiv context particularly the importance of community for ecclesiology, and pastoral ministry cannot be overemphasized.

By way of retrieving the declining image of community, Father Solomon Ukeyima has initiated an annual cultural fiesta for Tiv people called *Kyegh sha Shwa* KSS (chicken cooked with beniseed, [sesame indicum sauce]).[6] The gathering has been celebrated for the past three years on December 27. Thousands of people witness the fiesta. The huge population that participates at the festival shows how much the Tiv have embraced KSS.

Although many have embraced it, others are critical that the priest has deviated from his pastoral calling and taken to a practice that is more political than pastoral. Confronted by these critical voices, the

---

[3] See Bénézet Bujo, *Foundations of an African Ethic: Beyond the Universal Claims of Western Morality* (New York: Crossroad, 2001).

[4] Dzurgba, *On the Tiv of Central Nigeria*, 129.

[5] See Wilson Muoha Maina, "African Communitarian Ethics in the Theological Work of Bénézet Bujo," *Pacifica* 21 (June 2008): 193.

[6] See Hemba Stephen, "Kyegh Sha Shwa (KSS) a Huge Opportunity for Benue State," December 30, 2016. https://www.facebook.com/hemba.stephen?fref=nf&pnref=story. KSS is a traditional Tiv cuisine. It is served with pounded yam or any kind of fufu, a meal that is typically swallowed. To show how a visitor is appreciated and welcomed, he or she is entertained with such a meal.

priest argues that KSS goes beyond the food people come to share. It is rather a forum that expresses the unity of Tiv people where they experience community life, seek reconciliation for broken relationships, and explore ways of working towards what benefits the Tiv.

In the past, Father Adasu had called for a return to authenticity of Tiv culture.[7] Perhaps, the cultural innovation is a response to that call. This annual fiesta has started yielding practical results as politicians, and others who had strong disagreements among themselves have been seen discussing amicably, and sharing a meal from the same bowl at the forum.[8] Such a strategic pastoral action needs to be encouraged to reinforce community life among the Tiv.

Retrieving the relational value of community living among Africans in general and the Tiv in particular, is one way of sinking the faith in culture. An individual in an African traditional setting is always in communion with the community. An African community is made up of individual human beings who communicate and relate with each other. This communication is present in all areas of daily living.[9] Tiv society like other African societies is more important than individual persons. This concept needs to be emphasized in the context of pastoral ministry.

Just as the notion of community plays a cohesive role in the life of the African person, it can do the same in the life of the church. Excluded from the community, Africans are not fully persons. A person's personality and individuality are guaranteed only insofar as the individual is integrated in the community on the one hand, and the community serves and strengthens the individual on the other. The individual does everything possible to ensure that the community's health and survival are intact.[10]

---

[7] Hemba Stephen, "Kyegh Sha Shwa (KSS) a Huge Opportunity for Benue State."

[8] Solomon Mfa Ukeyima (a Catholic priest working at St Francis Catholic Mission, Daudu, Nigeria), in a phone interview on December 31, 2016.

[9] Maina, "African Communitarian Ethics in the Theological Work of Bénézet Bujo," 194.

[10] Magesa, *Anatomy of Inculturation*, 193.

The centrality of community does not in any way nullify the autonomy of the individual in African culture. Both are important. The philosophy of individualism is subordinated by a philosophy of collectivism. Even the individual's achievement is seen as the society's achievement.[11] The community is proud of people who bring honor and prestige through great achievements. As an open and close-knit society, the celebration of successful members serves as a positive reinforcement to others.

Secret societies or secret cult groups on campus are known to be influential, and close-knit,[12] but covert. The existence of secret societies was a healthy phenomenon in African societies that has taken a dangerous dimension in institutions of higher education in Nigeria. Emerging adults are quite familiar with campus life, and perhaps, the operations of secret cults on campus. Their implicit knowledge of the pervasive influence of the secret cult model of operation provides a means of rooting Catholicism in Tiv culture. This familiar terrain provides them, the requisite knowledge to begin evangelizing their peers on campus recognizing that young people are the best evangelizers to their peers.[13]

A secret cult group is an organization whose activities are kept away from the knowledge of others. These activities are essentially covert, disguised and are usually carried out behind closed doors. Cultism is a ritual practice by a group of people whose membership, admission, policy and initiation formalities as well as their mode of operations are done in secret and kept secret with their activities having negative effects on both members and non-members alike.[14]

Cult groups have a strong influence in the Nigerian society. They receive legal, medical and logistic support from older members who also enhance their government registration under false names in order to give legal backing to their operations within the academic

---

[11] Dzurgba, *On the Tiv of Central Nigeria,* 129.
[12] Kilani, The Changing Faces of the Terror of Cultism in Nigerian Society, 101.
[13] John Paul II, *Ecclesia in Africa* [Post-Synodal Apostolic Exhortation], sec. 93.
[14] Kilani, The Changing Faces of the Terror of Cultism in Nigerian Society, 98.

environment.[15] Nigerian educational institutions were not associated with secret cults until 1952, when the first secret cult group called the Seadogs confraternity (aka Pyrates) was formed at the University of Ibadan by a group of seven students. Their goal was to explore a front to fight all kinds of vices in the university community.[16]

Secret societies have both positive and negative elements. The negative elements including, their secret nature, and the overall harmful effects their activities have on members will possibly be discarded for the model to appeal to Catholicism. Retrieving the close-knit relationship, pervasive influence (older members supporting the younger ones on campus, and those on campus recruiting more members), and the determination to fight all kinds of vices can be helpful in Catholicism. This can be achieved if the close-knit concept of community is enforced in the Catholic Church.

For the African to live out the Christian message in a meaningful and contextual way, African communitarianism needs to be promoted. This practice finds expression in the Small Christian Communities (SCCs). SCCs situate one in one's milieu to confront the problems of life.[17] "They help the gospel to be part and parcel of people's lives. They help the people to find ways to live together in peace, love, and justice. In a sense, SCCs are the extended family, that is, the clan where people know each other well."[18]

The concept of SCCs is not familiar in Tiv church. However, the church in Tivland has a strong model of pious organizations and outstation churches in village settings that can be likened to SCCs. These are also known as Basic Christian Communities (BCC).[19] The establishment of pious organizations in the Catholic communities on campus provides an avenue to strengthen community life among emerging adults. These gatherings are important for support, solidarity and sharing.

---

[15]Kilani, The Changing Faces of the Terror of Cultism in Nigerian Society, 101-102.
[16]Kilani, The Changing Faces of the Terror of Cultism in Nigerian Society, 100. The seven students include Professor Wole Soyinka, a Nigerian noble laureate.
[17] Uzukwu, A Listening Church, 117.
[18] Magesa, Anatomy of Inculturation, 40.
[19] Moti, The Early Jerusalem Christian Community.

In a text message, Doosuur Tom revealed that members of her pious organization in the church were very helpful when she underwent a surgical procedure in the hospital. They sent financial support to assist in paying the medical bill.

Central to the notion of community life is the creation of worship communities that make the encounter with the effective and life-giving Christ possible, and so an indispensable means of giving meaning and value to the life of the believer.[20] Meaning and value can be found in mutual support succinctly expressed in Tiv symbols that make community life visible. The following expressions, as *avange waren iorov uhar hen tine kon ga* (a lizard does not escape two people at the trunk of a tree), or *kon mom ngu hingir kyô ga* (a single tree does not make a forest) convey a strong sense of community among the Tiv. These sayings convey a powerful image of close-knit relationships in pious organizations in the church.

As members of pious organizations, adults have always under-mined emerging adults as people who lack the requisite experience to provide leadership. The goal to root Catholicism in Tiv culture entails a critical reexamination of the need to incorporate emerging adults in leadership positions in the church.

The concentration of leadership in the hands of the clergy and adults denies young people the opportunity to express their leader-ship potentials. This structure sees leadership as the prerogative of the clergy and adults. Adults have a general feeling of distrust and discomfort when young people are entrusted with leadership re-sponsibilities.[21] This impression disconnects emerging adults from the Catholic Church and needs to be changed.

The evidence given by Ternadoo Ikpa of BSU supports the claim that emerging adults resent their exclusion from leadership posi-tions. In their chaplaincy, when students were to raise funds under the umbrella body of the Nigerian Federation of Catholic Students (NFCS), adults who are not members were given the responsibility to lead the organizing committee. He said members of the organiza-

---

[20] Moti, *The Early Jerusalem Christian Community,* 126.
[21] Mondo, mccj, Youth in the Heart of the Church, 26.

tion reject an attitude that undermines them. His facial expression while expressing this view showed a feeling of disappointment.[22]

One way to motivate emerging adults, encourage active participation, and challenge them to take up the duty of community theologians is by entrusting them with leadership responsibilities. In this way, young people will find themselves, not as spectators, but active participants in the mystery of salvation.[23] Tiv people believe that young people too can make meaningful contributions. This claim is demonstrated in the saying, *wanye kpa kaa er ibur yar tiôr* (Even a child advised that the best way to butcher a deer is to turn it upside down).[24]

When emerging adults' contributions are recognized, a task to act as community theologians will be vigorously pursued. To be effective community theologians, catechetical training offers an approach that facilitates a grounding of emerging adults in the faith. The next segment elucidates the importance of catechetical training as an effective strategy for evangelization.

Catechetical Training

In the years preceding the Second Vatican Council, the faith of the Catholic Church was commonly transmitted through Catholic education and catechism. Catholic education emphasized the relationship of the faith to the society. This view of Catholic education as an

---

[22] Ternadoo Ikpa (a twenty-seven years old student of Benue State University, Makurdi), in a one-on-one interview on May 19, 2014 at Makurdi.

[23] Mondo, mccj, Youth in the Heart of the Church, 19.

[24] Abraham Iorliam Gyata (85 years old father of the investigator), in a discussion in June, 2014. The discussion revealed that in the past, the Tiv believed that it took time for a deer that was struck with a weapon (dagger, arrow, or even a gun) to die. If it was struck at a particular spot, it would escape and die several miles away. Wherever it died, no one claimed ownership. It was a free for all meat. Anyone that came around had an unhindered access to it. There was a particular case of a deer that died hanging in a ditch with its back outside. Those who came at the spot were unable to butcher it due to the thickness of its skin. They stood watching the animal helplessly until a little boy appeared on the scene and told them that the only way to butcher the animal was to turn it upside down. They heeded the voice of the child, and when they turned it upside down, it became easy to butcher it. Since then, this saying has been associated with the wisdom of children implying that they too can make a meaningful contribution.

inclusive term that embraced Catholic schooling prevailed until the Second Vatican Council (1962-1965). After the ecumenical council, the term catechetics (or catechesis) emerged as the dominant terminology. Catechesis may be regarded as a focusing of Catholic education.[25]

Key ideas that led to the catechetical movement were the revised theology of the church that was expressed in the language of the Second Vatican Council. The trend of this council shifted from the earlier councils that were convened mainly to refute heresies or to defend the church against other errors and enemies. Rather than becoming obsessed with errors, the church must be open and welcoming.[26] A moment of renewal (aggiornamento) had come. This renewal led to the interpretation of the mysteries of the Catholic faith in light of the renewed understanding of the church fostered by the Second Vatican Council.

For instance, conversion was no longer understood as becoming a Catholic or returning to the church after having "fallen away," but as a deep change of one's life, a commitment to live a new life in Christ.[27] To effectively understand the truths of the Catholic tradition, required returning to the sources. It is this understanding that led to the catechetical movement.

Catechetics and catechism have sometimes been used interchangeably. The two terms are derived from the same root *catechein*, meaning to resound. In teaching the faith, catechism was for the most part in a question and answer format. Questioning is one dimension of doing theology. Questions are raised based on human experience. This is a practice of everyday life. For instance, why is it raining in the middle of the dry season? Why are some women barren? Why are some students able to pay their tuition, and others are unable?[28]

The present form of catechism is a question and answer format that is a product of post-Vatican I (1869) era that translated the council's truncated ecclesiology into simple categories and dissected much of

---

[25] Boys, *Educating in Faith*, 80
[26] Boys, *Educating in Faith*, 89.
[27] Boys, *Educating in Faith*, 91.
[28] Orobator, *Theology Brewed in an African Pot*, 6.

the narrative faith into stylized formulas for memorization. Its effectiveness was evident, but it was perhaps doubtful if pupils either knew or could explain the correct answers or not.[29] For the most part, this method still prevails in the Tiv church. As theological understanding developed, this propositional method of learning the faith increasingly became inadequate. In Tiv culture, it is grossly ineffective in facilitating the sinking of the faith. Realizing its inherent weakness, the church came to emphasize catechetics as a deeper way of teaching the faith.

Catechesis, its noun derivation is "that form of ecclesia action which leads both communities and individual members of the faithful to maturity of faith."[30] It is an educating in faith that involves the proclamation of the Good News taking into consideration the realities of life confronting the human person. Catechesis enhances the work of evangelization. Both catechesis and evangelization have a vital link since the goal was to return the person to his or her initial act of conversion. The duty of the catechist is to bring out the aspects of the Christian mystery as much as possible by their significance than by their explanation.[31]

In focusing on the significance of the Christian mystery, catechetics affirms the link between faith and culture, the church and the world, and can explain the faith using cultural texts. The mystery of the faith can also draw its significance from Tiv cultural practices. Cultural practices on the other hand can help to integrate the faith in Tiv culture.

In catechesis, it is necessary to connect with the people's language, as shaped by historical complexity of the past, if Gospel and sacrament are to be appropriated within their lives and cultural realities. Any people's own religious language provides stories and symbols

---

[29] Boys, *Educating in Faith,* 95. Children who were trained through the question and answer method in Tivland were articulate and efficient in recounting the propositions without understanding their real meaning.
[30] Boys, *Educating in Faith,* 98.
[31] Boys, *Educating in Faith,* 97.

of the holy, of links with the past, of bodily time and wholeness, or of cosmic and social harmony.[32]

Today, the church in Tivland is in need of a comprehensive cate-chetical approach that integrates the cultural texts. "Christian mission and sacramental worship may not have respected this language in the past, but may now draw on it in celebrating Christ."[33] Drawing on a person's language helps to address doctrines and practices of the Catholic Church that are often the subject of confusion and misunderstanding. Doctrines such as, the use of images, and role of the Blessed Virgin Mary in Catholic tradition can be addressed through seminars, conferences, and workshops.

Educated emerging adults can receive adequate catechesis that grounds them in the Catholic faith, and ultimately empowers them to interpret the faith to others including, unlettered population in rural communities. This discussion on doctrines in need of intensive catechesis turns to an exploration of the place of images in the worship of Catholics.

The Use of
Images at Worship

Emerging adults' criticism of images as objects of worship is a mis-construed perception of the role of images used in a Catholic worship. For emerging adults to be effective community theologians, they need to be adequately informed about the beliefs and practices of the Catholic Church. One way of facilitating this grounding in faith is by elucidating aspects of the Catholic faith that are most often misunderstood.

As seen in the previous chapter, emerging adults stated that people have different views of the Catholic Church. Some of the views are erroneous. However, they were unable to define the true position of the church on those issues that include, the use of incense, and the place of symbols and images in Catholic worship, and the role of

---

32 Power, *Sacrament*, 312.
33 Power, *Sacrament*, 312.

Mary in salvation history. These doctrines can be explicated through an integral catechetical approach.

The use of symbols and images is a composite of Catholic worship. Symbols represent the mysteries of the Catholic faith. The Eucharistic symbols of bread and wine, for instance, represent and participate in the God who is being worshipped. Catholics do not worship images but use them as means of offering worship. They are signposts of the Catholic faith. They are signs of the great mysteries of the Catholic tradition. Just as road signs and Global Positioning System (GPS) lead the navigator to a destination, in the same way, images lead Catholics on their pilgrim journey to God.

A symbol is not the same as a sign, although some people often use them interchangeably. A sign points to an object, for instance, an arrow shows the direction to a particular place, say a church building. On the other hand, a symbol not only indicates something, but represents it in some intrinsic manner. A cross would only be a sign for an unbeliever indicating an event in the past, but to believers it is a symbol because it invites them to participate in the many lessons the symbol teaches, even to the point of dying to defend the faith as Jesus did.[34] Catholics encounter God through the symbols of worship. Incense, for instance is used as a symbol of encounter with God through prayer.

Incense as
Symbol of Prayer

One of the most frequently asked questions in the Catholic tradition by Catholics and non-Catholics alike concerns the role of incense in Catholic liturgy. Incense is a granulated aromatic resin, obtained from certain trees in eastern and tropical countries, especially from those of the terebinth family. When sprinkled upon a glowing coal in the censer, it burns and emits abundant white fragrant smoke.[35] The censer is swung in honor of the objects of worship including human beings who participate at worship. The ascent that goes out

---

[34] See Arbuckle, *Culture, Inculturation, Theologians,* 21-22.
[35] John Asen, *Catholic Faith and Practice: Questions and Answers Volume One* (Makurdi: Religio, 2012), 37.

with the cloud of smoke signifies God's acceptance of the prayers of the worshipping community.

The use of incense is an ancient practice in the Catholic Church. It is analogous to a particular form of incantation in Tiv culture. In a healing ritual aimed at restoring the health and fortunes of a sick person or someone who is bedeviled with ill luck, the Tiv refer to God as the final arbiter. It is believed that such a misfortune may have befallen the person as a result of immoral behavior and neglect of tradition or may have been caused by someone else. In this context, *Aondo* (God) is called upon for healing. The ritual healer uses a live chicken and swings it several times over the head of the victim. The following incantation is uttered simultaneously with the ritual act, *ibo sen, ibo sen, ibo sen* (guilt descend or go downward, mentioned at each swing), *isho kondo, isho kondo, isho kondo* (innocence ascend or go upward mentioned at each swing).[36] This ritual act signifies the restoration to health and fortunes of the victims in the same way the smoke of incense signifies the ascent of the prayer of the worshipping community to God.

The first use of incense was recorded in the fourth century when the bishop led the vigil of the resurrection that usually took place on Saturday evening. The liturgy centered on the reading of the gospel account of the passion and resurrection of Christ. Perhaps, this was in line with the instruction given to Aaron to burn incense morning after morning, and in the evening twilight (Ex 30:7-8). In New Testament times too, incense was used in worship. It is often thought that incense had been introduced to represent the spices that the women took to the tomb of Jesus on Easter day.[37]

Today, the burning of incense at Catholic worship symbolizes the zeal with which the people of God should be animated. Its sweet fragrance symbolizes the smell of Christian virtue; and by its rising smoke, the ascent of prayer before the throne of the almighty.[38]

---

[36] Joseph S. Gbenda, "An Appraisal of Ethical Values in Tiv Religion," *Ate: Journal of African Religion and Culture* 1 (December 2010): 34.
[37] Paul F. Bradshaw, and Maxwell E. Johnson, *The Origins of Feasts, Fasts and Seasons in Early Christianity* (Collegeville: Liturgical Press, 2011). 26-27.
[38] Asen, *Catholic Faith and Practice*, 38.

Among Tiv Catholics, incense has often been used beyond the boundaries of worship. It has become an object of popular religiosity.

Tiv Catholics burn incense in their homes as a symbol of God's protection from evil spirits and satanic forces. The belief that every sickness, misfortune, and even death are caused by an external force has necessitated the use of incense to ward off evil forces. This symbolic act works for many Tiv Catholics and non-Catholics alike. Mnena Shilumun, a student of COE, responding to a question on what emerging adults say about the Catholic Church stated that some criticize the use of incense by Catholics as superstition. She stated, "I find that strange because incense works for me. Any time I begin to experience serial nightmares, I burn incense in my room, and consequently, I sleep peacefully."[39] One thing to consider while using incense is that, it is ineffective in itself. Incense, sacramentals, and icons draw their efficacy from the power of prayer.

Sacramentals & Icons

Sacramentals are sacred signs that bear a resemblance to the sacraments. They signify effects, particularly of a spiritual nature, which are obtained through the intercession of the Church. These sacramentals include, holy water, holy oils, vessels, and vestments. By these sacramentals, men and women are disposed to receive the chief effect of the sacraments, and various occasions in life are rendered holy.[40] Cultural practices such as *ifan i hamber* (clearing a curse), and *ikyôôr* (wearing a snail-shell) are analogous to holy water, and the relics of holy people Catholics wear on the neck respectively.[41]

---

[39] Mnena Shilumun (a twenty-six years old student of College of Education, Katsina-Ala), in a one-on-one interview on June 4, 2014 at Katsina-Ala.

[40] See *Catechism of the Catholic Church*, sec. 1667, 2014,
http://www.vatican.va/archive/ENG0015/__P58.HTM

[41] See Geri, *A History of Tiv Religious Practices and Changes*, 55.
Ikyôôr has resonance with the Christian practice of wearing sacramentals like medals and scapulars as a mark of dedication and Catholic identity, and also to enjoy the protection of the saints the images represent.

In connection with clearing a curse, Tiv people believe that, when a child is cursed by a parent or parents for his or her wrong-doing, that child cannot prosper unless the curse is cleared. A child who fights with a parent is sometimes cursed with the words *u yar u wua ga* (you will go hunting without killing a game). With these words, it is believed that ill-luck follows the child all through life. A child who regrets his or her action and begs for forgiveness enjoys the clearing of the curse. This was done by the parent stippling water from the gourd and using his mouth to splash the water on the feet of the afflicted child. Tiv people use water to clear a curse in the same way Catholics use holy water to invoke blessings and purification from sin. Other cultural practices such as *ikyôôr* resonate with Catholic symbols.

Young virgins in Tiv culture wore snail-shells just as Catholics wear sacred icons. *Ikyôôr* was a practice in Tiv society that mandated young girls to wear snail-shells as a symbol of their virginity. Virginity was sacred and was taken seriously in such a way that a man who got involved in an illicit sex had to make reparations through a ritual called *saa akôôr,* (untying the snail). If the ritual was not performed, it was believed the man suffered from impotency, and the girl suffered from barrenness or regular miscarriages.

The sprinkling of holy water particularly, is a practice that signifies blessing, and recalls baptism. Tiv cultural practices helped to promote friendliness and good character and were taken seriously in Tiv communities. The impact of formal education, and migration from rural communities has greatly led to the decline of these practices in a way that young people cannot see them as having a link with practices of the Catholic Church.

In the past, Tiv parents were worried when their female children started manifesting signs of puberty such as the appearance of breasts. As a way of preserving their virginity, every girl was expected to tie *ikyôôr* (snail-shell) round her neck. This was done to prevent young men who were paying attention to her from seducing her.[42] When formal education came to Tivland, parents were

---

[42] East, trans., *Akiga's Story: The Tiv Tribe as Seen by One of Its Members,* 309. The old woman threaded a shell on to a piece of cotton, and tied it round the girl's neck, thus

scared of sending their female children to school as a way of protecting them from obscene behavior. The girl grew up with the emblem as a symbol of virginity. Shortly before going to live with her husband in the event of marriage, her spouse untied the snail as part of the marriage ceremony by giving the parents a tender female goat that had not given birth.

On the first night of their marriage, if the husband discovered her virginity was broken before marriage, he would send a perforated cloth to show the parents the infidelity of their daughter. It was a serious violation of the Tiv moral code for a girl to lose her virginity before marriage.[43] The practice was understood to promote moral character, but it was intrinsically discriminatory as it excluded the partner responsible for the broken virginity.[44] The act left the woman with a stigma in the eyes of the husband and the community, and allowed the male partner the freedom to insidiously cajole more girls into sex before marriage.

Cultural practices that fail to appreciate the dignity of women as being made in the image and likeness of God (Genesis 1:27), assault the equality of human dignity, and the creator. The snail shell as a symbol of virginity, and moral conduct resonates with sacred icons, not as objects of worship, but as symbols of virtue.

The separated brethren criticize Catholics for worshipping images building their argument on the divine command that forbids this practice. "You shall not have other gods besides me. You shall not carve idols for yourselves in the shape of anything in the sky above or on the earth below or in the waters beneath the earth; you shall not bow down before them or worship them" (Genesis 20:3-5).[45]

---

putting a guard on her. The young men would fear to have intercourse with her, and she would come to full puberty without sexual violation.

[43] Gbenda, "An Appraisal of Ethical Values in Tiv Religion," 33.

[44]*New American Bible* (Nashville: Catholic Press, 1991). See the story of the woman caught in the act of adultery in John 8:1-11. No evidence to show that the male partner was accused of the crime.

[45]*New American Bible* (Nashville: Catholic Press, 1991). Their criticism that Catholics worship images fails to recognize that some biblical passages approve the use of images. For instance, in Numbers 21:8-9 God told Moses to make seraph to serve as an image that would bring healing to the afflicted Israelites who were bitten by a serpent.

Catholics do not worship, but venerate sacred images in line with the teaching that sacred images in Catholic churches and homes are intended to awaken and nourish the faith of Catholics in the mystery of Christ.

Through the icon of Christ and his works of salvation, it is he whom Catholics adore. Through sacred images of the holy Mother of God, of the angels and of the saints, Catholics venerate the persons represented.[46] The Tiv concept of ancestors as the living dead members of the community also resonates with the icons representing holy men and women in the Catholic tradition.

The Council of Nicea (787) approved that the figure of the precious and life-giving Cross and the venerable and holy images and pictures of Jesus, Mary, the saints, and pious people can be displayed in churches, and on sacred vessels and vestments. When they are frequently seen, they lift Catholics in their memory to long after them. These should be given salutation and honorable reverence.[47] Catholics venerate images, but honor and revere Mary considering her role in salvation history.

Mary as a
Symbol of Motherhood

What the Catholic Church believes about Mary is based on what it believes about Christ, and what it teaches about Mary illumines in turn its faith in Christ. As the church believes and teaches that Jesus is God, it follows that Mary is the mother of God. Catholics honor Mary recognizing her role in the economy of salvation. Most often this role has been misunderstood by others who accuse Catholics of deifying Mary. Her position as mother of God and mother of the church resonates with the role of the mother in an African family.

In most African societies, parents provide for their children as long as they are not yet independent. Sometimes, the father and the mother support their children separately. A child who is returning

---

[46]*Catechism of the Catholic Church*, sec. 1192.
[47] John H. Leith, ed., *Creeds of the Churches: A Reader in Christian Doctrine from the Bible to the Present Third Edition* (Atlanta: John Knox, 1982), 55.

to school may benefit from the generosity of both parents. In a situation where the mother is not in the position to augment the support given by the father, she is always pleading with her husband to attend to the needs of the children particularly at a time when he refuses to grant the children's request. African mothers are known for pleading and winning favors on behalf of their children.

The intercessory role of African mothers is supported by the biblical evidence of the story of James and John in Matthew 20: 20-23. The mother of the sons of Zebedee is the model of a typical African mother who knows what is good for her children, and she appears determined to ensure that the children receive their benefits for working for the master.[48]

What African mothers do for their children is similar to what Mary does for the church. In recognizing the role of Mary in salvation history, the church promotes the cult of Mary. Hence after the Synod of Ephesus the cult of the people of God toward Mary wonderfully increased in veneration and love, in invocation and imitation, according to her own prophetic words: All generations shall call me blessed, because He that is mighty hath done great things to me (Luke 1:48-49). The cult of Mary is essentially identified with the recitation of the rosary. This cult is zealously promoted by Tiv Catholics, and indeed the global Catholic community. The cult, as it always existed, differs essentially from the cult of adoration which is offered to the Incarnate Word, as well to the Father and the Holy Spirit.[49]

The separated brethren criticize this cult, accusing Catholics of worshipping Mary. Critics use the image of an envelope to describe the role of Mary arguing that when one receives a parcel, it is the content of the envelope that matters, not the envelope itself.[50] Judging from this understanding, the role of Mary supposedly terminated after she "parceled" the son of God into the world. Those who refer

---

[48] Orobator, *Theology Brewed in an African Pot*, 4-5.
[49]*Vatican Council II*, "Lumen Gentium [Dogmatic Constitution on the Church]," sec. 66, http://www.vatican.va/archive/hist_councils/ii_vatican_council/documents/vat-ii_const_19641121_lumen-gentium_en.html
[50] Teryila Aba (a twenty-six years old student of University of Agriculture, Makurdi), in a one-on-one interview on June 3, 2014 at Makurdi.

to Mary as an envelope, as well reduce their biological mothers to the image of an envelope. The image of the mother as envelope has no basis in Tiv culture. Tiv mothers continue to be deeply involved in the lives of their children as long as they live. They are always supporting and interceding for the children like Mary who intercedes on behalf of the people at the wedding feast at Cana (John 2: 1-11).

Tiv mothers provide a model to understanding the cult of Mary in the Catholic Church. Mary stands out in eminent and singular fashion as exemplar both of virginity and motherhood.[51] The value attached to virginity demonstrated in the practice of wearing a snail shell, and the intercessory role of the mother in Tiv culture meet the criterion of appropriateness with the cult of Mary in the Catholic tradition.

Jesus promoted her intercessory role by giving her as mother of the church (John 19: 27). Since then, Mary has been deeply involved in the life of the church. She aided the beginning of the church with her prayers, when shortly before the coming of the Holy Spirit she was in fellowship with the Apostles in prayer and patient waiting (Acts 1:14). The entire body of the faithful pours forth instant supplications to the Mother of God and Mother of men that she, who aided the beginnings of the Church by her prayers, may now, exalted as she is above all the angels and saints, may continue to intercede for humanity.[52] Mary, incense, sacramentals, icons, and other critical mysteries of the Catholic faith can be taught, discussed, and explained in catechism classes and conventional gatherings such as seminars, conferences, and workshops.

Catechism

The rote learning of Catechism should be confined to children who have high capacity to memorize. These may be children who were christened as infants, and they are preparing to complete the initiation process with the sacraments of the Eucharist and Confirmation. At the level of the children mostly below the age of ten, the ques-

---

[51]*Vatican Council II,* "Lumen Gentium," sec. 63.
[52]*Vatican Council II,* "Lumen Gentium," sec. 69.

tion-and-answer formula focuses on basic knowledge of God and the Catholic faith. For example, the following questions introduce one to the knowledge of God. *Aondo ka ana?* (Who is God?). *Aondo ka Jijingi u hemban u a lu tswen iyol na, man hanma kwagh na ngu a ikuren ga* (God is a Supreme Spirit who exists alone in himself and everything of his has no end).

To deepen this creedal proposition, the catechist may explore various images children have about God particularly from their experience of culture and people around them. A parent who threatens an errant child with divine punishment of hell fire spurs the child to view God as a policeman.[53] Various images may be considered for children to have a true picture of the personality of God.

Concerning the purpose of one's creation, the simple catechism delivers the faith in the following question and corresponding answer. *Hii nan man Aondo a gbe we?* (Why has God made you?). *Aondo gbam sha aci u m fa un, man mcivir un shin tar ne man m ember un gbem ken tartor u sha* (God created me to know him, to worship him in this world and to be happy with him forever in heaven).[54]

The church also delivers the creed to the catechumens with a focus on the sacraments. *Baptisma ka nyi?* (What is Baptism?). *Baptisma ka sacramentu u wanger se amishe a kwaghbo, man u eren se mbalumun mba Kristu, mbayev mba Aondo, man u lun nongu u Kristu* (Baptism is the sacrament that washes away our original sin, and makes us adopted children of God, and members of the church). This answer shows that baptism reorients the Catholic and defines his or her Christian identity by adopting a new name.

---

[53] Felix Koikara ,SDB, and Joe Mannath, SDB, *Do it Learn it Live it: Sessions with Youth* (Bangalore: Asian Trading Coorporation, 2010), 65.

[54] Moti, *The Early Jerusalem Christian Community,*119. Also see *The Simple Tiv Catechism of Christian Doctrine* (Enugu: Eastern Nigeria Printing Corporation, 1962) for the overall question and answer method. The question and answer theory was very much used in the fourth century. It was believed that the creed was a secret formula, which could not be written down, but must be memorized by the faithful. On the day of baptism, catechumens were expected to render the creed in the same way it was delivered to them. Delivering and rendition were called *traditio symboli,* and *redditio symboli* respectively. See J.N.D. Kelly, *Early Christian Creeds* (New York: David Mckay Company, Inc., 1976), 32.

To connect this identity with culture and Catholicism means taking names from Tiv culture that are meaningful, and resonate with Catholicism.[55] Although the propositional definitions are appropriate for beginners, it is germane to concretize and deepen the understanding by linking resonating images in culture that are familiar to children, and help to integrate children both in faith and in culture.

In Tivland today, catechists are failing to expound the mysteries of the Catholic faith to learners in its simplest form of the question and answer method. Even those who take their job seriously don't seem to advance catechism with appropriate cultural symbols and images to integrate faith and culture. The main duty of catechists as teachers of catechism is gradually eroding, with a shift to a mandate by the pastor to collect and collate the finances of the parish. Their commitment to the financial aspect of parish life has made some people to derogatorily refer to them as "revenue collectors."

Pastoral agents will have to resist the temptation to place undue emphasis on money or stole fees at the expense of catechesis because the shift constitutes a danger to the contextualization of the faith. The faith cannot take root in Tiv culture if money is the goal. Most priests demonstrate trust in their catechist, and they are most comfortable allowing them to handle the parish finances. Since most of the catechists are occupied with finances, volunteer catechism instructors some of whom are not well educated in the faith have taken up the duty of teaching catechism.

In parishes where members of the Confraternity of Christian Doctrine (CCD),[56] volunteer to teach catechism, most priests fail to

---

[55] See Cahalan, *Introducing the Practice of Ministry*, 25-26. A name is forged with an identity of a life time. Jesus' name is derived from Josiah, which means God saves. His identity is deeply tied to his identity as one who came to save. A child's naming at baptism signifies a new identity in Christ, and in the Christian community. During baptism, most Tiv Catholics take Christian names from other cultures without knowing what exactly those names mean. In some cases, those names are identified with the saints that bore them. Though a good practice, names from Tiv culture with sound theological meaning advance the grounding of Catholicism in Tiv culture.

[56] See Boys, *Educating in Faith*, 86. This organization was founded in 1536 in Milan by Castello de Castellano, and was given a great impetus by Charles Borromeo, the cardinal archbishop of Milan. Its purpose was to organize schools of Christian doctrine conducted by trained teachers, where youth and unlettered men and women

closely monitor and supervise their work. The task of educating in faith is a serious issue that must be taken seriously by the teachers who must be supervised. When people are grounded in the faith, they will voluntarily donate time, talent, and treasure to the church.

The pastor is the first catechist of the parish. It is incumbent on him to monitor and supervise catechism classes to ensure doctrines are correctly interpreted for children to grow in the knowledge of the faith in the most meaningful ways. As children grow to emerging adulthood, and then to adulthood, the method of teaching the faith can be expanded to catechetics. One way of creating a robust and comprehensive approach to catechetics is by organizing seminars.

Seminars

A seminar is a formal gathering of people to receive training or information on a particular subject or topic. Seminars are effective ways of training Catholics to deepen their knowledge of the practices and the doctrinal life of the church. The best way to learn is by doing. In a seminar, participants interact and participate actively by engaging in activities, and sharing ideas from different perspectives. Of particular importance is the *scaffolding* program.

A scaffold is a temporary structure constructed to support a person working high above the floor or ground to either stand or sit on it while working. It is used in the context of ministry with young people as a metaphor for support. *Scaffolding* program has been developed to train young people of Africa to build life skills from the Christian perspective. It is an exercise that says at the beginning of learning, learners need a great deal of support, but the support is gradually taken away to allow the young people rely on their independence.

The development expected from such learning also applies to the growth of a young person as a Christian. *Scaffolding* translates the Catechism of the Catholic Church into life skills. The benefit of this translation is that, it uses familiar images to integrate young people

---

may be instructed in the truths of the faith. By 1710 it spread to Europe, and years later, it reached other parts of the world including Nigeria.

in the faith of the church. One of the general objectives of *scaffolding* is to provide young people with opportunities to learn more about themselves and God's role in their lives.[57] The learning is effectively carried out through a well-defined method.

The Scaffolding program uses a method that is participatory and learner oriented. The format of a typical session includes, an ice-breaker (demonstrates a small activity related to the topic); introduction (a time to introduce the theme in few words); activity (main part of the session that lets learners do individual activities or work in groups, the activity must achieve the objectives); general conclusion (has two parts, the various groups report back to the assembly, and the facilitator gives his/her input based on what the groups reported); soup for the soul (a time of prayer or Bible reading that relates to religious experience that is critical in forming convictions, and also to develop a symbol that fits the theme); and scaffolding for life (learners evaluate their learning by responding to a questionnaire, and may also share their responses before leaving finally).

The overall seminar format gears toward explaining issues of human life in relation to the Catholic faith. The concept of the Trinity, for instance, has a mutual enforcement with the concept of the family. To understand how the family and the Trinity are related, every participant may draw his or her family tree, and view the family from the perspective of persons in relationship. The family tree brings together the parents, the children, and the grandchildren in a horizontal relationship.[58] Just as each person of the Trinity has an influence on the created world, in a similar way, each family member has a particular influence on the family. The understanding of family leads to the concept of the Christian family.

The Christian family is a communion of persons, a sign and image of the communion of the Father and the Son and the Holy Spirit.[59] "The Christian family constitutes a specific revelation and realization of ecclesial communion, and for this reason it can and should

---

[57] Sahaya G. Selvam, sdb, *Scaffoldings: Training Young People in Christian Life Skills: Student's Workbook* (Nairobi: Paulines Publications Africa, 2008), 7.
[58] Selvam, sdb, *Scaffoldings*, 68.
[59] Selvam, sdb, *Scaffoldings*, 71.

be called a domestic church."[60] As noted in chapter five, the positive influence of the family on emerging adults helps to realize the purpose of the domestic church. They are influenced to the degree that has connected them with the Catholic Church, ultimately enrolling as members of pious organizations.

In Tiv Catholicism, pious organizations on campus are avenues to facilitate the contextualization of the faith. A way to do this is by organizing scaffolding seminars on critical areas of the Catholic faith either on weekly, bi-monthly, or monthly basis. Scaffolding empowers members of these societies to discuss issues that make Catholicism meaningful to the Tiv in the contemporary world. This method of catechesis introduces young people into a living community and helps them to take root in it. Undertaken in a seminar, the catechetical approach is more than a forum to share ideas. It is a relationship,[61] which again supports the notion of community life among emerging adults. Like seminars, workshops too can offer such training to emerging adults.

Workshops

A workshop is a series of meetings in which a large gathering of participants break up into small groups to learning the methods and skills of doing something. Every workshop uses a particular method to impact skills capable of solving a problem. The pastoral circle used as a method to explore the link between faith and culture can be applied in a workshop situation to explore different pastoral issues impeding the grounding of the Catholic faith in Tiv culture. This method has been most effectively used in solving problems concerned with social justice. It has also been used to transform parishes.[62]

---

[60]*Catechism of the Catholic Church,* sec. 2204, *http://www.vatican.va/archive/ENG0015/_P7S.HTM#4Z*
[61] Selvam, sdb, *Scaffoldings,* 23.
[62] See Christine Bodewes, "Can the Pastoral Circle Transform a Parish?" in *The Pastoral Circle Revisited: A Critical Quest for Truth and Transformation,* ed. Frans Wijsen, Peter Henriot, and Rodrigo Mejia (New York: Orbis, 2005), 56-72.

The pastoral circle has been helping Christian communities to live contextually for over twenty-five years. It continues to help activists and theologians serve their communities.[63] Its transforming capacity underscores its importance in the context of emerging adults in Tiv society. Just as workshops and seminars are fruit bearing catechetical approaches, retreats specifically designed to meet the faith needs of young people is another valid catechetical approach capable of yielding practical results in contextualizing the faith.

Retreats

The term retreat is often identified with the military. It refers to a withdrawal in a war situation to launch better strategies of attacking and defeating the offensive enemy who poses a threat to the rival combating group. In Catholic parlance, retreat is a special and solitary period Catholics set aside for spiritual exercises so they can most effectively take stock of their lives. It is a period of time they re-examine their relationship with God, and with one another. The period of retreat that usually lasts for several days, can certainly advance the taking root of faith in a culture.

In the context of young people, the idea of Youth Encounters the Savior (Y.E.S) retreat was introduced to address the faith needs of young people that would yield practical results. The idea originated from the US. The Ugandan church later embraced it, and it was introduced in Kenya in 1994. The retreat is basically designed to last for three days. The proclamation of the Christian message is at the core of the three-day program.[64]

The proclamation is imbued with catechetical principles including the following principles.

- The first principle is a fourfold presentation of the faith through liturgy, the Bible, systematic teaching and the testimony of Christian living. This underlying principle constitutes the

---

[63] See Johannes Banawiratma, "The Pastoral Circle as Spirituality," in *The Pastoral Circle Revisited: A Critical Quest for Truth and Transformation,* ed. Frans Wijsen, Peter Henriot, and Rodrigo Mejia (New York: Orbis, 2005), 73.
[64] Piet Verhagen, MHM, and John Ogola, eds., *Youth Encounters the Saviour: Behaviour Change Retreat* (Nairobi: Paulines Publications Africa, 1997), 9.

method of Y.E.S retreats. All four expressions of the Catholic faith are intricately woven into each of the three days of the Y.E.S retreat.

- In the second principle, catechesis introduces the youth into a living community and helps them to take root in it.

- Thirdly, catechesis proclaims the wonderful works of God, which show forth the truth, and especially the love contained in them moving the heart and inspiring the whole of life.

- The process of inculturation enunciated in the fourth principle says, catechesis adapts itself to the life and thoughts of peoples, shows due appreciation of their laudable views and customs and integrates them into a Christian way of life.[65]

The goal of the retreat is to be faithful to Christ's gospel. The gospel is addressed to the community of young people in a way that they will hear and experience the gospel in a version that is contextual to the present times and circumstances.[66] As the implementation of this retreat strategy was successful in Kenya, for instance, it can as well succeed in the context of Tiv emerging adult Catholics.

Using the setting of pious organizations, Chaplains can organize such retreats in line with the above principles. Every pious society is responsible to plan their group retreat. The chaplain may organize at least two general retreats during Advent and Lenten seasons that would accommodate all emerging adults including, registered and non-registered members of pious societies. Participation at these gatherings would be unrestricted to promote community life at the broader level of the Catholic community.

Community life among emerging adults is the gateway to the grounding of the faith in Tiv culture. It is much easier to organize catechetical training (seminars, workshops, and retreats) when a community is already formed. These programs enliven the faith of Catholics. These patterns of engaging emerging adults ultimately lead to an emergence of community theologians well-grounded to

---

[65] Verhagen and Ogola eds., *Youth Encounters the Saviour*, 10.
[66] See Verhagen and Ogola eds., *Youth Encounters the Saviour*, 12.

take the faith to rural communities. Apart from the contextual ways of transmitting the faith to emerging adults, they are endowed with charisms that can impact the rooting of the Catholic faith in Tiv culture.

Charisms Associated with Emerging Adults

Charism comes from the Greek word *charis* rendered grace in English. It means a free gift that brings joy, love, gratitude, pleasure, and kindness. Charisms are fundamental gifts for service. They are capacities or qualities that people express through activities, actions, and speech. Today, charisms are generally referred to as practices such as teaching, preaching, offering care, prayer and worship, social justice, and leadership and administration. Charisms are not private, internal qualities, meant for self-improvement. They are embodied actions lived out and expressed in word and deed.[67]

In his theology, Paul identifies that gifts of faith, hope, and love are common to all members of the believing community. He distinguishes these with charisms, which are gifts given to individual members for service for the community.[68] The central argument of Paul concerns the diversity of gifts needed for the common good and the building up of the Christian community that ultimately unifies the community. No Christian is charism-exempt (1 Pet 4:10). At the same time, no single person receives all the gifts. Each person is a unique combination of charisms, and no two people hold exactly the same constellation (1 Corinthians7:7).[69] A discourse on charism raises the question of its relationship with talent.

Both charism and talent have subtle nuances. A gift is something one receives without merit. One cannot be praised or blamed for it, but one can only accept and praise (or blame) the giver. In this sense, charisms and talents are experienced in much the same way.

---

[67] Cahalan, *Introducing the Practice of Ministry*, 33.
[68] See Cahalan, *Introducing the Practice of Ministry*, 32. Also see Romans 12: 3-8; 1 Corinthians 12:4-11; Ephesians 4:11-16. In these passages, Paul argues that charisms are particular and unique gifts granted by the Spirit to each person for the purpose of building up the community.
[69] Cahalan, *Introducing the Practice of Ministry*, 33.

However, many people experience a talent as something "natural," a particular attitude to do something that one did not acquire, but it's inborn. It can be argued that charisms and talents are experienced to some extent as given whether through nature or grace.

In Christian perspective, no distinction exists between the two terms, and both have a divine source.[70] Again, nuances characterize the development of a talent and a charism. People exert themselves in various ways to gain both knowledge and skill in a talent over time before they develop a certain level of competence. In the case of charisms, because they are potential, not fully developed, they require personal awareness, discernment, and acceptance. This too needs skills and abilities for the charism to develop to fuller capacity.[71] This background leads to the understanding of gifts and talents associated with emerging adults in Tiv society.

Present day young people are gifted in significant ways. What distinguishes them from the past generation is their level of education, and their access to local and global cultures through modern means of transportation and communication. These factors enable them to effectively develop their charisms, not for personal good, but for the rooting of Catholicism in Tiv culture.

In Tivland today, emerging adults can boast of effective use of the media for evangelization. Aaron Abo a student of Uniagric said:

> In our evolving world, the internet is the place to establish contact with young people. Some of them wake up, and even before praying, pick up their cell phones and begin to access Facebook and other social networks to know what is new on the web. As a Computer Science student, I will take advantage of this opportunity and post daily readings from the lectionary on the web.[72]

Many young people are familiar with how the social media works. Some connect the social media with their experience of the Catholic faith. One young person posted on her Facebook page a saying that,

---

[70] Cahalan, *Introducing the Practice of Ministry,* 35.

[71] Cahalan, *Introducing the Practice of Ministry,* 36.

[72] Aaron Abo (a nineteen years old student of University of Agriculture, Makurdi), in a one-on-one interview on June 1, 2014 at Makurdi.

"God does not use wifi, but he connects everyone. He has no telephone, but I talk to him, he is not on Facebook, but he is my friend. God is not on twitter, but I follow him." Generally, the social media provides an avenue to evangelize young people, who are potential evangelizers of rural communities.

To effectively evangelize rural communities entails garnering skills in the practice of ministry. For instance, some emerging adults have been identified as inspirational preachers. John Igbana, a student of Uniagric acknowledged that he is blessed with the gift of preaching. As the president of the Young Catholic Students of Nigeria (YCSN) in his high school days, anytime he gave a spiritual talk to members, they were moved with tears. "When I noticed that I have such a gift, I worked hard to develop it. Today I go out to preach to other people as a member of the Legion of Mary society.[73] Full involvement, and commitment to religious communities, helps to improve the talents and skills of young people. While some are inspirational preachers and speakers, others have the gift of acting.

As people who watch diverse movies that come with new experiences, some emerging adults have developed skills for acting. In a skillful way, they reenact the passion of Christ that attracts fresh memories of the passion event among Tiv Catholics. The public dramatization of Christ's passion and death on Good Friday draws more meaning and often creates emotional sensitivities in people whose hearts are moved with tears. In the same way, Tiv Catholics will draw more meaning from Catholicism if biblical stories are dramatized frequently. It will yield practical results if Sunday readings are dramatized on weekly basis. Dramatization makes biblical stories meaningful, visible and coherent. In the same way, songs that build on biblical stories, and harmonize the experiences of the Tiv can make Catholicism a concrete reality in Tiv culture.

Singing as an aesthetic of worship is a key factor that determines the degree to which emerging adults are connected to worship. In Tanzania, young people have demonstrated their prowess, innovating the choir by introducing new ideas in music. The choir group has

---

[73] John Igbana (a twenty-seven years old student of Benue State University, Makurdi), in a one-on-one interview on May 19, 2014 at Makurdi.

187

set aside the "secular words" from the rhythm of the *twanga pepeta* and replaced them with religious words. They also did the same to hi-pop music. Young people inculturated the songs by substituting the secular words with religious relics. Their music has made tremendous impact. People like their songs because they propagate an important message to everyone in the community.[74]

In Tiv society, emerging adults have the gift to make the choir attractive and meaningful. They constitute membership of choir groups. Some individual members of choir groups have the talent to play the keyboard and other musical instruments. They place their gifts in voluntary service of the church.

The church expects emerging adults to continue to offer voluntary service[75] especially now that foreign aid has declined. Christian missionaries contributed majorly to the development of mission areas in Tivland with very little contribution from the neophytes. The old Makurdi diocese benefitted greatly from foreign funding agencies for the building of churches, schools, hospitals, and the training of personnel.[76] These agencies include, *Missio, Propaganda Fide, Church in Need, Little Way, and Miserior*.

The church in Tivland relied heavily on foreign aid that is no longer forthcoming. Catholicism can take root in Tiv culture with improvised strategies for self-reliance. To achieve this goal, modern evangelization among the Tiv should bring out a morality in which the

---

[74] Magesa, *Anatomy of Inculturation: Transforming the Church in Africa*, 42.

[75] See Cahalan, *Introducing the Practice of Ministry*, 41. Voluntary work is not connected to financial remuneration. Volunteering is an important form of service in the US in both secular and religious communities. It is a practice whereby many people give time and talent generously to meet the needs of others. Volunteering covers a wide range of activities. Tiv Catholics also help their faith communities by volunteering in different ways including, cleaning the environment, supplying physical labor during the construction of a church project, and teaching catechism. They need to be motivated to continue giving such services to make the church in Tivland a self-reliant church.

[76] Godwin A. Bagu, "Makurdi Diocese at Fifty: The Imperative of a Self-Reliant Church," *Catholic Diocese of Makurdi at 50: A Celebration of Service to Humanity*, Ed. Shagbaor F. Wegh (Makurdi: Selfers Academic Press Ltd., 2010), 258-259.

ecclesia community is not just a believing and worshipping community, but also a community of service.[77]

In this way, young people can place their gifts including, their physical energy at the service of the church by assisting in the construction of buildings, and other projects. Those who are capable can donate money as well including, giving their tithes. Most importantly, educated emerging adults who volunteer as catechetical instructors will be doing a great deal of service to the church as well.

Conclusion

This chapter has responded to the issue concerning the contextualization of the Catholic faith in Tiv culture. The response is based on three main strategies. The first is the formation and promotion of community life among emerging adults. These communities are capable of producing community theologians who will take the faith to rural communities. The second strategy underscores the importance of catechesis as the best approach to teach emerging adults, and adults truths of the Catholic faith. Catholicism can take root in Tiv culture if catechesis adopts catechetical approaches that integrate images in Tiv culture with Catholic categories. The third strategy acknowledges that emerging adults are endowed with gifts and talents they place at the service of the church.

These strategies, if effectively implemented by those who work closely with emerging adults can make Catholicism alive, active, and rooted in Tiv culture.

---

[77] Yuhe, "The Encounter of Tiv Religious and Moral Values with Catholicism in the Time of Secularization", 91.

9

TOWARD A GOAL-ORIENTED THEOLOGY

T his last segment summarizes the central argument of this theological work. Building on the summary, the next section
makes practical suggestions that would enhance the grounding of
Catholicism in Tiv culture if effectively implemented. Drawing a
reprise from what has been discussed, this chapter shows that theology cannot be limited to a theoretical, transcendental or ivory-
tower discipline. It is a practical enterprise, carried out within a
particular context with a goal to achieve practical results. The general conclusion caps the author's main argument.

Synopsis

This summary is based on three basic questions. What is the problem at stake? Why is the situation this way? How can the problem
be solved?

The issue at stake is that the Catholic faith is yet to take concrete
root in Tiv culture since Catholicism came to Tivland in 1930. The
issue of the contextualization of Catholicism is a universal problem
that has affected different societies across the globe. It has raised
serious concerns among theologians. Catholicism did not take root
in North Africa (even though the territory was part of the origins of
the Catholic faith), because it did not take into consideration the
culture of the people in transmitting the gospel message.

The story of the split of faith with culture was also true of Japan that experienced a lack of sufficient or sustained contact. Many cultures including Tiv society of central Nigeria have experienced the distant relationship between faith and culture. The question that readily comes to mind is, what was responsible for this state of affairs?

The model of transmitting faith in a culture determines to a large degree how it is received. Scholars identify the translation, adaptation, and contextual models as the three basic models that missionaries often use in their missionary work. Most foreign missionaries caught up in a new pastoral situation adopt the translation model as the first approach to evangelization. Adaptation models too have their weaknesses because cultures are not static, and in addition, a symbol that resonates with a particular culture may not fit another culture. This suggests that both the translation and adaptation models are inadequate in rooting the gospel in a culture. Contextual models are the most enduring of the three models. Contextual models are the most favored in the context of theology in Tiv culture because such models dialogue with faith and culture. They are embedded in inculturation and incarnation approaches.

In response to the theological problem under consideration, three contextual models were used. A combination of Browning's strategic practical theological method, Tracy's method of analogical correlation, and the circle method were used to effectively bring faith and culture in a reciprocal dialogue. Tiv society was known for profound cultural practices such as the practice of community life. The concept of community life, and other practices were potent analogical tools that were capable of bringing faith and culture in dialogue. For reasons probably of language, and lack of integration in Tiv culture, the missionaries were unable to incorporate these practices in their missionary work. Today, Tiv society has changed greatly with the advent of colonialism, cross-cultural contact, and the introduction of modern means of transportation and communication. With these changes, the task of rooting Catholicism in Tiv culture can be explored in different spheres including, the context of the worship experiences of educated emerging adults in Catholic communities on campus.

The predilection to adopt emerging adults as theological subjects arises from two main reasons. Firstly, they represent the future of Catholicism in Tivland as people who will act as unconventional community theologians by taking the faith to rural communities. Secondly, history is replete with instances of young people spearheading changes in most societies, which supports the view that they can bring enduring change to Catholicism in Tivland.

In Tiv society too, influential young people were very proactive. Before the advent of colonialism in Nigeria, many rituals were associated with them. They organized themselves on the basis of age-grades, and carried out farming, and social activities in a cooperative manner.

During the colonial administration, the colonial officers elevated those who were influential to the position of tax officers to enforce the administrative policy that required eligible Tiv people to pay taxes. Generally, young people played an active role in the colonial government that exposed the positive and negative consequences of colonialism. Positively, colonial rule raised the standard of living of the Tiv that exposed them to formal education, foreign medicine, and better ways of relating. The introduction of money in the economy on the other hand, led to the collapse of exchange marriage that was intrinsically problematic, and promoted monogamy that was preached by the Christian missionaries. On the negative side, the value of community life declined as money was introduced in the economy, and young people began to take individual responsibility in achieving their set goals. It can be argued that when money became the medium of exchange for goods and services, individualistic tendencies started creeping into Tiv society. Community life declined considerably, effects of which are conspicuous in Tiv society today.

How can the experiences of emerging adults at worship in the contemporary Tiv culture bridge the gap between faith and culture? In response to the above question, the theological inquiry was broken down into the issue of what most connects emerging adults with Catholic worship, and what the Catholic Church needs to know about them. This was achieved within a descriptive theological framework that used three praxis-oriented methods. The circle method provided the tools that helped in exploring the context of emerging adults in three institutions of higher education. The circle method also helped to explore the investigation in a systematic manner.

The information that was obtained through participant observation, and interviews was analyzed from the perspective of social and cultural analysis. It was discovered that family and education are symbols that impact the worship experiences of educated emerging adults in either negative or positive ways. The positive impact of these symbols enhances their understanding of Catholic worship and practices with a commitment to remain Catholics for life. On the other hand, the negative impact of the symbols have rather plummeted their understanding of basic Catholic doctrines and practices.

Emerging adults who demonstrated limited knowledge about beliefs and practices of the Catholic Church raised questions concerning Catholic doctrines and practices including, the role of incense at worship, sacramentals, the use of images in the life of the church, and the role of Mary in Salvation history. Interestingly, a demonstration of strong belief in the Eucharist was outstanding among these young people. All recognized the Eucharist as the real presence of Jesus in the symbols of bread and wine. For some, the mystery of the Eucharist enlivens their faith, and gives them the impetus to keep moving in the midst of life challenges. They drew analogies between the Eucharist, and Tiv cultural rituals such as *imborvungu* and *igbe*, and observed that like the Eucharist, these practices are also exclusive for initiates. Despite the capacity of emerging adults to establish a relationship between the Eucharist and Tiv ritual practices, they lacked the knowledge to explain the depth of this relationship.

Analogies between Tiv cultural practices and Catholic doctrines and practices were further explored using Tracy's analogical framework by specifically identifying the similarities and differences between the Eucharist, the cross, and *imborvungu*. As the Eucharist flows from the atoning sacrifice of Jesus on the cross, it was analogously examined with *imborvungu* as both meet the criteria of appropriateness. *Imborvungu* was examined both as a symbol of reparation and as a symbol of torture, adumbrating the Christian cross. The challenge to bring Tiv cultural practices in dialogue with the Catholic faith is to enhance a mutual reinforcement of faith and culture, and ultimately ground Catholicism in Tiv culture.

The goal of grounding Catholicism in Tiv culture can be achieved by offering a pastoral response to the theological problem in the form of practical solutions. The response was based on three strategic actions. These strategies include, firstly, the building of communities among emerging adults that will produce community theologians, secondly, the training of emerging adults through an intensive catechesis that integrates images in Tiv culture to make them effective interpreters of the faith in Tiv culture, and lastly, identifying the charisms and talents of emerging adults, and to place these gifts at the service of the community to make the Catholic faith alive, active, and rooted in Tiv culture. The following are key areas to note while implementing the strategies.

The Way Forward

The divorce between faith and culture made Catholicism to appear as a foreign religion in many cultures. Their harmony today has brought a reciprocal dialogue between the two. In this regard, the story of Catholicism in Zaire is a success story.[1] How can faith and culture establish a mutual enrichment in Tiv culture? The following recommendations are germane in realizing this goal.

Intentional Communities

Pastors and chaplains that minister to young people need to encourage them to register to at least one pious organization in the religious community, be it a chaplaincy or a parish. This is a step toward establishing intentional communities. These communities create avenues to discuss faith, and other experiences that may en-

---

[1] Elochuckwu E. Uzukwu, *Worship as Body Language Introduction to Christian Worship: An African Orientation* (Collegeville: The liturgical Press, 1997), 297-316.

hance the cohesiveness of members in each pious society. Members should be encouraged to establish relationships with each other.

The pastor, chaplain, or officials of each organization must keep track especially of dormant members. Catholics have often been criticized for failing to connect with their members even when those members are perpetually absent from the group. A follow-up on such members either by telephone, physical contact or any other preferred means will help to identify their challenges, and if the need arises, offer the needed care and support. It will be helpful for group members to demonstrate the value of being each other's brother or sister's keeper (see Gen. 4:9).

To be a brother or a sister's keeper means getting involved in the person's life. One way of connecting with the other is to identify the person's feelings and passions. It is also helpful to recognize that emerging adults have their distinctive idiosyncrasies, and to effectively minister to them entails connecting with their world. They love music, sports (soccer), their dress code is different, and sometimes they speak in symbolic ways. The word of God provides a means to strengthen their community living, and equally address their unique experiences as individuals.

The Word of God

The need to strengthen emerging adults, and above all to strengthen community life among them with the word of God underscores the importance of scripture reading. Catholics have been criticized for having a poor attitude toward the reading, and study of the Bible. In addition, Catholic priests in Tivland are criticized for failing to prepare adequately before delivering their homilies.

As a teacher, every priest is to regard preaching as an essential duty and must take this duty with utmost seriousness. They are to prepare adequately for it both by prayer and study, not only when they go to the pulpit to preach, but may take the word to classrooms, and in other ways including the presentation of the word of God to various groups.[2] In the course of preparation, the priest may think of

---

[2] *Guidelines on Pastoral Ministry in the Catholic Diocese of Makurdi,* 14.

cultural resources that resonate with the Catholic tradition recognizing that the purpose of every homily is to explain the readings and make them relevant to the circumstances of the people.[3] A priest who is at home with the culture of the people where he serves does not lack homiletic materials. A well-prepared homily draws the worshipping community closer to the mystery of Christ. A homily edifies the people of God, but catechesis deepens knowledge of the faith.

Catechesis

Catechesis as the most effective approach to deepen knowledge about the Catholic faith cannot be treated with levity. The Pastor is the catechist of the parish. He delegates the duty to the catechist whose primary duty is to offer catechetical instructions. The priest is to ensure that the catechist does his/her job, and those who volunteer as catechetical instructors are competent people, highly knowledgeable about the Catholic faith. Catechumens preparing for the reception of the sacraments must possess a certain level of cognate experience of the Catholic faith before they are accepted to receive the sacrament(s).

Most times, catechumens demonstrate a lack of seriousness at attending catechetical lessons. Some are perpetual absentees from catechetical classes. Such people take advantage of the financial needs of the parish, and make comments such as, *me na fada nyaregh tso una erem baptisma* (I will give the priest money and he will baptize me). Priests must stand firm on matters of catechesis, deemphasizing the stole fee required for the sacrament, and emphasizing what catechumens need to know about the faith of the Catholic Church.

Most importantly, the understanding that catechesis is associated with people preparing for the sacraments needs to be discouraged. Catechesis is an ongoing process for all members of the church. Emerging adults who take advantage of this opportunity deepen their knowledge that helps them to effectively explain the faith to others. It is incumbent on pastors to continually organize seminars,

---

[3] See *Guidelines on Pastoral Ministry in the Catholic Diocese of Makurdi*, 14.

conferences, and retreats for emerging adults with a forum for questions and answers. Above all, priests must closely supervise catechetical lessons to bring out beauty, not only in worship, but in the Catholic community in general.

Aesthetics of Worship

Worship in the Catholic Church is not a forum for entertainment, but of prayer. Aesthetics conveys the notion of beauty. Music is an aspect that gives beauty to worship. Music is the primary mode through which the worshipping community expresses her experience at worship. It moves the human heart. Not every kind of music has a place in Christian worship. A standard music that forms part of worship is tailored on the word of God. Lyrics are very important in music.

The Holy Spirit can lead to the composition of the music that serves the word of God,[4] and appeals to the experiences of the worshipping community. Songs were the most beautiful expressions of the experiences of the slaves in North America.[5] Music that draws from the word of God and the experiences of the people makes worship meaningful to the worshipping community.

Spirituals are a distinctive brand of African American songs that were a source of inspiration and natural means of responding to and communicating with God. Spirituals are a pastoral liturgical resource for any community of worshippers. They are analogous to theological documents, carefully and thoughtfully presented in simple and often symbolic language of a particular people.[6]

Most Tiv people are moved by Catholic music. Above all, they are moved by the lyrics of the songs and spirituals. For instance, the following song, drawn from the experience of Job in the book of Job, gives hope to the sufferings of the Tiv.

---

[4] Joseph Cardinal Ratzinger, *The Spirit of the Liturgy* (San Francisco: Ignatius Press, 2000), 151.

[5] Melva Wilson Costen, *African American Christian Worship* (Nashville: Abindgon Press, 1993), 32.

[6] Costen, *African American Christian Worship*, 85.

Ior mba ve suur sha Ter vea ya kunya ga
Shi vea va ahenge ga
Yobu suur sha Ter Yobu zua a kunya ga
Chan yo Yobu ya
Kpa chan i Yobu la hingir iember

The English translation of the song is as follows:

People who count on the Lord shall not be humiliated
And they shall not be disappointed
Job was not humiliated because he counted on the Lord
Even though Job suffered
But Job's suffering later turned to Joy

Songs that integrate the word of God and human experience are congenial to the worship experiences of emerging adults, and they can make worship lively and meaningful. By carefully selecting worship songs, and preparing adequately during choir rehearsals, such songs will surely move the hearts of worshippers.

Musical instruments contribute greatly toward boosting the aesthetics of worship. Talents of emerging adults can be harnessed by allowing them to act as key players of musical instruments. The poor condition of musical instruments and public address systems in some Catholic Churches in Tivland needs to be addressed. Catholics can learn from the separated brethren whose public address systems are always effective even where there is a small congregation. Paying attention to aesthetics of worship is helpful in drawing people to the mystery of God.

This is a collaborative ministry of all Catholics. In particular, priests, catechists, and those who work closely with emerging adults are key agents that will ensure the implementation of these recommendations that are critical in harmonizing Catholicism with Tiv culture.

Conclusion

The above discussion is a practical theological investigation that explored the harmonious relationship between faith and culture. It is specifically a local theology because it springs from particular contexts of higher education institutions in Tivland. It explored the worship experiences of emerging adults in those contexts. The worship experiences of emerging adults demonstrate the need for faith to initiate a dialogue with culture.

The dialogue between faith and culture helps to explain symbolic categories, and Catholic doctrines and practices that are often misunderstood in the language and practices of the Tiv. It also enriches culture to view the Catholic faith not as an encroachment on the cultural heritage of the Tiv, but as a religion that has primal religious foundation in Tiv culture. This reciprocal dialogue enriches emerging adults in both faith and culture and makes them community theologians who will effectively articulate the faith for the grounding of Catholicism in Tiv culture.

ACKNOWLEDGEMENTS

"What shall I say unto the Lord,
all I have to say is thank you Lord."

This is part of a song that captures my sentiment of gratitude to God for the grace to put together this material. I am grateful to my parents late Abraham Iorliam Gyata and my mom Mrs. Agatha Iorliam for the values they thought me. My depth of gratitude goes to late Bishop Athanasius Atule Usuh, my Local Ordinary, William A. Avenya, Bishops Robert McElroy, John Dolan, Peter Adobo, and Wilfred Anagbe.

I acknowledge the support of the faculty and staff, of the school of Theology and Ministry, St Thomas University. I thank in a special way Professors Bryan T. Froehle, Mary Carter Waren, Joe Holland, Ted Whapham, and Beth Stovell. Dr. Joe Holland in particular made immeasurable sacrifices toward the publication of this book. Dr. Josee Gregoire on her part painstakingly read my manuscripts and made useful comments.

My brother priests too supported me in significant ways. Fr Daniel Asue read the manuscript and made useful comments. I acknowledge the support of Fathers Kenneth Agede, Daniel Melaba, Gabriel Gberikon, Pius Ajiki, Didacus Kajo, Michael Ikyem, Emmanuel Nyinya, Cosmas Jooli, Michael Jaki, Simon Ikpum, Donald Komboh, Nicholas Tarbo, Emmanuel Abela, Simeon Iber, Gabriel Wankar, Godwin Bagu, Benjamin Vesue, Alex Iorhii, Samuel Tarvihi and Abraham Alueigba. Others include late Chris Utov, Augustine Igbum, Moses Iorapuu, Remigius Ihula, Vitalis Torwel, Samuel Tumba, Christopher Bologo, Boniface Achabo, Vincent Ahar, John Asen, Vincent Jijingi, Celestine Aayongu, Clement Ugoh,

Michael Bull, Anthony Akaatenger, Thomas Dekaa, Fidelis Nwankwo, Emmanuel Ahua, Boniface Ayoo, and many others.

I am higly indebted to Fr. Franky Jean, and the parishioners of Holy Family Catholic Church in the Archdiocese of Miami, Florida, USA for their support and encouragement. Of particular mention are Elsie Franzil, Djenié Prato, Ginnette and Matheu Louis, Hubert Lejuene, Elizabeth Semeah, the family of Desir, the family of Forte, the Family of Townsend, and the family of Ferer Chapenteur. You are always in my thoughts and prayers.

I deeply appreciate the support I received from Msgr. Steve Callahan, Fathers Pat Mulcahy and Michael Tran, and the parishioners of St Brigid's Catholic Church, St Francis of Assisi Catholic Church, Vista, and St Joseph Cathedral, all in the Diocese of San Diego, California. I also acknowledge the support I received from Sisters of different congregations including Madelin Fitzgerald.

The vision of Christ prayer group in Miami provided spiritual nourishment. The families of Deacon Valentine and Philo Onuigbo, Richard and Justina Mendy, Mr. and Mrs. David Odiwo, Merci and Henrieta Rivière, the family of Edwards, were simply wonderful. Thank you all for being inspirational and supportive.

My lay friends that contributed immensely to this project include, Professor and Dr. Mrs Victor Igbum, Dr. and Dr. Mrs. Genyi, Dr and Mrs Simon Kene, Accountant and Mrs. Gbayan, Gabriel Arubi, Dooshima Ayoo, Mr. and Mrs. Kaase Aye, Mr. and Mrs. Ipevnor, Emmanuel Vanger, Shima Nachia, Emmanuel Amua, and the management, staff, and the Catholic community of College of Education Katsina-Ala.

To you, and many others too numerous to mention, including those who responded to my questions, I say, your different contributions enriched this work. Words cannot adequately communicate the depth of my gratitude. May God bless you richly.

CLEMENT TERSEER IORLIAM
San Diego, California, 2018

BIBLIOGRAPHY

Achebe, Chinua. *Things Fall Apart.* New York: Anchor, 1994.

Adasu, Moses Orshio. *Understanding African Traditional Religion.* Part One. Sherborne, England: Dorset, 1985.

Adega, Andrew Philips. "Ate: (Living Room) As the Centre of Unity in Tiv Compounds." *Ate: Journal of African Religion and Culture* 1 (December 2010): 1-9.

Adi, Nguemo, and Ngove Peter Pever. "Student Enrolment at Benue State University, Makurdi." In *Benue State University at 20: Achievements, Challenges and Prospects.* Edited by Oga Ajene, Mathieu A. Adejo, and Member-George Genyi. Makurdi: SAP Publishing House, 2012.

Adoboh, Peter Iorzuul. "Diocese of Katsina-Ala." Accessed March 17, 2014. http://www.catholic-hierarchy.org/diocese/dkats.html

Adzege, John Atagher. *Blaming the Victim: The Tiv and Ethnicity in Nigeria.* Makurdi: Benue Printing and Publishing Company, 1997.

"Africa Population 2014." *World Population Review.* Accessed January 27, 2015. http://worldpopulationreview.com/continents/africa-population/

Agaba, John, and Ezekiel A. Hanior. "The Goodnews Chapel, Origin, Growth and Development 1993-2012." In *Benue State University at 20: Achievements, Challenges and Prospects.* Edited by Oga Ajene, Mathieu A. Adejo, and Member George-Genyi. Makurdi: SAP Publishing House, 2012.

Ajiki, Pius T. T. "The Good Shepherd Chaplaincy Benue State University." In *Benue State University at 20: Achievements, Challenges and Prospects.* Edited by Oga Ajene, Mathieu Armstrong Adejo. Makurdi: SAP Publishing House, 2012.

Akper, Godwin I. "Prosperity Gospel: A Case Study of Benue State in North-Central Nigeria," *Journal of Reformed Theology* 1 (2007): 41-49.

Aliegba, Eugene T. "Violence Against Women: Its nature and Manifestations." In *Perspectives on Violence Against Women in Nigeria.* Edited by Charity Angya. Makurdi: Aboki, 2005.

Alli, Yusuf, and Sanni Onogu. "I Joined Politics out of Circumstances — Suswam at 50." *The Nation,* November 14, 2014. Accessed November 14,

2014. http://thenationonlineng.net/new/i-joined-politics-out-of-circumstances-suswam-at-50/

Arbuckle, Gerald A. *Culture, Inculturation, Theologians: A Postmodern Critique.* Collegeville: Liturgical Press, 2010.

Angya, Charity. "Early Marriage in Tivland and its Social Consequences." In Review *of Gender Studies in Nigeria.* Vol. 2. Edited by C. Angya. Makurdi: Black Heritage Publications, 2003.

Arnett, Jeffrey Jansen. *Emerging Adulthood: The Winding Road from the Late Teens through the Twenties.* New York: Oxford University Press, 2004.

Asen, John. *Catholic Faith and Practice: Questions and Answers.* Volume One. Makurdi: Religio, 2012.

Astin, Alexander W., Helen S. Astin, and Jennifer A. Lindholm. *Cultivating the Spirit: How College Can Enhance Students' Inner Lives.* San Francisco: Jossey-Bass, 2011.

Asue, Daniel Ude. "Catholic Sexual Ethics and Tiv Women: A Case-study of Pastoral Practice in Regard to HIV/AIDS." Ph.D dissertation, St Thomas University, Miami, 2012.

Asue, Daniel Ude. "Remodeling Catechesis in Post Vatican II African Church." *Asian Horizons* 6, no 3 (September 2012):528-541.

Atel, Edward Terkula. *Dynamics of Tiv Religion and Culture: A Philosophical-Theological Perspective.* Lagos: Free Enterprise Publishers, 2004.

Avenya, William. "Diocese of Gboko." Accessed March 17, 2014. http://www.dioceseofgboko.org/about-us/.

Ayres, Lewis. "Deification and the Dynamics of Nicene Theology: The Contribution of Gregory of Nyssa." *St Vladimir's Theological Quarterly* 49, no. 4 (2005): 375- 394.

Bagu, Godwin A. "Makurdi Diocese at Fifty: The Imperative of a Self-Reliant Church." In *Catholic Diocese of Makurdi at 50: A Celebration of Service to Humanity.* Edited by Shagbaor F. Wegh. Makurdi: Selfers Academic Press Ltd., 2010.

Banawiratma, Johannes. "The Pastoral Circle as Spirituality." In *The Pastoral Circle Revisited: A Critical Quest for Truth and Transformation.* Edited by Frans Wijsen, Peter Henriot, and Rodrigo Mejia. New York: Orbis, 2005.

Bediako, Kwame. *Jesus in Africa: The Christian Gospel in African History and Experience.* Glasgow: Regnum, 2004.

Bell, Catherine. *Ritual Perspectives and Dimensions.* New York: Oxford University Press, 1997.

Benedict XVI. "Message of His Holiness Pope Benedict XVI for the Celebration of World Day of Peace." Vatican, 2010. Accessed November 26, 2012. http://www.vatican.va/holy_father/benedict_xvi/messages/peace/documents/hf_ben-xvi_mes_20091208_xliii-world-day-peace_en.html.

"Benue State University." Accessed December 12, 2013. http://www.campusflava.blogspot.com/2009/11/benue-state-university.html.

Bevans, Stephen. *Models of Contextual Theology.* New York: Orbis, 2002.

Bodewes, Christine. "Can the Pastoral Circle Transform a Parish?" In *The Pastoral Circle Revisited: A Critical Quest for Truth and Transformation.* Edited by Frans Wijsen, Peter Henriot, and Rodrigo Mejia. New York: Orbis, 2005.

Bourdieu, Pierre. *Outline of a theory of Practice.* Translated by Richard Nice. Cambridge: University Press, 1999.

Boys, Mary C. *Educating in Faith: Maps and Visions.* San Francisco: Harper & Row, 1989.

Bradshaw, Paul F., and Maxwell E. Johnson. *The Origins of Feasts, Fasts and Seasons in Early Christianity.* Collegeville: Liturgical Press, 2011.

Branch, Edward B. "Multiculturalism and Campus Ministry in a Changing University Culture." In *The Gospel on Campus: A Handbook of Campus Ministry Programs and Resources.* Second Edition. Edited by Michael Galligan-Stierle. Dayton: Catholic Campus Ministry Association, 1996.

Browning, Don S. *A Fundamental Practical Theology: Descriptive and Strategic Proposals.* Minneapolis: Fortress, 1991.

Browning, Don. "Practical Theology and Political Theology." *Theology Today* 42, no. 1 (1985): 15-33.

Bujo, Bénézet. *Foundations of an African Ethic: Beyond the Universal Claims of Western Morality.* New York: Crossroad, 2001.

Cahalan, Kathleen A. *Introducing the Practice of Ministry.* Collegeville: Liturgical Press, 2010.

Cartledge, Mark J. *Practical Theology: Charismatic and Empirical Perspective.* London: Paternoster, 2007.

Catechism of the Catholic Church. Second Edition. "Respect for Human life." Accessed November 4, 2014.

http://www.vatican.va/archive/ENG0015/_P7S.HTM#4Z

Catechism of the Catholic Church. Second Edition. "Sacramentals." Accessed November 17, 2014. http://www.vatican.va/archive/ENG0015/__P58.HTM

Catechism of the Catholic Church. Second Edition. "The Christian Family." Accessed November 28, 2014. http://www.vatican.va/archive/ENG0015/_P7S. HTM#4Z

Chidili, Barth. *Inculturation as a Symbol of Evangelization.* Jos: Mono Expressions, 1997.

Chopp, Rebecca. *The Power to Speak: Feminism, Language, God.* Oregon: Wipf and Stock, 2002.

Chryssavgis, John. *Cosmic Grace Humble Prayer: The Ecological Vision of the Green Patriarch Bartholomew 1.* Grand Rapids: William B. Eerdmans, 2003.

Chupungco, Anscar J. "Inculturation of Worship: Forty Years of Progress and Tradition." Valparaiso University, Indiana. Accessed January 28, 2015.

http://scholar.valpo.edu/cgi/viewcontent.cgi?article=1109&context=ils_pape rs

The 1983 Code of Canon Law. Accessed October 22, 2014. http://www.vatican.va/archive/ENG1104/_INDEX.HTM.

Cone, James H. *God of the Oppressed.* Mary Knoll: Orbis, 1997.

Cone, James H. *The Cross and the Lynching Tree.* Maryknoll: Orbis Books, 2011.

Costen, Melva Wilson. *African American Christian Worship.* Nashville: Abindgon Press, 1993.

Doki, Gowon Ama. "Images of Womanhood in Tiv Society: A Critical Appraisal." In Review *of Gender Studies in Nigeria.* Vol. 2, Edited by C. Angya. Makurdi: Black Heritage Publications, 2003.

Dorney, Kathleen CND. "Aspects of Campus Ministry: Forming Faith Communities." In *The Gospel on Campus: A Handbook of Campus Ministry Programs and Resources.* Second Edition.Edited by Michael Galligan-Stierle. Dayton: Catholic Campus Ministry Association, 1996.

Dzeremo, Baver. *Colonialism and the Transformation of Authority in Central Tivland: 1912-1960.* Makurdi: Aboki, 2002.

Dzurgba, Akpenpuun. *On the Tiv of Central Nigeria: A Cultural Perspective.* Ibadan: John Archers, 2007.

Dzurgba, Akpenpuun. *The Tiv and Their Culture.* Ibadan: John Archers, 2011.

East, Rupert, trans. *Akiga's Story: The Tiv Tribe as Seen by One of Its members.* London: Oxford University Press, 1965.

Elsener, Josef. "Pitfalls in the Use of the Pastoral Circle." In *The Pastoral Circle Revisited: A Critical Quest for Truth and Transformation*. Edited by Frans Wijsen, Peter Henriot, and Rodrigo Mejia. New York: Orbis, 2005.

"Emerging Youth Cultures: Preparatory Document for the Plenary Assembly of the Pontifical Council for Culture, 2013." Accessed December 9, 2013. http://www.cultura.va/content/dam/cultura/docs/pdf/events/Plenary2013/p reparatorydocument.pdf

Éla, Jean-Marc. *My Faith as an African*. Maryknoll: Orbis, 1993.

Eze, Mary Dorothy. "A Christian Response to Gender Inequality Against Women." *Religion, Violence and Conflict Resolution in Nigeria*. Edited by Cyril Obanure. Makurdi: Aboki Publishers, 2008.

Farley, Edward. "Interpreting Situations: An Inquiry into the Nature of Practical Theology." In *The Blackwell Reader in Pastoral and Practical Theology*. Edited by James Woodward and Stephen Pattison. Malsen: Blackwell Publishers, 2000.

Freire, Paulo. *Pedagogy of the Oppressed*. Translated by Myra Bergman Ramos. New York: Continuum, 2000.

Ganss, George E., SJ. *Ignatius of Loyola: Spiritual Exercise and Selected Works*. Mahwah: Paulist, 1991.

Gbenda, Joseph S. "An Appraisal of Ethical Values in Tiv Religion," *Ate: Journal of African Religion and Culture* 1 (December 2010): 30-36.

Gebara, Ivone. *Out of the Depths: Women's Experience of Evil and Salvation*. Translated by Ann Patrick Ware.Minneapolis: Fortress Press, 2002.

Geertz, Clifford. *The Interpretation of Cultures*. New York: Basic Books, 1973.

Gennep, Arnold van. *The Rites of Passage*. London: Routledge, 2004.

Geri, Godfrey Tor. *A History of Tiv Religious Practices and Changes: A Focus on Imborvungu, Poor and Ibiamegh*. Makurdi: Aboki Publishers, 2012.

Graham, Elaine, Heather Walton, and Frances Ward. *Theological Reflection*. London: SCM, 2005.

Grenz, Stanley J. *Theology for the Community of God*. Nashville: Broadman & Holman, 1994.

Guidelines on Pastoral Ministry in the Catholic Diocese of Makurdi. "Holy Matrimony." Makurdi: Office of the Chancellor, 2012.

Gutiérrez, Gustavo. *A Theology of Liberation*. New York: Orbis, 2010.

Healey, Joseph, mm, and Donald Sybertz, mm. *Toward an African Narrative Theology*. Maryknoll: Orbis, 1996.

Hemba, Stephen. "Kyegh Sha Shwa (KSS) a Huge Opportunity for Benue State." December 30, 2016. https://www.facebook.com/hemba.stephen?fref=nf&pnref=story. KSS is a traditional Tiv cuisine.

Hoge, Dean R., William D. Dinges, Mary Johnson, SND. de N., and Juan L. Gonzales, Jr. *Young Adult Catholics: Religion in the Culture of Choice*. Notre Dame: University of Notre Dame Press, 2002.

Holland, Joe. "Pacem in Terris Global Leadership Initiative" (Unpublished Manuscript, April, 2012).

Holland, Joe. "Roots of the Pastoral Circle in Personal Experiences and Catholic Social Tradition." In *The Pastoral Circle Revisited: A Critical Quest for Truth and Transformation*. Edited by Frans Wijsen, Peter Henriot, and Rodrigo Mejia. New York: Orbis, 2005.

Holland, Joe, and Peter Henriot. *Social Analysis: Linking Faith and Justice*. New York: Orbis, 1983.

Heitink, Gerben. *Practical Theology: History, Theory, Action Domain*. Translated by Reinder Bruinsma.Grand Rapids: William B. Eerdmans, 1993.

"History of Benue State University." Accessed December 12, 2013. http://bsum.edu.ng/dwnloads/BSU_Brief_History.pdf.

Iber, Simeon Tsetim. *The Principle of Subsidiarity in Catholic Social Thought: Implications for Social Justice and Civil Society in Nigeria*. New York: Peter Lang, 2010.

Igbum, Victor. "Charismatic/Pentecostalism: Its Impact on Christianity in Tivland." *Ate: Journal of African Religion and Culture* 1 (December 2010):54-60.

Ioannes Paulus II. *Laborem Exercens* [On Human Work], sec. 21. Accessed October 4, 2014. http://www.vatican.va/holy_father/john_paul_ii/encyclicals/documents/hf_j p-ii_enc_14091981_laborem-exercens_en.html.

Ioannes Paulus II. *Sollicitudo Rei socialis*. Accessed September 18, 2014. http://www.vatican.va/holy_father/john_paul_ii/encyclicals/documents/hf_j p-ii_enc_30121987_sollicitudo-rei-socialis_en.html.

Iorliam, Clement T. "Recreating Community Life Among Young People in Tiv Society, Nigeria: "The New Heavens and the New Earth" (Is 65:17-25)." *International Journal of African Catholicism* 3, no. 2 (Summer, 2012):1-24.http://www.saintleo.edu/media/411882/young_people_in_nigeria_final.pdf.

John Paul II. *Ecclesia De Eucharistia* [Encyclical Letter on the Eucharist in its Relationship to the Church]. Accessed December 9, 2013. http://www.vatican.va/holy_father/john_paul_ii/encyclicals/documents/hf_j p-ii_enc_20030417_eccl-de-euch_en.html.

John Paul II. *Ecclesia in Africa* [Post-Synodal Apostolic Exhortation]. Accessed October 1, 2014. http://www.vatican.va/holy_father/john_paul_ii/apost_exhortations/docum ents/hf_jp-ii_exh_14091995_ecclesia-in-africa_en.html.

John Paul II. *Ecclesia in America* [Post-Synodal Apostolic Exhortation on the Encounter with the Living Jesus Christ: The Way to Conversion, Communion and Solidarity in America]. Accessed September 18, 2014. http://www.vatican.va/holy_father/john_paul_ii/apost_exhortations/docum ents/hf_jp-ii_exh_22011999_ecclesia-in-america_en.html.

John Paul II. *Centesimus Annus.* Accessed September 18, 2014. http://www.vatican.va/holy_father/john_paul_ii/encyclicals/documents/hf_j p-ii_enc_01051991_centesimus-annus_en.html.

John Paul II. "Homily at the Mass for the Beatification of Father Cyprian Tansi." Accessed December 14, 2014. http://www.vatican.va/holy_father/john_paul_ii/travels/documents/hf_jp-ii_hom_22031998_nigeria-beatification_en.html

Kakwagh, Venatus, and Agnes Ikwuba. "Youth Unemployment in Nigeria: Causes and Related Issues." *Canadian Social Science* 6, no. 4 (2010): 231-237. http://proxy.stu.edu/docview/756031488/fulltextPDF/1370F6DfE94569D6B2 C/1?accountid=14129.

Kelly, J.N.D. *Early Christian Creeds.* New York: David Mckay Company, Inc., 1976.

Kilani, Abdulrazaq. "The Changing Faces of the Terror of Cultism in Nigerian Society: An Islamic Perspective." *Comparative Islamic Studies* (2010): 98-111. Accessed November 28, 2014. doi:10.1558/cis.v4il-2.97.

Koikara, Felix, SDB, and Joe Mannath, SDB. *Do it Learn it Live it: Sessions with Youth.* Bangalore: Asian Trading Corporation, 2010.

Labelle, Jeffrey, SJ, and Daniel Kendall, SJ. *Catholic Colleges in the 21st Century.* Mahwah: Paulist, 2011.

Lartey, Emmanuel Y. "Globalization, Youth and the Church: Views from Ghana." In *Youth Religion and Globalization: New Research in Practical Theology.* Edited by. Richard R. Osmer and Kenda Creasy Dean.New Brunswick U.S.A/London UK: Transaction Publishers, 2006.

Leith, John H. *Creeds of the Churches: A Reader in Christian Doctrine from the Bible to the Present*. Third Edition.Atlanta: John Knox, 1982.

Luna, Juan José. "The Pastoral Circle: A Strategy for Justice and Peace." In *The Pastoral Circle Revisited: A Critical Quest for Truth and Transformation*. Edited by Frans Wijsen, Peter Henriot, and Rodrigo Mejia. New York: Orbis, 2005.

Lupande, Joseph M., Joseph G. Healey, and Donald F. Sybertz. "The Sukuma Sacrificial Goat and Christianity: An Example of Inculturation in Africa." *Worship* 70 no, 6 (1996): 506-516.

Magesa, Laurenti. *Anatomy of Inculturation: Transforming the Church in Africa*. Maryknoll: Orbis, 2004.

Maina, Wilson Muoha. "African Communitarian Ethics in the Theological Work of Bénézet Bujo," *Pacifica* 21(June 2008): 192-209.

Mato, Clement. "*The* Catholic Church in Tivland." In *Catholic Diocese of Makurdi at 50: A Celebration of Service to Humanity*. Edited by Shagbaor F. Wegh. Makurd: Selfers Academic Press, 2010.

Mbefo, Luke. "Theology and Inculturation: Problems and Prospects – The Nigerian Experience." *The Nigerian Journal of Theology* 1, no.1 (December 1985): 54-69.

Mbiti, John S. *African Religions and Philosophy*. London: Heinemann, 1985.

Metz, Johann Baptist. *Faith in History and Society: Toward a practical Fundamental Theology*. New York: Crossroad, 2007.

Mitchell, Nathan D. "History of the Relationship between Eucharist and Communion." *Liturgical Ministry* 13 (Spring 2004): 57-65.

Mitchell, Nathan D. "New Direction in Ritual Research." In *Foundations in Ritual Studies: A Reader for Students of Christian Ritual*. Edited by Paul Bradshaw and John Melloh. Grand Rapids: Baker Academic, 2007.

Moltmann, Jürgen. *The Trinity and the Kingdom: The Doctrine of God*. San Francisco: Harper and Row, 1981.

Mondo, Paulino Tuesigye, mccj. "Youth in the Heart of the Church: Steps in a Journey of loving Family [The Approach of the African Church to Youth from *Gaudium et Spes* to the Third Millennium]." *Bringing the Church to Youth or Youth to the Church*. Makuyu: Paulines Publications Africa, 2006.

Moti, James Shagba. *The Early Jerusalem Christian Community: A Biblical model for Basic Ecclesial Communities*. Rome: Urbaniana University Press, 1983.

Moti, James and Francis S. Wegh. *An Encounter between Tiv Religion and Christianity.* Enugu: Snaap Press Limited, n.d.

Nthamburi, Zablon. "Making the Gospel Relevant Within the African Context and Culture." *AFER* 25, no. 3 (1983): 162-171.

Ogar, Augustine. "Inculturation of African Traditional Reconciliatory Values." *Abuja Journal of Philosophy and Theology* 2 (2012): 49-62.

Ojore, Aloys Otieno."Helping Young People Identify their Vocation in Life and Service to the Community." In *Ministry to Youth and Young Adults.* Nairobi: Paulines Africa, 2001.

Orobator, Agbonkhianmeghe E. *Theology Brewed in an African Pot* Maryknoll: Orbis Books, 2008.

Orobator, Agbonikhianmeghe E. "Why is Boko Haram Succeeding?" *Commonweal,* March 3, 2015. Accessed March 15, 2015. https://www.commonwealmagazine.org/why-boko-haram-succeeding?utm_source=Main+Reader+List&utm_campaign=53dc39f726-July+18_The_Week_at_Commonweal&utm_medium=email&utm_term=0_407bf353a2-53dc39f726-91226109.

Parks, Sharon Daloz. *Big Questions Worthy Dreams: Mentoring Emerging Adults in Their Search for Meaning, Purpose, and Faith.* San Francisco: Jossey-Bass, 2011.

Paul VI, *Evangelii Nuntiandi* [Apostolic Exhortation]. Accessed January 12, 2014. http://www.vatican.va/holy_father/paul_vi/apost_exhortations/documents/hf_p-vi_exh_19751208_evangelii-nuntiandi_en.html.

Paul VI. *Populorum Progressio* [The Development of Peoples]. Accessed September 6, 2014. http://www.vatican.va/holy_father/paul_vi/encyclicals/documents/hf_p-vi_enc_26031967_populorum_en.html.

Poupard,Paul Cardinal. "The Dialogue Between Faith and Culture: Keynote Address at the University of Santo Tomás" (Manila: Colloquium of the Federation of Asian Bishops' Conferences, January 14, 1996). Accessed March 23, 2014. http://www.inculturacion.net/phocadownload/Autores_invitados/Poupard,_The_dialogue_between_faith_and_culture.pdf.

Pecklers, Keith F. *Worship: A Primer in Christian Ritual.* Collegeville: Liturgical Press, 2005.

Pius XI. *Quadragesimo Anno* [on Reconstruction of the Social Order]. Accessed September 18, 2014.
http://www.vatican.va/holy_father/pius_xi/encyclicals/documents/hf_p-xi_enc_19310515_quadragesimo-anno_en.html.

Pontifical Council for Justice and Peace. *Compendium of the Social Doctrine of the Catholic Church.* Washington: United States Conference of Catholic Bishops, 2005.

Power, David N. *Sacrament: The Language of God's Giving.* New York: Crossroad, 1999.

Ratzinger, Joseph Cardinal. *The Spirit of the Liturgy.* San Francisco: Ignatius Press, 2000.

Reader, John. *Reconstructing Practical Theology: The Impact of Globalization.* Hamsphire: Ashgate, 2008.

Rogers, Jack. *Presbyterian Creeds.* Louisville: Westminster John Knox Press, 1991.

Ross, Susan A. *Extravagant Affections: A Feminist Sacramental Theology.* New York: Continuum, 1998.

Scharen, Christian, and Aana Marie Vigen, eds. *Ethnography As Christian Theology and Ethics.* New York: Continuum, 2011.

Scharfenberger, Kimberly. "Pope Francis Encourages Europe to Invest in Education and Family." *The Cardinal Newman Society.* December 3, 2014. Accessed December 9, 2014
http://www.cardinalnewmansociety.org/CatholicEducationDaily/DetailsPage/tabid/102/ArticleID/3759/Pope-Francis-Encourages-Europe-to-Invest-in-Education-and-Family.aspx#

Schneible, Ann. "Cardinal Dinardo on Youth and the Digital World: Plenary Assembly for Young People Continues in Vatican City." *Zenit News,* February 8, 2013. Accessed November 7, 2013.
http://www.zenit.org/en/articles/cardinal-dinardo-on-youth-and-the-digital-world.

Schreiter, Robert J. *Constructing Local Theologies.* New York: Orbis, 2006.

Schroeder, George M. "The Quest for Wisdom: Reflections on Campus Ministry and the Relationship Between the Church and Higher Education." In *The Gospel on Campus: A Handbook of Campus Ministry Programs and Resources.* Second Edition.Edited by Michael Galligan-Stierle. Dayton: Catholic Campus Ministry Association, 1996.

Sedmak, Clemens. *Doing Local Theology: A Guide for Artisans of a New Humanity.* Marynoll: Orbis, 2002.

Selvam, Sahaya G., sdb. *Scaffoldings: Training Young People in Christian Life Skills Student's Workbook.* Nairobi: Paulines Publications Africa, 2008.

Setran, David P, and Chris A. Kiesling. *Spiritual Formation in Emerging Adulthood: A Practical Theology for College and Young Adult Ministry.* Grand Rapids: Baker, 2013.

Speciale, Alessandro. "Vatican Admits it Doesn't Fully Understand Youth Culture." *Religion News Service* January 31, 2013.

http://www.religionnews.com/2013/01/31/vatican-admits-it-doesnt-fully-understand-youth-culture.

Smith, Christian, and Patricia Snell. *Souls in Transition: The Religious and Spiritual Lives of Emerging Adults.* New York: Oxford University Press, 2009.

Stanley, Brian. "Inculturation: Historical Background, Theological Foundations and Contemporary Questions." *Transformation,* 24, no 1 (2007): 21-27.

Stinton, Diane B. "African Christianity." In *Jesus the Complete Guide.* Edited by Leslie Houlden. London: Continuum, 2003.

Swinton, John, and Harriet Mowat. *Practical Theology and Qualitative Research.* London: SCM, 2007.

Sullivan, Francis A., SJ. *Creative Fidelity: Weighing and interpreting Documents of the Magisterium.* Eugene, Oregon: Wipf and Stock, 2003.

The New American Bible. Nashville: Catholic Press, 1991.

The Simple Tiv Catechism of Christian Doctrine. Enugu: Eastern Nigeria Printing Corporation, 1962.

Tillich, Paul. *Dynamics of Faith.* New York: HarperCollins, 2009.

Tracy, David. *The Analogical Imagination: Christian Theology and the Culture of Pluralism.* New York: Crossroad, 1981.

Tseayo, Justin Iyorbee. *Conflict and Incorporation in Nigeria: The Integration of the Tiv.* Zaria: Gaskiya Corporation Limited, 1975.

Turner, Victor. *The Forest of Symbols: Aspects of Ndembu ritual.* London: Cornell University Press, 1967.

Udaa, Godwin. "The History of Education in the Catholic Diocese of Makurdi." In *Catholic Diocese of Makurdi at 50: A Celebration of Service to Humanity.* Edited by Shagbaor F. Wegh. Makurd: Selfers Academic Press, 2010.

University of Agriculture, Makurdi. "2013/2014 Admission List," http://uam.edu.ng/Resources/Downloads/2013-2014-Admission-List.

Unongo, Paul Iyorpuu, OFR. "The Imperative of Youth Leadership Development in the Current Millenium." A lecture delivered to the community of Tiv Students (CTS) and the community of the Benue State University, Makurdi. October 16, 2010.

Usuh, Athanasius A. "A Brief History of Makurdi Diocese." Accessed March 17, 2014. http://www.makurdidiocese.com/about_us.php.

Uzukwu, Elochukwu E. *A Listening Church: Autonomy and Communion in African Churches.* Eugene, Oregon: Wipf & Stock, 1996.

Uzukwu, Elochuckwu E. *Worship as Body Language Introduction to Christian Worship: An African Orientation.* Collegeville: The liturgical Press, 1997.

Van der Ven, Johannes A. *Ecclesiology in Context.* Grand Rapids Eerdmans, 1996.

Vasquez, Manuel A. *More Than Belief: A Materialist Theory of Religion.* New York: Oxford University Press, 2011.

Vatican Council II. *"Ad Gentes* [On the Mission Activity of the Church]." Accessed October 6, 2014.
http://www.vatican.va/archive/hist_councils/ii_vatican_council/documents/vat-ii_decree_19651207_ad-gentes_en.html.

Vatican Council II, *"Dei Verbum* [Dogmatic Constitution on Devine Revelation],"

sec 21. Accessed November 8, 2014.
http://www.vatican.va/archive/hist_councils/ii_vatican_council/documents/vat-ii_const_19651118_dei-verbum_en.html.

Vatican Council II, *"Gaudium et Spes,* [Pastoral Constitution of the Church in the Modern world]." Accessed January 24, 2014.
http://www.vatican.va/archive/hist_councils/ii_vatican_council/documents/vat-ii_const_19651207_gaudium-et-spes_en.html.

Vatican Council II, *"Lumen Gentium* [Dogmatic Constitution on the Church]," sec. 66. Accessed November 19, 2014.
http://www.vatican.va/archive/hist_councils/ii_vatican_council/documents/vat-ii_const_19641121_lumen-gentium_en.html

Vatican Council II, *"Sacrosanctum Concilium* [Constitution on the Sacred Liturgy]," sec. 47. Accessed November 14, 2014.
http://www.vatican.va/archive/hist_councils/ii_vatican_council/documents/vat-ii_const_19631204_sacrosanctum-concilium_en.html

Veling, Terry. *Practical Theology: On Earth as it is in Heaven* New. York: Orbis, 2005.

Verhagen, Piet MHM, and John Ogola. *Youth Encounters the Saviour: Behaviour Change Retreat.* Nairobi: Paulines Publications Africa, 1997.

Weems, Renita J. *The Women's Bible Commentary.* Edited by Carol A. Newson and Sharon H. Ringe. Louisville: John Knox, 1992.

Wegh, Shagbaor F. *Between Continuity and Change: Tiv Concept of Tradition and Modernity.* Enugu: Snaap Press, 2003.

Wegh, Shagbaor F. *Marriage, Family and the Church in Tivland.* Makurdi: Dekon Computer Services, 1994.

White, James F. "Moving Christian Worship Toward Social Justice." *Christian Century* 104 19 (1987): 559.

Wijsen, Frans. "The Practical Theological Spiral: Bridging Theology in the West and the Rest of the World." In *The Pastoral Circle Revisited: A Critical Quest for Truth and Transformation.* Edited by Frans Wijsen, Peter Henriot, and Rodrigo Mejia. New York: Orbis, 2005.

Williams, Andrea S., and James D. Davidson, "Catholic Conceptions of Faith: A Generational Analysis," *Sociology of Religion,* 57 no 3 (Fall 1996): 273-289.

Yuhe, Dominic V. "The Encounter of Tiv Religious and Moral Values with Catholicism in the Time of Secularization." Ph.D dissertation, Pontifical St Thomas University, Rome, 1978.

Zinkuratire, Victor. "Isaiah 1-39: Life Context of the Interpretation." In *The Global Bible Commentary.* Edited by Daniel Patte. Nashville: Abingnon Press, 2004.

BOOKS FROM

PACEM IN TERRIS PRESS

AFRICANA STUDIES

AFRICAN ENCOUNTER OF FAITH & CULTURE
Ritual & Symbol for Young People
in Tiv Society of Central Nigeria
Clement Terseer Iorliam, 2020

BOTTOM ELEPHANTS
Catholic Sexual Ethics & Pastoral Practice in Africa:
The Challenge of Women Living within Patriarchy
& Threatened by HIV-Positive Husbands
Daniel Ude Asue, 2014

HUMANITY'S AFRICAN ROOTS
Remembering the Ancestors' Wisdom
Joe Holland, 2012

CATHOLIC SOCIAL TEACHING STUDIES

CATHOLIC LABOR PRIESTS
Five Giants in the United States Catholic Bishops Social Action Department
Volume I of US Labor Priests During the 20th Century
Patrick Sullivan, 2014

CATHOLIC SOCIAL TEACHING & UNIONS
IN CATHOLIC PRIMARY & SECONDARY SCHOOLS
The Clash between Theory & Practice within the United States
Walter "Bob" Baker, 2014

PACEM IN TERRIS
Its Continuing Relevance for the Twenty-First Century
(Papers from the 50th Anniversary Conference at the United Nations)
Josef Klee & Francis Dubois, Editors, 2013

PACEM IN TERRIS
Summary & Commentary for the Famous Encyclical Letter
of Pope John XXIII on World Peace
Joe Holland, 2012

100 YEARS OF CATHOLIC SOCIAL TEACHING
DEFENDING WORKERS & THEIR UNIONS
Summaries & Commentaries for Five Landmark Papal Encyclicals
Joe Holland, 2012

THE "POISONED SPRING" OF ECONOMIC LIBERTARIANISM
Menger, Mises, Hayek, Rothbard: A Critique from
Catholic Social Teaching of the Austrian School of Economics
Pax Romana / Cmica-usa
Angus Sibley, 2011

BEYOND THE DEATH PENALTY
The Development in Catholic Social Teaching
Florida Council of Catholic Scholarship
D. Michael McCarron & Joe Holland, Editors, 2007

CATHOLIC STUDIES

ROMAN CATHOLIC CLERICALISM
Three Historical Stages in the Legislation of a Non-Evangelical,
Now Dysfunctional, and Sometimes Pathological Institution
Joe Holland, 2018

CATHOLIC PRACTICAL THEOLOGY
A Genealogy of the Methodological Turn to Praxis,
Historical Reality, & the Preferential Option for the Poor
Bob Pennington, 2018

SAINT JOHN OF THE CROSS
His Prophetic Mysticism in the Historical Context
of Sixteenth-Century Spain
Cristóbal Serrán-Pagán y Fuentes, 2018

POSTMODERN ECOLOGICAL SPIRITUALITY
Catholic-Christian Hope for the Dawn of a Postmodern Ecological Civilization Rising
from within the Spiritual Dark Night of Modern Industrial Civilization
Joe Holland, 2017
JOURNEYS TO RENEWED CONSECRATION
Religious Life after Fifty Years of Vatican II
Emeka Obiezu, OSA & John Szura, OSA, Editors, 2017

THE CRUEL ELEVENTH-CENTURY IMPOSITION OF
WESTERN CLERICAL CELIBACY
A Monastic-Inspired Attack on Catholic Episcopal & Clerical Families
Joe Holland, 2017

PETER MAURIN'S
ECOLOGICAL LAY NEW MONASTICISM
A Catholic Green Revolution Developing
Rural Ecovillages, Urban Houses of Hospitality,
& Eco-Universities for a New Civilization
Joe Holland, 2015

GLOBAL GOVERNANCE & UNITED NATIONS STUDIES

SEEKING GLOBAL JUSTICE & PEACE
Catholic-Inspired NGOs at the United Nations
Emeka Obiezu, 2019

BRETTON WOODS INSTITUTIONS & NEOLIBERALISM
Historical Critique of Policies, Structures, & Governance of the International Monetary Fund
& the World Bank, with Case Studies
Mark Wolff, 2018

PROTECTION OF RELIGIOUS MINORITIES
A Symposium Organized by Pax Romana at the United Nations
and the United Nations Alliance of Civilizations
Dean Elizabeth F. Defeis & Peter F. O'Connor, Editors, 2015

PERSONAL WITNESS STORIES

"BETTER FOR BEING WITH YOU"
A Philosophy of Care
Sister Bernadette Kenny, MMM with Tauna Gulley, 2019

RUINED FOR LIFE
Post-Missionary Immersion, Reintegration, & Conversion
David Masters, 2019

PADRE MIGUEL
A Memoir of My Catholic Missionary Experience in Bolivia
amidst Postcolonial Transformation of Church and State
Michael J. Gillgannon, 2018

Books from Pacem in Terris Press,
are available for purchase from Amazon.com
and from Amazon outlets in other countries.

Made in the USA
Las Vegas, NV
10 November 2022

59166790R00129